AMERICAN

RELIGIOUS

HUMANISM

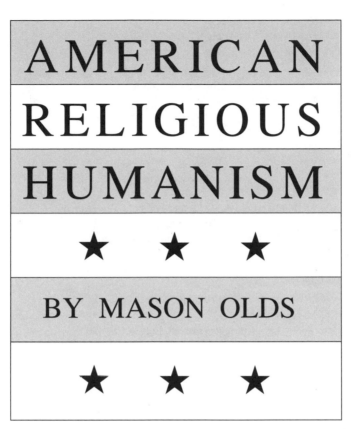

AMERICAN
RELIGIOUS
HUMANISM
★ ★ ★
BY MASON OLDS
★ ★ ★

Revised Edition

FRH

FELLOWSHIP OF RELIGIOUS HUMANISTS

originally published as
Religious Humanism in America: Dietrich, Reese, and Potter
© 1977 University Press of America

Revised edition

Published by the Fellowship of Religious Humanists
c/o First Unitarian Society
900 Mt. Curve Avenue, Minneapolis, MN 55403-1186

Library of Congress Catalog Card Number: 95-83834

ISBN 0-9616216-1-3

book and cover design by Jane Baker

Acknowledgements

American Religious Humanism (1995) is a revision of an earlier text completed in 1972, entitled *Three Pioneers of Religious Humanism: Dietrich, Reese and Potter*. There are significant differences between the first and second edition. The revised text contains more historical background: for example, the conflict between the "orthodox" Congregationalists and the "rational Christian" Congregationalists; a brief section on the anti-religious thought of Friedrich Nietzsche; and the significance of the Free Religious Association in paving the way for religious humanism. The revised text also adds a significant chapter on "Religious Humanism Today," noting that the legacy of the pioneers is to be found in such contemporary institutions as the Ethical Culture Societies, the American Humanist Association, the Fellowship of Religious Humanists, Humanistic Judaism, and the North American Committee on Humanism.

A study of this scope and complexity could not be accomplished without the aid and encouragement of many others. First, I was assisted by the library staffs at Harvard Divinity School, Meadville Theological School, Yale Divinity School, Tufts University, Brown University, and Springfield College. At each of these libraries, I was cordially received, allowed unlimited access to their holdings, and provided with machines for making copies of pertinent materials. Second, I am indebted to several Unitarian ministers who knew the three pioneers. They provided instructive reactions to the study as it developed, and even shared resources from their private libraries. Notable among these were the Reverends Edwin H. Wilson, Raymond B. Bragg, and R. Lester Mondale. In addition to their assistance, I was allowed by the Department of Ministry of the Unitarian Universalist Association to examine the ministerial files of the three pioneers.

Fourth, I am greatly indebted to the members of the Department of Religious Studies at Brown University. They have been my teachers and my critics. I mention especially Professors Wendell S. Dietrich and John G. Milhaven who directed me through the original version of my study.

Fifth, I am much obligated to Jane Baker for both her good judgment and technical skills in getting the manuscript into publishable format for the revised edition. Sixth, I am indebted to the officers of the Fellowship of Religious Humanists, who had great interest in the original work, who have encouraged me to revise the study and to deal with the more recent developments, and who have underwritten the costs of the revised edition.

Seventh, I owe much to my wife, Marjorie, who has been a constant support and encouragement in my scholarly endeavors. It was she who typed the first draft of the original study before the days of the word processor, and she has assisted by reading the revised text and often forcing me to put a somewhat complicated text into a more accessible style.

As helpful as the various forms of assistance and encouragement have been, I realize there are still shortcomings. I thank publicly everyone mentioned here for making the study better, and for its limitations I must plead *mea culpa.*

Mason Olds
Springfield, Massachusetts
Winter 1996

Contents

Introduction

John H. Dietrich, minister of the Unitarian Society of Minneapolis, on 8 December 1929 spoke to his congregation on the subject "Religion without God." In this address Dietrich stressed the difference between humanism and theism. For the latter, he quoted from Cardinal Newman, the nineteenth-century Anglican who converted to Roman Catholicism: "By religion I mean a knowledge of God and of our duties toward him." Using this statement of Newman's as a definition for theism, Dietrich defined humanism in the following way: "By religion I mean the knowledge of man and our duties toward him." Dietrich reminded his congregation that in an earlier age all of life was interpreted from the theistic perspective. Subsequently, a conflict between the doctrine of the "divine right of kings" and the rights of man—and between the religious and the secular order—had arisen. Through this struggle, the political order had freed itself from the religious, and the secular order had extricated itself from ecclesiastical control. It was no longer necessary to appeal to theological principles for understanding politics, nor for a scientist to believe in the existence of God in order to be effective in his work. Dietrich therefore asked, If a man can be a good citizen and a good scientist without belief in God, can he also be religious without God?

Dietrich argued that life is a process of the constant adjustment of the organism to its environment. He maintained that religion was developed by humans to help them adjust to their environment. The historical connection of religion with the concept of God may thus simply be a historical manifestation of something more basic; if so, humans may well have reached a stage in their development where the concept of God can be discarded without affecting religion as an eternal tendency toward adjustment. Dietrich concluded, "one does not need to believe in God in order to be religious."

The views expressed by Dietrich were not new, for he had been speaking in such a fashion for well over a decade; but by 1929 the expression "religion without God" was a favorite subject for discussion. In fact, Harry Emerson Fosdick, the well-known minister of the Riverside Church in New York, had published an article in *Harper's* in December 1929 entitled "Religion without God." Fosdick later reprinted these remarks in his book *As I See Religion* (Grosset & Dunlop, 1932). Although the liberal Fosdick could not wholeheartedly embrace the views of such radicals as Dietrich, he did agree with many of the criticisms the humanists leveled against traditional religion, and he accepted much that the humanists could affirm in the area of ethics. However, Fosdick believed that the humanistic evaluation of human personality had developed out of the underlying premises of theism; he thought that, lacking these theistic premises, the humanists ultimately would be unable to sustain "high morality." Fosdick therefore considered humanism a temporary stage through which some must pass in order to work out a more meaningful theism. Unlike Dietrich, Fosdick thought that high religion and morality could not be sustained without God.

The year before the appearance of Dietrich's address and Fosdick's article, Fulton J. Sheen, the Roman Catholic theologian, had published *Religion without God* (Longmans, Green, 1928), in which he lumped the non-theistic humanists together with such advocates of the philosophy of organism as A. N. Whitehead. He saw the roots of such "revolutionary" views reaching back to the sixteenth-century movement that began under the leadership of Martin Luther. After Sheen had presented the doctrines of the advocates of "religion without God" and had traced the historical development of this movement, he critically evaluated the movement from the perspective of Thomistic philosophy. Sheen saw the movement of "religion without God" as something both new and revolutionary. He said: "And what is this new idea of religion? It is briefly a religion without God, that is, God as traditionally understood. Religion, according to the twentieth century philosophers and theologians, centres not about God but man."

Just before Sheen's work appeared, A. E. Dieffenbach, editor of the Unitarian publication the *Christian Register*, had reviewed Julian Huxley's book *Religion without Revelation* under the heading "Religion without God." Dieffenbach viewed Huxley's work as representative of humanism "proceeding from its groping beginning to intellectual preciseness." Dieffenbach maintained that there is a *Zeitgeist* and the trend toward humanism reflected it; in the main, he supported the trend.

From these remarks, we can see that as the third decade of the twentieth century drew to a close there was a movement within American religious thought that was labeled "religion without God" and that it was generally identified as humanism, in contrast to theism. On this point, Dietrich, Fosdick, Sheen, and Dieffenbach were in accord; but as to the validity of the movement, each had his own particular reactions. The purpose of this study, then, is to examine this movement of "religion without God." In order to do this, we shall divide the study into three major parts. In the first part, we shall examine some of the important antecedents to religious humanism, especially in the areas of humanism, Protestant liberalism, and Unitarianism. In Part Two, we shall look at the formative period, focusing primarily on the thought of three pioneers of the movement and considering criticisms offered by their contemporaries. In Part Three, we shall examine the legacy of religious humanism, especially as it continues to live on in humanist institutions today. We venture first to locate the movement; as its point of view is both religious and humanistic, we shall locate it both within humanism and within religion.

PART I

★ ★ ★

ANTECEDENTS

OF

RELIGIOUS

HUMANISM

★ ★ ★

CHAPTER 1

Religious Humanism and Humanism

"Man is the measure of all things, of the things that are, that they are, and of the things that are not, that they are not."—Protagoras

ALTHOUGH HUMANISM HAS A LONG AND DISTINGUISHED HISTORY, the meaning of the term has depended on the historical context. Hence a kind of ambiguity surrounds the subject. In order to resolve this ambiguity and understand precisely the nature of religious humanism, we must examine it in relationship to other types of humanism: how are they alike, and how do they differ? Specifically, we shall examine the relationship of religious humanism to Greek and Renaissance human-ism, and then we shall compare it to two contemporaneous humanistic movements, literary and naturalistic humanism.*

The first generation of religious humanists—John Dietrich, Curtis Reese, and Francis Potter—were aware of a nonwestern religious humanist tradition, to be found in certain types of Taoism, Confucian-ism, and Buddhism. This awareness enabled them to argue convinc-ingly that humanism could be a religion, although they had to acknowl-edge that the West had not been greatly influenced by these eastern religious traditions. To discover the roots of the earliest expression of humanism in the West, they turned to Greece of the fifth century before the Christian era and to Italy of the fourteenth century of the present era. As Charles Francis Potter, the founder of the First Humanist Society in

---

*It might be stressed that religious humanism should not be confused with the "integral" humanism of Jacques Maritain, and it is obviously different from the existential humanism of Jean-Paul Sartre and the Marxist humanism of the New Marxists.

New York City, said, "It is from the Greek Humanists, however, and through the Renaissance, that modern western Humanism derives."[1] We shall glance first at the early Greeks and then look at the Renaissance in order to begin to locate the position of religious humanism.

Greek Humanism

Although the religious humanists traced their spiritual ancestry back to the Greek humanists, this does not mean that the Greeks had worked out an extensive, systematic statement about the nature of humanism; rather, various Greeks had struggled with embryonic problems and concepts that the religious humanists reappropriated, developed, and systematized some twenty-five centuries later.

As the religious humanists looked back to their Greek forebears, they found many affinities to their own time and concerns. Such men as Anaxagoras (b. ca. 500 B.C.) and Protagoras (b. ca. 481 B.C.) also had questioned the superstitious beliefs of their age (in fact, Anaxagoras has been called the "father" of free thought). The religious humanists found their interest in science foreshadowed by the primitive attempts of Anaxagoras and Democritus (b. 470 B.C.). They discovered skepticism about the nature of the gods in Protagoras and about personal immortality in Democritus. Like the religious humanists, Protagoras had grappled with the problem of an ethics of convention versus an absolute standard; and they continued to seek, as had Democritus, the meaning of happiness. In other words, the religious humanists were not seeking a new orthodoxy in Greek humanism; rather, they saw the Greeks as having had the questing, adventurous spirit they exemplified in their own age. Moses Hadas captured the respect of the contemporary religious humanists for their earlier counterparts:

> What the world has admired in the Greeks is the remarkably high level of their originality and achievements, and this high level premises a deeply held conviction of the importance of individual attainment. . . . The whole outlook, in other words, is anthropocentric: man is the measure of all things.[2]

Renaissance Humanism

Advocates of religious humanism also claimed that their form of humanism was "a lineal descendant of the Renaissance Humanism,"[3] a movement that began in the fourteenth century and continued into the sixteenth, starting in Italy and spreading north into the continent and finally over to England. This was a time when humanists engaged in language study, rediscovered the Greek and Roman classics, revamped their educational system, and created great art and architecture.

The Renaissance humanists revolted against the other-worldliness of medieval Christianity, turning their focus away from a preoccupation with personal immortality and toward making the best of life in the world. The ideal man was no longer the ascetic monk but the universal man of the world. They also reacted against the religious restrictions placed on knowledge; instead, they increasingly relied on reason instead of faith.

Such men as Petrarch returned to the study of classical literature for both its literary form and its understanding of humanness; Pietro Pomponazzi doubted the doctrine of personal immortality and maintained that the highest forms of ethics need not be predicated on belief in a future life; Lorenza Valla used textual and historical criticism for interpreting religious and literary documents. It was during this period that Leonardo da Vinci and Michelangelo were painting their masterpieces.

The religious humanists claimed the Renaissance humanists as their spiritual forebears in that they advocated such things as enjoying this life to the full, developing well-rounded personalities, getting away from the religious control of knowledge, and using textual and historical criticism for studying religious documents. But on two counts the religious humanists differed from their predecessors in the Renaissance. First, the Renaissance was basically an aristocratic movement; art and beauty were to be enjoyed only by an elite few. The twentieth-century religious humanists were much more democratically inclined; they sought to restructure society so that all humans might release their powers and develop their potentialities. Second, the Renaissance humanists threw out the medieval view of reality and substituted for it the view of Plato and the Neo-Platonists. In this move they were traditionalists turning to the past for their answers, rather than innovators enthusiastic about the embryonic sciences. In contrast, the religious humanists of the twentieth century embraced science and the scientific method as the means for arriving at the truth. John H. Dietrich made the point this way: "Five hundred years ago people became Humanists through the study of classical literature, but today they become Humanists as a result of the application of the scientific method."[4]

Literary Humanism

We move now to two types of humanism that were contemporaneous with religious humanism. One of these was literary humanism as advocated by such men as Irving Babbitt, Paul Elmer More, and Norman Foerster.[5] Literary humanism arose in the United States near the end of the 1890s, reached its peak in the 1920s and 30s, and has practically disappeared from the present scene. Sometimes called "the new humanism," it must be distinguished from"the new humanism" of men like John H. Dietrich. Dietrich's might be labeled "religious humanism," and that represented by Babbitt, "literary humanism."[6]

Babbitt thought that literary criticism was in a bad state because modern critics lacked a clear view of literary standards. Many seemed preoccupied with novelty simply for its own sake, with no idea of novelty as an expression of humanness. The trouble, said Babbitt, originated in Rousseau's preoccupation with the eccentric and with a return to nature. Babbitt also blamed science for forcing scientists constantly to make new discoveries.

The answer Babbitt suggested to humanity's problems was similar to what thinkers of the Renaissance proposed: namely, to return to the past, especially the Greek past. Babbitt thought that the Greeks had answered the problem of humanness by advocating a harmonious balance among the various aspects of human personality. The function of the writer, he thought, should be to follow the Greek tradition and to point out how we can attain humanness. Rather than telling the ugly naked truth, as H. L. Mencken did, writers should point to human possibilities. Where Rousseau had gone astray was in allowing emotions to dominate reason, thus throwing us out of harmonious balance.

It should be stressed that Babbitt did not advocate a mechanical repetition of the past, for this would bring sure death to civilization, but he did think that one should stand within the tradition of the Greeks—and all of the great writers of the past—and use them as models for writing in the present. He believed that knowledge of the classics and a good education in the humanities would make us more human.[7]

The religious humanists were certainly aware of the literary humanists, who dwelt primarily in the eastern United States, and they even acknowledged their right to use the term *humanism*. Furthermore, they welcomed their attempts to help people become more human. There was, however, an important difference: the way each group evaluated science. The literary humanists tended to disparage it and to embrace a return to the classics, whereas the religious humanists threw out the Bible and substituted science as their new norm. In other words, the former were critical of science, and the latter viewed it as the modern saviour. Moreover, the literary humanists encouraged humans to turn inward, to be introspective in order to balance the various aspects of personality. The religious humanists, on the other hand, encouraged humans to turn outward and transform the world through humanitarian projects. The literary humanists had very little interest in projects involving social action.

Nietzschean Humanism

In the modern period the ideas of several European philosophers crossed the Atlantic and influenced American intellectuals. Charles Darwin, Karl Marx, and Sigmund Freud come immediately to mind. But a person frequently overlooked in this context, especially in the years between the two world wars of this century, is Friedrich Nietzsche (1844–1900).

Long before the publication of *Thus Spake Zarathustra,* Nietzsche had proclaimed the death of God. In many respects the constructive aspects of Nietzsche's philosophy were an attempt to interpret and to offer a way of being, even living, in a world devoid of God. His study of ancient Greece revealed that as that great culture rose, so did the vitality of its Olympian gods. But as that culture declined, so did these once great deities. So intimately were the Olympian gods connected to their culture, they could not survive its downfall. Along with other commentators of his age, Nietzsche considered western Christian culture—and its God—to be in decline.

Since people believe in God without good reasons, Nietzsche felt it futile to refute the hypothesis of his existence through reason; an irrational belief will not yield to rationality. Instead Nietzsche used "psychological dissection." He contended that prevaricating poets had created the gods. They told parables of clouds, and like a herd of sheep, humans looked up to their creations. Moses and the author of the Gospel of John were as much poets as Homer and Hesiod.

Priests followed the poets and picked up where they had left off. Their God is not based on knowledge, but is used to exploit human ignorance. Events not immediately explicable are declared to be the work of God. Gaps in human knowledge enabled the priests to create the parable of their redeemer. According to Nietzsche, that parable is a delusion, for it involves "a stopgap, which they call God."[8]

At best, belief in the existence of God is conjecture. The idea is certainly thinkable, but believers allege that God is also visible and feelable. Because such claims cannot be confirmed, Nietzsche considered belief in God to be a bad conjecture. It leads to the conviction that the few human perfections that exist are, in fact, corrupt. God is "the thought which makes crooked all that is straight," said Nietzsche. For instance, priests often proclaim the most autonomous, creative people of their age to be heretics, forcing them to recant their teachings or be doomed to hell. Nietzsche saw all talk about an unmoved Mover, the One, and the Permanent as detrimental parables invented by lying priests.

God did not create humans; humans, through their poets, created their gods out of human need. Zarathustra explains that humans encounter an indifferent universe full of unbearable suffering. They feel impotent, so it is comforting to believe that the universe has ultimate meaning, that God works in his infinite wisdom through human suffering and privations, that humans endure pain for their own good—if not in this life, certainly in the afterworld. Unlike the herd, Zarathustra sees the gods for what they are, the flitting ghosts of poets, and dispenses with them.

The death of God came not swiftly, but over a long time. The old gods, of course, came to an end long ago. In the ancient Near East, their deaths resulted from the jealousy of the Hebrew God who decreed, "There is no God but me." In one fell swoop, divine command consigned all the old gods to oblivion. This jealous God was anthropomorphic, but over time the poets discarded his more human characteristics and declared him to be spirit. This declaration constituted the largest leap toward disbelief. Zarathustra merely affirmed what the God of Judeo-Christian tradition had already announced: gods, both old and new, are dead.

Unlike humans, gods do not die a single death; they die in various ways in different times and places. The last pope, a character in *Zarathustra,* described the divine death he "witnessed." The God he knew was concealed, addicted to secrecy. The old rascal even conceived his son in a sneaky way, through adultery, by seducing a young virgin already betrothed to another. The herd believed God to be loving; the last pope saw he could also be harsh and vengeful, especially in his youth. He could have spoken more clearly to people, but refused, thus wreaking havoc on those who could not understand him. Any fair-minded person must concede such behavior to be in bad taste. This God enjoyed judging, even creating a hell for those he judged harshly, although real love transcends reward and retribution. But as he aged, he mellowed, even became soft. In the end, this did him in. This old God,

8

seated on his throne at the apex of the universe, looked down upon his creation, perceived the ubiquitous pain and suffering, and simply could bear it no longer; he died of pity.

Yet the details of God's death are less clear than they might appear. According to another character, the "ugliest man," God died not of natural causes, but was murdered! In fact, he audaciously confesses, it was he who committed the deicide. His motive was simple: God knew everything about him—not just every hair on his head, but his every thought, word, and deed—and this was unbearable. He took revenge on the cosmic voyeur and did him in.

Although Nietzsche dropped various other hints throughout his philosophical poem, we now understand an encounter in the prologue between Zarathustra and the old saint. After meditating on a mountain for ten years, Zarathustra descends to the forests, where he meets an old saint who confesses that he cannot love humans because they are sinners, but he can love God, presumably because he is ignorant of God's sins. Zarathustra is puzzled; does the old saint not know that God is dead? The saint cannot love humans who are alive, and the object of his love is dead; he is an absurd character who loves in vain. That is also true of all those who follow the saint's path. The death of God is a theme not only running throughout *Thus Spake Zarathustra,* but pervading all of Nietzsche's thought.

As we shall see, each of the three pioneers discussed in this study had some knowledge of Nietzsche's thought, especially his concept of the death of God. John H. Dietrich preached sermons about Nietzsche's ideas. Curtis W. Reese edited and saw through its posthumous publication a work on Nietzsche by Burman Foster, a professor at the University of Chicago. Evidences of Nietzsche's thought crop up in Charles F. Potter's theory of the "creative personality," and Potter occasionally used the term *Superman.* In his assessment of religious humanism in 1929, Willard Sperry of Harvard Divinity School noted the importance of Nietzsche's thought to the doctrines of religious humanism.

Naturalistic Humanism

The final type of humanism we shall consider in our attempt to locate religious humanism within the general context of humanism is "naturalistic humanism." This point of view was advocated by a number of professors associated with Columbia University. Men such as John Dewey, John Herman Randall, Jr., and Corliss Lamont are representative of this position. Randall, after reflecting on fourteen essays by eminent philosophers who were proponents of the philosophy of naturalism, described the "Nature of Naturalism."[9]

As Randall observed, philosophers often have argued that there are two realities, neither of which is reducible to the other. Such dualism has taken many forms. The Greeks saw nature in opposition to art; medieval thinkers contrasted the natural with the supernatural; empiricists saw an antithesis between nature and experience; idealists distinguished the natural from the transcendental. More recently, some moderns have spoken of nature and humans as if they were different types of reality.[10]

In contrast to these dualists are the monists, who maintain that dualism is an incorrect interpretation of reality, for reality is one. Among monists, those who argue that reality is composed of ideas are called idealists; those who maintain that the natural world is the real one are called naturalists. To the contemporary naturalist, "Nature" is an all-inclusive category, somewhat as "Being" was for the Greeks and "Reality" was for the idealists. The naturalistic humanists deny the validity of various dualistic ways of interpreting reality and repudiate the idealistic monist. They maintain that the world of nature is the sum total of reality. Lamont has said of naturalistic humanism that it is "a world-view in which Nature is everything, in which there is no supernatural and in which man is an integral part of Nature and not separated from it by any sharp cleavage or discontinuity."[11] Or as Randall contended: "...there is no room for any Supernatural in naturalism—no supernatural or transcendental God and no personal survival after death."[12]

According to the naturalistic humanist, the most useful method for helping humans understand their world has proven to be the scientific method. The naturalist believes that the scientific method should not be restricted—in fact, it should be extended to every area of human concern.[13] This does not mean that the naturalists have reduced everything to science, for they realize that the nature of almost anything is perhaps more than it is empirically thought to be, but, at least, it is what it is given in experience as being. The naturalists, therefore, do not wish to reduce anything; they seek to apply a method to all areas of human concern in order to understand them.

In contrast to the mechanical naturalism of the nineteenth century, the contemporary naturalist seeks to extend the scientific method to such areas as religion and ethics. In the "new naturalism" there is room for religion because it is a fact of human experience. The naturalist,

10

however, does not accept religion as a good within itself, for while certain aspects of religion enrich human life, others are harmful. Religion must be critically evaluated and reformed on the basis of its social usefulness. In this view, "there is room for celebration, consecration, and clarification of human goals."[14] Randall opined that in the past the naturalists appreciated the insights of the supernaturalists, for some of them had been helpful, but he maintained that their explanations were incorrect; rather than providing, for instance, a supernatural interpretation for the origin of values, a naturalistic one is not only possible but also more accurate. To insist on an antinaturalistic basis for values "is faulty metaphysics; standards have their natural setting, in terms of which they are warranted."[15] Through the use of the scientific method the naturalists can determine those aspects of religion and values of use to humans and then bring their best critical thought "to bear on organizing and adjusting them within the pattern of the Good Life."[16]

Although there are varieties within the contemporary American naturalist framework as well as within the religious humanist, we have now reached the point where we can identify the religious humanists. They stand within the general position of naturalistic humanism. This is true in their understanding of the universe, of the importance of the scientific method, and of the place of religion and values in human life. The relationship of religious humanism to naturalistic humanism is that the former is a sub-type within the latter larger type. In other words, the religious humanist is a naturalistic humanist, but a naturalistic humanist need not be a religious humanist. The religious humanists accept the framework of the naturalistic humanists and they use the religious institution for preaching, teaching, and promoting their understanding of religion from the naturalistic humanist perspective. Rather than interpret life from the dualistic perspective of one of the various kinds of supernaturalism, they view life strictly within the context of nature. Lamont said:

> One of the most important groups believing in naturalistic Humanism calls itself religious Humanists. These derive their main strength from the ranks of Unitarian clergymen, such as John H. Dietrich, formerly minister of the First Unitarian Church in Minneapolis; Charles Francis Potter, long head of the now defunct First Humanist Society of New York City; Curtis W. Reese, former Dean of the Abraham Lincoln Centre in Chicago. . . . [17]

CHAPTER 2

Religious Humanism and Protestant Liberalism

"What the gods have been expected to do, and have failed to do through the ages, man must find the courage and intelligence to do for himself. More needful than faith in God is faith that man can give love, justice, peace and all his beloved moral values emobodiment in human relations. Denial of this faith is the only real atheism."—A. Eustace Haydon

WE HAVE LOCATED RELIGIOUS HUMANISM WITHIN NATURALISTIC humanism; we shall now attempt to locate it within established religious thought. From the clues already acquired in our study, we shall begin our search within that tradition known as "Protestant liberalism." First, we shall list a few of the obvious characteristics of this movement; and second, we shall attempt to distinguish at least three different perspectives within the general movement of which religious humanism is one, and indicate its relationship to the other two.

Historically, Protestant liberalism began early in the nineteenth century with the thought of the German theologian Friedrich Schleiermacher (1768-1834) and reached its apex early in the twentieth century. Usually it is maintained that, theologically, the nineteenth century did not end in the United States until the Great Depression in 1929. The publication of Karl Barth's *The Epistle to the Romans* in 1918 signaled the end of the liberal era and inaugurated the advent of neo-orthodoxy in Europe; Reinhold Niebuhr had a similar effect in the United States with the publication of his *Moral Man and Immoral Society* in 1932.

Features of Protestant Liberalism

As the nineteenth-century theological movement known as Protestant liberalism has been dealt with at some length in numerous studies, we shall not retrace that familiar ground here. In order that our context is sufficiently understood, however, we mention the book by John Dillenberger and Claude Welch entitled *Protestant Christianity,* which contains an excellent summary of this movement. The authors maintain that four separate influences or features converged to become "liberal theology": (1) Friedrich Schleiermacher and his theology of religious experience; (2) biblical criticism, as evidenced in Old Testament thought in the documentary hypothesis of the Pentateuch and in the New Testament in the efforts to solve the synoptic problem; (3) Albert Ritschl (1822-1889) and his theology of moral values; (4) religion and science, especially as they focus on the problem of a geo-centric world-view versus the modern one and on "special creation" versus evolution. [1]

These features tended to affect the liberals' understanding of Christian doctrine. Liberals sought to embrace the most modern discoveries in science, yet at the same time maintain their religious faith. If Christian doctrine conflicted with knowledge of the modern world, then doctrines had to be adjusted. This meant that God was thought to work within the laws of nature, for it would be inconsistent to assume a rational God who violated his own created order. They emphasized the immanence of God at the expense of the traditional belief in his transcendence. They thought of humans as higher animals trying to cast off the vestiges of their bestial ancestry. If there were a "golden age" for humans it lay not in some past mythical Garden of Eden, but in the future. As for Jesus, he was the great moral teacher, whose uniqueness resided in his teaching and ethical example. Moreover, the liberals stressed practical rather than metaphysical questions. Generally, arguments for the existence of God, which preoccupied the medieval Scholastics, were of little concern to the liberals, whose understanding of God was alleged to be based upon personal experience. The liberals saw little connection between their understanding of God and rational arguments for the existence of a "Final Cause," a "Prime Mover," or a "Necessary Being." [2] They saw the universe as a cozy, one-story structure that revealed more continuity and wholeness than discontinuity and fragmentariness. Yet, it must be emphasized that, with few exceptions, the liberals never codified these views into a specific dogma; rather, their position reflected a spirit and direction that was tentative, tolerant, and flexible.

From this general context we turn next to more specific aspects of Protestant liberalism, to distinguish three types: "evangelical liberalism," "empirical philosophy of religious liberalism," and "humanistic liberalism." [3] Evangelical liberalism is represented by Harry Emerson Fosdick (1878–1969), the former famous minister of Riverside Church and at the time a member of the Union Theological Seminary faculty in New York City. The empirical type is reflected in the thought of Henry Nelson Wieman (1884–1975), who for many years was a member of the Department of Philosophy at the University of Chicago. Humanistic liberalism is expressed in a controversial document, published in 1933, entitled "A Humanist Manifesto." The first two types are without question representative of Protestant liberalism; the third can at least be said to have grown out of it. [4] One's generosity in drawing the liberal theological circle determines whether humanistic liberalism has gone beyond the general bounds of Protestant liberalism.

Evangelical Liberalism

Harry Emerson Fosdick, especially in the 1920s and 1930s, was considered the chief popular exponent of Protestant liberalism. It was his type of thought that the revival of fundamentalism in the 1920s sought to destroy. A sermon in 1922 entitled "Shall the Fundamentalists Win?" [5] is illustrative of those turbulent theological years. Yet with the rise of "humanistic liberalism," Fosdick had another theological flank to defend, and in response to this new threat he wrote *As I See Religion* in 1933. Although Fosdick's thought subsequently underwent significant changes, we shall examine the basic theology of this work and indicate in what ways religious humanism or "religion without God" differs from it. [6]

In *As I See Religion* Fosdick asked, What is Christianity? (33). He believed the time was past for dividing the world into those who accept the orthodox Christian tenets and those who are considered heathen because they have other beliefs and forms of worship. If the simple dichotomy of the sheep and goats was no longer viable, then it was time to rethink the significance of Christianity. Fosdick, however, did not wish to maintain that all of the world's religions are basically the same, for although each religion bears similarities to others, each also is unique. Fosdick therefore wished to avoid too simplistic a differentiation of Christians from non-Christians as well as a too simplistic identification based on similarities, for neither seemed to fit the facts.

15

Fosdick argued that Christianity cannot rest on the beliefs held by a few orthodox Christians, for many of their beliefs are superficial. In other words, he did not believe that the essence of Christianity lies in certain beliefs—in the Bible as an inspired book, in certain alleged miracles, in the deification of the founder of Christianity, in the founder's miraculous birth, in the second coming of Christ, in the sacraments, in blood atonement, in prayer, or even in philanthropic love. None of these alone is adequate, because Christianity does not have a monopoly on such beliefs. Fosdick found at least one parallel, if not several, in the other religions of the world. Yet, Fosdick did not think that the reason for the widespread belief in various doctrines necessarily means that the different religions have copied from each other; rather, they originate in "similar emotional reactions to the mystery of the world" (39).

If Fosdick found most of the orthodox tenets superfluous, then what did he consider the essence or the uniqueness of Christianity? He said that the uniqueness of the Christian faith "lies in reverence for personality" (40). Jesus was the champion of personality, for he "thought of personality as the central fact in the universe and used it as the medium of interpretation for all other facts" (42). Fosdick suggested that the criterion for determining a Christian is not the acceptance or rejection of orthodox beliefs, but the acceptance or rejection of Jesus' attitude toward personality.

According to Fosdick, Jesus' high regard for personality determined both his attitude toward other people and his attitude or understanding of the "Creative Power in the universe." To Jesus, personality was supremely sacred, which meant that he cared about people and believed in them. This emphasis on personality has driven Christians to social action because whatever demeans personality must be removed or changed. Furthermore, the Christian approaches God in personal terms. Fosdick, however, saw little evidence that the universe is under the efficient supervision and control of a personal God; to the human mind, the universe is a mystery, and because of this mysteriousness anything that is affirmed about God can be only a partial and inadequate symbol. To ascribe the important symbol of personality to God, therefore, is to think inadequately about him. Yet personality appears to be the best symbol available, since Christians discover God most significantly in their personal lives (57).

Obviously Fosdick found little significance in the orthodox doctrine of the hypostatic union of Jesus with God. He did reason that if God is to be symbolized by personal life, then Jesus is an appropriate symbol because he is the "best" expression of personal life known to humans. This, according to Fosdick, was what the church meant when it spoke of the divinity of Jesus. The uniqueness of Jesus, then, resides in his being the leading representative of a philosophy of life that grasps the personal nature of the universe.

The central significance of personality finally leads to the question of the personal immortality of individuals. Fosdick admitted that the personal survival of the individual after death goes beyond the evidence; the belief is incredible, and the outward appearance of the corpse counts against life after death. Yet he argued that the Christian's hope of immortality is based on the importance of personality as taught by Jesus, as revealing the nature of God, and as describing the nature of the believer's experience of God (58–60).

Fosdick acknowledged that some of these beliefs are held by other world religions; while he considered that a good thing, he felt that Christianity has these beliefs in "a greater form" and "in a better balance." He also admitted that among the large numbers of people who claim the name Christian, only a few have taken seriously Jesus' reverence for personality.

Obviously Fosdick was attempting to reconcile the Christian faith with the modern world, especially with science. But rather than fixing on the scientific method as the only valid method for discerning truth and falsehood, he seemed content to allow faith and science to complement each other. While he was careful not to contradict science openly, he was willing to move beyond the evidence with respect to the kind of God he believed in and his hope of personal immortality. God did not violate the laws of nature in working miracles; he worked within the limitations of the laws of the universe. Also implied in Fosdick's view is the belief that in some sense, because of the personal character of God, God is able to enter into a personal relationship with humans. This may not be mysticism as it has been traditionally understood, but it is a form of "religious experience" whose object, namely God, cannot be verified by use of the scientific method. Moreover, Fosdick laid great stress on the importance of Jesus. He may not have been miraculously conceived, or performed miracles, or have been the second person of the trinity, or the "sacrifice" for the sins of the whole world, but he was the "Master" who understood the value of personality and who best grasped the personal nature of God.

Religious humanism was in general agreement with Fosdick in (1) emphasizing the importance of human personality; (2) seeking to make religion relevant in the modern world; (3) seeing the importance of social action in removing obstacles to personality development; (4) being aware of the existence of other world religions (although drawing different inferences from this knowledge); (5) attacking orthodox Christian doctrine and fundamentalism; and (6) believing that reverence for personality is more important than accepting certain traditional doctrines.

However, the religious humanists were not in complete accord with Fosdick, for they thought him timid in not following through with the scientific method for determining truth. They also argued that there is no evidence for the personal nature of God; the claims of religious experience can and should be interpreted within a naturalistic framework and in psychological terms. Fosdick's theistic inference was therefore not valid, and he placed too much emphasis on the importance of Jesus. Moreover, his view of personal immortality implied a mind-body dualism that is more Platonic than Christian, and that is unsupported by the "new naturalism."

Empirical Philosophy of Religion

Henry Nelson Wieman represents a second trend within the American liberal theological tradition.[7] Sometimes referred to as "religious realism," this trend also goes by the name of the "empirical philosophy of religion." Wieman sought an interpretation of religion that would not conflict with the world of science and felt that many theologians stopped short of taking the scientific method seriously. He therefore objected to any attempt to exempt religion from scientific scrutiny. Religion cannot claim to have a specific channel for obtaining its knowledge. Religious knowledge, argued Wieman, must be established in the same way as other kinds of knowledge, namely through the scientific method; only through the scientific method is it possible to distinguish truth from falsehood.

Even the problem of the existence of God must be resolved by the scientific method. Just as humans can resolve arguments about the chemical composition of water, they can resolve arguments about the existence and nature of God. Wieman thought that people in the past had been unable to resolve the problem of the existence of God because they failed properly to define the term *God*. Wieman tried to define God in such a way that his existence could be verified by the scientific method.

Through the years Wieman offered a number of definitions; they do not necessarily contradict each other, but they indicate the difficulty of obtaining the precision demanded by the scientific method.

From empirical observation, Wieman noted that humans can be led toward the best or toward the worst; that fact raises such questions as What is the best? Where is the agency that can transform humans? Wieman believed that humans, through their minds, can be creatively transformed to seek the best and avoid the worst. Anything that hinders the creative enrichment and the expansion of the human mind is therefore "evil." In contrast, a "creative interchange" can increase both understanding between individuals and human freedom. "Evil interchanges" such as manipulation and maliciousness stand in the way of creative interchange. The religious problem becomes how to enhance such creative interchange so that it can overcome the destructive, restricting types.[8]

Wieman saw that adherents to the Judeo-Christian tradition claim that love has the power to creatively transform the human mind—and even the larger society—so that the individual and society can attain the best they are capable of. The truth of this claim can be determined by a critical examination of the evidence. If love can legitimately be identified with the creative interchange, it is the value to be emphasized above all others. Creative interchange took place in Jesus' relationship with his disciples, who were thereby transformed. It continued even after his death, and the disciples interpreted this continuous transformation as the presence of the resurrected Christ in their lives (262).

Although it might go by other names, creative interchange is acknowledged in other cultures and religions. In this context Wieman finally proposed a definition of God: the power of creativity or "source of human good" that enhances and transforms human life. Wieman said, "I have tried to answer the question about God by describing the place of creativity in human life. I think that there is no other word in the English language fit to designate the religious significance of creativity except the word 'God'" (271).

Although Wieman made a bold attempt to reinterpret the tenets of the Christian faith in such a way that persons of faith can affirm the faith of the fathers and at the same time affirm the modern world in which the scientific method is the instrument for determining truth, his position was not widely accepted. Both those to his theological right and left contended that his reinterpretation distorted the historic faith. The religious humanists, to his left, maintained that his understanding of

19

God was not what the Christian church meant by the term; therefore, his interpretation was dishonest and would lead to confusion. God should either be used in the traditional sense or dropped altogether from religious vocabulary. However, the humanists endorsed Wieman's use of the scientific method as the means for arriving at the truth, and they appreciated his concern with the problem of transforming human personality so that both individuals and society can be improved.[9]

Humanistic Liberalism

A third trend in liberalism was "humanistic liberalism," as John H. Dietrich designated it in the early 1920s, but usually referred to as "religious humanism." This is the same kind of humanism we encountered under the heading of naturalistic humanism, especially that of the religious type. Roy Wood Sellars, who was a professor in the philoso–phy department at the University of Michigan during the early decades of this century, represents this point of view. In 1918, in *The Next Step in Religion,* Sellars maintained that religious humanism was that decisive next step, and a decade later, in *A Religion Come of Age*, he again argued that mature religion will be humanism.[10]

In 1928 the Humanist Fellowship was organized. It was made up mostly of students at the University of Chicago, and in April 1928 the fellowship began publication of a journal entitled the *New Humanist*. A few years later, in 1933, some members of the fellowship suggested that Sellars draft "A Humanist Manifesto."[11] He did so, and passed the draft on to Curtis W. Reese, Raymond Bragg, Edwin H. Wilson, and others, who revised and edited it for publication in the journal. This document caused quite a stir when other magazines republished it and debated its tenets.[12]

The opening statements of the Manifesto made clear that the time was past for a revision of traditional religious beliefs. This was so because twentieth-century people have a larger understanding of the universe, they have made great accomplishments through science, and they have a deeper appreciation of world brotherhood. Taking into account these developments, the religious humanists offered their Manifesto so "that religious humanism may be better understood."

The Manifesto contained fifteen short theses:

1. Religious humanists regard the universe as self-existing and not created. Of course, this is an attack on traditional theism: if the universe is eternal, there is no need for a Creator or a First Cause; there is no empirical evidence for a Necessary Being, nor does the universe reveal any teleological plan.[13]

2. *Humanism believes that man is a part of nature and that he has emerged as the result of a continuous process.* This repudiation of any doctrine of the "special creation of humans" affirms belief in the theory of evolution, which the humanists considered "a well-established theory," although they admitted some of the details needed to be worked out.

3. *Holding an organic view of life, humanists find that the traditional dualism of mind and body must be rejected.* Sellars realized that this was the most controversial thesis as well as one of the most fascinating philosophical problems. Yet its intent was to deny any belief in personal immortality. According to Sellars, this was in opposition to Christianity, which had advocated two types of dualism. First, Roman Catholicism advocated a "Christian Aristotelian" dualism that infers a bodily resurrection through God's power; since the soul is the organized form of the body, it is incomplete without it—hence the resurrection of the body. The second type of dualism is the "Platonic-Cartesian" advocated by Protestant Modernists, who were usually vague on this point but who tended to advocate an immortal soul that leaves the body behind. The humanists repudiated both types of dualism and held to the belief that consciousness is a function of the brain; when the brain is destroyed, consciousness is also, so it is impossible for consciousness to continue beyond the death of the organism.[14]

4. *Humanism recognizes that man's religious culture and civilization, as clearly depicted by anthropology and history, are the product of a gradual development due to the interaction with his natural environment and with his social heritage. The individual born into a particular culture is largely molded by that culture.* The implication here is that religions are created by humans trying to adjust to their environment. When social situations change, religion evolves accordingly. Furthermore, one belongs to a particular religious tradition because of the culture one is born into, not as a result of the "truth" of one metaphysical religious system over another.

5. *Humanism asserts that the nature of the universe depicted by modern science makes unacceptable any supernatural or cosmic guarantees of human values. Obviously humanism does not deny the possibility of realities as yet undiscovered, but it does insist that the way to determine the existence and value of any and all realities is by means of intelligent inquiry and by the assessment of their relations to human*

21

needs. Religion must formulate its hopes and plans in the light of the scientific spirit and method. This thesis denies the doctrine that God has revealed his will to humans and that good is what God commands and evil is disobedience to his will. On the contrary, humans create values and they must create a world in which people live by values. If good predominates in the world, it is because people have created good, and if evil predominates, people also have created it. There is no cosmic guarantee that good will win out, either in this life or in a world to come. In other words, people are responsible for the morality (or lack of it) in the world; furthermore, virtue is its own reward, for we are not good to please God or to gain heaven.

6. *We are convinced that the time has passed for theism, deism, modernism and the several varieties of "new thought."* The humanists believed that new interpretations of Christianity had moved so far away from the original faith, in order to save it, that misunderstanding and deception had crept in. To avoid this problem, they advocated discarding the old faith entirely and developing a new one based on a naturalistic understanding of the universe and the place of humans within it.

7. *Religion consists of those actions, purposes, and experiences which are humanly significant. Nothing human is alien to the religious. It includes labor, art, science, philosophy, love, friendship, recreation—all that is in its degree expressive of intelligently satisfying human living. The distinction between the sacred and the secular can no longer be maintained.* This statement is self-explanatory; it simply denies a dichotomy between the secular and the religious, a point of view that came of age in the 1950s and '60s through the thought of such men as Dietrich Bonhoeffer and Harvey Cox.

8. *Religious Humanism considers the complete realization of human personality to be the end of man's life and seeks its development and fulfillment in the here and now. This is the explanation of the humanist's social passion.* In contrast to the Christian churches, which often interpreted their missions as saving people for a future life in heaven, humanists sought to create a world in which all individuals could develop and live the best lives they are capable of living.

9. *In place of the old attitudes involved in worship and prayer the humanist finds his religious emotions expressed in a heightened sense of personal life and in a cooperative effort to promote social well-being.*

10. *It follows that there will be no uniquely religious emotions and attitudes of the kind hitherto associated with belief in the Supernatural.*

Sellars took theses nine and ten together and said their importance lies in altering the framework and outward character of religion. They propose a shift from supernaturalism to naturalism, from heaven to earth; with this new emphasis will come new attitudes, aims, and procedures. Prayer, for example, rather than being petitionary, will be meditative.[15]

The remaining theses briefly state social concerns that might be consistent with views other than those of humanists; they follow without explanatory comment:

11. Man will learn to face the crises of life in terms of his knowledge of their naturalness and probability. Reasonable and manly attitudes will be fostered by education and supported by custom. We assume that humanism will take the path of social and mental hygiene and discourage sentimental and unreal hopes and wishful thinking.

12. Believing that religion must work increasingly for joy in living, religious humanists aim to foster the creative in man and to encourage achievements that add to the satisfactions of life.

13. Religious humanism maintains that all associations and institutions exist for the fulfillment of human life. The intelligent evaluation, transformation, control, and direction of such associations and institutions with a view to the enhancement of human life is the purpose and program of humanism. Certainly religious institutions, their ritualistic forms, ecclesiastical methods, and communal activities must be reconstituted as rapidly as experience allows, in order to function effectively in the modern world.

14. The humanists are firmly convinced that existing acquisitive and profit-motivated society has shown itself to be inadequate and that a radical change in methods, controls, and motives must be instituted. A socialized and cooperative economic order must be established to the end that the equitable distribution of the means of life be possible. The goal of humanism is a free and universal society in which people voluntarily and intelligently cooperate for the common good. Humanists demand a shared life in a shared world.

15. We assert that humanism will: (a) affirm life rather than deny it; (b) seek to elicit the possibilities of life, not flee from it; and (c) endeavor to establish the conditions of a satisfactory life for all, not merely for a few. By this positive morale and intention humanism will be guided, and from this perspective and alignment the techniques and efforts of humanism will flow.

Those who signed the "Manifesto" were mostly professors, writers, and ministers. The most renowned signer was John Dewey of the philosophy department at Columbia University. Other important professors were J. A. C. Fagginger Auer of the Harvard Divinity School, A. Eustace Haydon, professor of comparative religions at the University of Chicago, Edwin A. Burtt, professor of philosophy at Cornell University, and John Herman Randall, Jr., professor of philosophy at Columbia University. One Reformed Jewish Rabbi, Jacob K. Weinstein, signed.

Most of the ministers who signed had a Unitarian affiliation; among them were John H. Dietrich, Curtis W. Reese, and Charles Francis Potter.

Sellars believed the significance of the religious humanist movement, as represented by the "Manifesto," was that it challenged the traditional Christian theistic tradition and offered a constructive alternative. He also argued that, although without God, humanism is a religious point of view; it has similarities to both Buddhism and Confucianism, neither of which in its early development had a belief in a supreme being. This particular Far Eastern tradition is in contrast to the Near Eastern, which almost always had doctrines of gods, heaven, and salvation, as witnessed by Judaism, Christianity, Zoroastrianism, and Islam. Sellars argued that to exclude the Far Eastern view by complete acceptance of the Near Eastern view is the height of religious provincialism; therefore, if the view of the Far East is accepted, humanism can make a legitimate claim to being a religion. Sellars concluded, "I doubt that any other religious movement has as fine a foundation in method and knowledge."[16]

As might be expected, publication of the Manifesto set off a barrage of editorial activity. The nondenominational magazine the *Christian Century* is perhaps representative of the reaction.[17] It responded with a long editorial critically evaluating each of the theses of the "religion without God." Unlike the well-reasoned editorials that have been a hallmark of the magazine through the years, this particular editorial was an impassioned outburst. Its emotional tone aside, the editorial was in agreement with several of the theses, especially those related to social betterment. But the editorial was highly critical of the denial of a mind-body dualism, which it viewed as throwing into grave question the doctrine of personal immortality. It also stated that without a "Cosmic Partner," social idealism is "sophomoric and philosophically meaningless." The writer of the editorial was not about to dispense with God, and thought any doctrine that relied only on human effort was bound to fail. Finally, the editorial questioned the legitimacy of John Dewey's support of the "Manifesto," revealing a misunderstanding of Dewey's philosophy during this period.

From this controversy, we can conclude that religious humanism grew out of the cultural milieu of American Protestant liberalism. The religious humanists thought they were leading liberalism to its logical conclusions. They thought liberals like Fosdick and Wieman were dragging their feet; they had used the scientific method up to a point and then discarded it. The religious humanists were convinced that the times demanded a move from modernist and liberal theism to naturalistic humanism. In a sense the humanists exceeded the bounds of Protestant liberalism, because in contrast to both Fosdick and Wieman, who attempted to return to the doctrines of the past, to separate the essential from the nonessential, to bring the essential into the present, and to interpret it in a way consistent with modern knowledge, they broke with an important part of the past. The religious humanists saw the Judeo-Christian tradition not as normative, but as merely one of several equally valuable traditions. To the humanists, the Jewish-Christian past was evidence of the evolutionary character of religion; it was not a norm for guiding the present, which should be guided by contemporary norms. No longer did they see a need to make the Christian faith relevant to the modern world; now the question was, What does it mean to be religious in a world of science and technology without Christian doctrines—even without belief in God? In other words, what is religion without God?

We have located religious humanism within the general field of humanism, and we have located it within an area of religious thought known as Protestant liberalism. In the next chapter we shall narrow our focus even more and examine it within the context of Unitarianism. We shall deal with the problem that has been called "the humanist-theist controversy" within the small denomination called Unitarian. The pursuit of this subject will greatly enhance our understanding of "religion without God" or religious humanism, for, as Fred G. Bratton has written, "Yet it is also true that the Protestant Revolt gave birth to the most radical of modern forces (from the Church of England came American Congregationalism, from which came Unitarianism from which came religious Humanism)...."[18]

CHAPTER 3

Religious Humanism and Unitarianism

"Any activity pursued in behalf of an ideal end against obstacles and in spite of threats of personal loss because of conviction of its general and enduring value is religious in quality."—John Dewey

UNITARIANISM IN THE UNITED STATES GREW OUT OF THE LIBERAL WING of Congregationalism, mostly in the Boston area, early in the nineteenth century.[1] In a sense, therefore, Unitarianism is a forerunner of Protestant liberalism.[2] Whereas the mainline Protestant churches contained liberals within their ranks, the Unitarians may be said to have denominationalized liberalism. As Paul Tillich said:

. . .in this country liberalism took the form of a church, Unitarianism. This never happened in Europe. There liberalism was a theological movement in the established churches, but it never established itself as a church. Perhaps this was a better solution because it seems that Unitarianism in this country suffers from its separation. It tends to be less flexible than liberal theology in Europe because it becomes bound to a church tradition.[3]

The Rise of Unitarianism in the United States

In the United States, Unitarianism began in the latter half of the eighteenth century, especially in and around Boston and, to a lesser extent, Philadelphia.[4] At that time there were two major religious movements in the colonies. One emphasized emotionalism and found its expression in the revivals of the Great Awakening. The other emphasized reason and found its expression in "rational Christianity" and deism, both products of the American Enlightenment.[5]

27

The Great Awakening revivals started in the Middle Atlantic colonies, spread into New England, and finally flourished in the South. Jonathan Edwards (1703–58), minister of the Congregational church in Northampton, Massachusetts, and an advocate of revivalism, was best known for a sermon entitled "Sinners in the Hands of an Angry God." Most revivalists were Calvinists, advocating a theory of revelation, a trinitarian doctrine of God, a substitutionary theory of atonement, and doctrines of original sin and of election or eternal damnation. Edwards himself could be self-critical, but other revivalists pandered to emotionalism to persuade people to experience "saving grace." Often they accused ministers who opposed the revivals of being unconverted.

Charles Chauncy (1705–87), minister of First Church in Boston, became especially critical of Calvinist theology and of the revivals sweeping New England. He began to formulate a more liberal theology, which was dubbed Arminianism. Jonathan Mayhew (1705–66), who had become minister at West Church, also began advocating liberal views. At about the same time, a few around Philadelphia began to promote universalist beliefs; notable mong them was John Murray (1741–1815), who later came to New England and founded the First Universalist Society in America at Gloucester, Massachusetts, in 1779. Elmo Robinson says about this period, "At first there were itinerant preachers who spread the gospel of universal salvation wherever they could find an audience to listen. Then, if a group of believers accepted the message wholeheartedly, they might organize a Universalist church, or as they preferred to call it, a Universalist society."[6] However, the growth of these societies was slow; by 1800 there were only five.

Liberal religious thought, of both Unitarian and Universalist varieties, arose as a reaction to the theological doctrines associated with Puritanism (Calvinism) and to the excesses of the Great Awakening. The liberals attacked the trinitarian doctrine of God and the notion of God's wrath. They spoke instead of the unity of God, "the Monarch of the Universe," who sought to communicate his goodness to humanity on earth. They also repudiated the doctrine of original sin, believing that individuals were neutral, not evil, at birth. Furthermore, they argued, revelation must be validated by reason. Rather than relying on faith alone, they advocated good works. They saw Jesus as a son of God, not God the son; but although he was not divine, God dwelt in him in a special way. Instead of interpreting Jesus' death as evidence of a wrathful God's seeking vengeance for human sin, the liberals were more concerned about the psychological effects of his death on human beings.

For instance, by seeing how humans had participated in the death of an innocent Jesus, they might understand how their own actions resulted in the suffering of others and repent. The liberals also denied the doctrine of particular election, maintaining that Jesus had lived and died for the whole world, not just for the elect, and that all souls were capable of salvation. Liberals viewed the revivals not as a great awakening but as a time of great terror, keenly aware of the negative psychological effects of such doctrines as an "angry God" and "eternal damnation" on families of the deceased.

As the eighteenth century wore on, a serious theological rift developed within the Standing Order of the Established Churches in Massachusetts. Since shortly after the founding of Plymouth Colony in 1620 and Massachusetts Bay Colony in 1630, the Congregational church, which had developed out of the Puritan movement in England, had been the established church. It maintained its privileged position until 1833. Following the revivals of the Great Awakening, it was evident that at least three different views had developed in the Standing Order: Calvinists who were strong advocates of the revivals; "old Calvinists" who opposed them; and a third, liberal faction, often called "Arminians," who were critical of both Calvinist theology and the revivals.[7] Most liberal churches were located around Boston, and Harvard College had become the breeding ground for "Unitarian moral theology." By 1787, King's Chapel, an Anglican church, had become Unitarian, and nine years later the First Unitarian Church in Philadelphia was organized with support from Joseph Priestley (1733–1804).

Schism in the Standing Order was precipitated by the appointment of a liberal, Henry Ware (1764–1845), to the Hollis Chair of Divinity at Harvard. Jedidiah Morse and other conservatives thought the new appointee should be a moderate Calvinist, but the majority of liberals on the committee prevailed. Morse responded by organizing the conservatives to do battle against the liberals. In 1808 they founded Andover Theological Seminary to insure that young men studying for the ministry could receive an orthodox theological education.

Morse's faction kept up the attack on the liberals until William E. Channing, the liberal minister of Federal Street Church in Boston, responded. In 1819 Channing had been invited to give the sermon at the installation of Jared Sparks, a recent Harvard graduate, at the new Unitarian church in Baltimore. Channing used this occasion to explain and promote the basic tenets of "Unitarian Christianity." In many respects, his theology simply continued the liberal thought of men such as Chauncy and Mayhew. Other liberals viewed the sermon as a fair statement of their beliefs, and the conservatives saw it as a focal point for their attacks. The sustained and bitter controversy that followed caused a rupture in the Standing Order. By 1825, the liberals had decided to form their own organization and created the American Unitarian Association. Its constitution defined the purpose of the new organization: "to diffuse the knowledge and promote the interests of pure Christianity."[9] Immediately 125 churches, 100 of them in Massachusetts, joined the new association. In Boston, only Old South Church refused to join. The members of these churches were the educators, judges, statesmen, businessmen, and leading writers of America, and many had been educated at Harvard, which had come under the control of the liberals.

For a brief period during their formative stage, the Unitarian churches along with the (trinitarian) Congregational churches enjoyed the privileges and benefits of the established Standing Order. The still separate Universalists, along with Baptists, Quakers, and Methodists, were dissenters. Universalists, however, like the Unitarians, were opposed to the Calvinist doctrine of election. They believed that Christ had died for the sins of the whole world; therefore all sinners would be saved, not just the elect. Their denominational roots went back to a group of New Englanders who, along with representatives from New York, met in Oxford, Massachusetts, on 4 September 1793.

In time these dissenting groups, led by the Baptists, joined forces, and together they were able to bring about disestablishment in Massachusetts in 1833. Although the Unitarians were limited primarily to eastern Massachuetts, their world view and values dominated that region from early in the nineteenth century until the end of the Civil War. But as changes in the broader society resulted from the growth of immigration, industry, and pluralism, the Unitarians gradually became just another denomination among many. With this change in status, they became staunch defenders of Thomas Jefferson's concept of a "wall of separation" between church and state.

The Free Religious Association

To bring the story of religious humanism up to date, we must place it in an earlier and broader context. At the end of the Civil War in the United States a number of liberal and even radical religious movements had arisen, most because of the issues raised by science, especially Darwinism and the application of the scientific method to historical documents. Eventually the scientific mode of thinking was applied to religion and even the Bible, giving rise to biblical criticism. Some utopian movements arose because they became disenchanted with mainline religion, finding a discrepancy between what people said they believed and how they actually lived. These utopians created communities in which they could live according to the doctrines they espoused. In the realm of ideas, in one way or another the impact of science was influencing the more liberal thinkers to reconcile the various conflicts between science and religion. Sometimes they reinterpreted the old doctrines of the faith in terms of the new thought, but at other times they broke away from the historic faith of their fathers and developed various theories of "scientific" theism.

Henry Bellows, the minister of All Souls Unitarian Church in New York, had served as president of the United States Sanitary Commission (a kind of forerunner of the Red Cross) during the Civil War.[10] In this position he came to appreciate the advantages of clearly and carefully thought out programs and the importance of good organization and administration in effectively implementing them. Since its founding in 1825 the American Unitarian Association had been a rather low-key and loosely organized denomination with little growth or expansion. Although Bellows thought the association had carried out the limited mission assigned to it, he also felt that it was too much a clerical operation and in outlook too restricted to Boston provincialism. He thought the time had come for some bold new thinking and that the association could benefit from a well-organized program of action. In order to carry out his plan for organization, a National Convention of Unitarian Churches was called for April 1865, to be held in All Souls Church in New York City. Up until this time, Unitarian churches had been strongly noncreedal, but at the meetings Bellows and his "Broad Church" supporters sought to have the convention accept what a group of "radicals" interpreted as a creed affirming allegiance to "Our Lord Jesus Christ." For those Unitarians who identified with the Christian tradition, such a creed simply expressed what they believed; but others found the creed objectionable, especially those who had opted for transcendentalism and those who had accepted a non-Christian "scientific theism." Among the objections of the radicals were the two following: first, Unitarians had created a noncreedal church that allowed the individual "free inquiry" and the right to private judgment in matters of religious faith; saddling Unitarians with a creed violated the principle of private judgment. Second, they agreed that religion was a universal phenomenon found among all people. However, they had an interest in and had even begun serious study of the various world religions. They knew about such founders as Buddha, Zoroaster, and Muhammad. To pledge allegiance to Jesus was perceived as "an act of sectarianism" inconsistent with their vision of a wider world fellowship. They advocated a "scientific study" of religion, but thought belief should be left to the private judgment of the individual.

The meetings in New York provided a beginning for the organization of the American Unitarian Association, albeit with some controversy. A second National Conference of Unitarian Churches was held in Syracuse during the second week of October 1866. The radicals tried to have the "creed" dropped, but failed. The name of the organization was revised to "The National Conference of Unitarian and Other Christian Churches," which of course did not appease those who did not think of themselves as Christians. The radicals left Syracuse greatly dissatisfied, believing "that Unitarians had removed forever [the] ancient principle of free inquiry and henceforward Christianity and freedom must be irreconcilable foes."[11]

Following the meetings in Syracuse, the radicals met in Boston to decide how they would respond to the trend in Unitarianism to express its faith in an exclusively Christian creed. The outcome was that, in 1867, they organized the Free Religious Association; Ralph Waldo Emerson was the first to place his name on the membership list. Most members maintained their affiliations with the American Unitarian Association, but a few, of whom Octavius Brooks Frothingham was perhaps the most prominent, withdrew and carried their churches with them. The controversy over the Unitarians adopting a Christian creedal statement continued until, at the National Conference meetings at Saratoga, in September of 1894, a compromise acceptable to the conservatives, the Broad Church group, and the radicals was finally reached. The editor of the *Unitarian* described the scene: "Many clasped hands; while others, who remembered similar debates with sadly different results, shed tears of gratitude. Such a scene has never occurred before in the history of Unitarianism."[12] The statement agreed upon reduced the religion of Jesus "to love of God and love to man," emphasized congregational polity, and cordially invited to "our fellowship any who, while differing from us in belief, are in general sympathy with our spirit and practical aims."[13] Once again Unitarians affirmed their noncreedal principle and refused to exclude any persons from membership based on the content of their belief. This decision was important, for it would open the way for the development of humanism within Unitarianism.

Although the Free Religious Association appealed to various kinds of theological and philosophical radicals within Unitarianism, it also attempted to be more inclusive. At one time the Reform rabbi Isaac M. Wise was a member. It was Wise who spearheaded efforts to organize Reform Judaism into a national Jewish denomination (the Union of American United Hebrew Congregations), to create the first school for the training of rabbis in the United States (Hebrew Union College in Cincinnati), to reform the Prayer Book, and to found and serve as editor of *American Israelite,* a weekly magazine promoting the programs of Reform Judaism.[14] A few members of the Ethical Culture movement also became members of the Free Religious Association, the most prominent being Felix Adler (1851-1933). Adler joined in 1876, even served as president from 1878-82, and remained an honorary vice-president for the next thirty years.

The significance of the Free Religious Association for understanding contemporary humanism is that it insisted that Unitarians remain true to their noncreedal policy. In the period between the two world wars this made it difficult, if not impossible, to exclude humanists from their churches.

In the early part of the present century most of the mainline Protestant churches experienced what has been called the modernist-fundamentalist controversy and were torn by bitter strife. Unlike the mainline churches, the Unitarian denomination was spared this particular controversy, but another one had a tremendous impact on it: what is generally referred to as the humanist-theist controversy. It raged over a score of years, from 1918 to 1937, and its highlights will help illuminate the relationship between religious humanism and Unitarianism.

The Beginnings of Religious Humanism in Unitarianism

Two points should be made about the period before 1918. First, the Reverend John H. Dietrich, who was minister of the Spokane, Washington, First Unitarian Church before becoming minister of the First Unitarian Society of Minneapolis in 1916, had been deliberately using the term *humanism* to refer to the message he was preaching.[15] Second, in 1917, at the annual meeting of the Western Unitarian

Conference, held in Des Moines, Iowa, Dietrich and Curtis W. Reese, minister of the Des Moines Unitarian Church, discovered that each had been preaching a similar message. While Dietrich had been speaking of "humanism," Reese had been referring to a "religion of Democracy." Reese eventually was forced by circumstances to accept Dietrich's term. In a sense the humanist movement began with this meeting between Dietrich and Reese, for the term *humanism* was subsequently used to refer to the thought of both these men as well as many others who embraced similar points of view. In 1926 Reese published a book he had originally entitled "Democratizing Religion" under the title "Humanism."

In 1916 Reese had preached a sermon in Des Moines entitled "A Democratic View of Religion." This sermon was the basis for his original conversation with Dietrich at the Western Unitarian Conference. In this sermon, Reese had compared "theocratic" or "autocratic" religion with "democratic" religion:

The theocratic view of the world order is autocratic. The humanistic view is democratic. In the theocratic order God is the autocrat; and under him are various minor autocrats, called divinities, angels, spirits, fairies, demons and the like. In the democratic order the people are the rulers of their own affairs, and above them are no autocrats, supreme or minor, whose favor they must curry.[16]

Reese explained that theocratic religion looks to God for aid in solving problems, whereas democratic religion says that humans must solve their own problems: "the method of conveyance in democratic religion is human effort, not divine intervention." Whereas theocratic religion seeks the kingdom of God beyond history, democratic religion seeks the "democracy of humanity" in history; democratic religion seeks human welfare, disagreeing with the Westminster divines that "the chief end of man is to glorify God, and to enjoy him forever."

Reese concluded that autocratic religion is primarily concerned with "other-worldliness" in contrast to democratic religion's concern with "this worldliness." Democratic religion advocates: "seize the 'eternal-now,' live in the 'eternal-now,' for the 'eternal-tomorrow' never is. The chief end of man... is to promote human welfare here and now."

During this period the attention of Americans was focused on the First World War, and the Unitarian denomination was in a state of lethargy. Within Unitarianism the Midwest had generally been more theologically radical than the more conservative East. Even so, Reese and Dietrich had ventured dangerously far from the Protestant liberalism preached from most Unitarian pulpits. If they continued to preach their radicalism, it was bound to become public and to cause controversy.[17]

The first sign of a gathering storm came when the *Christian Register,* the Unitarian magazine published in Boston, carried a short article by Dietrich on its front page.[18] Dietrich's title had been "The Religion of Man," but in order to make it less offensive Albert C. Diffenbach, the editor, changed it to "The Religion of Experience." However, not only the title but the content proved controversial, for an officer of the American Unitarian Association reproved Diffenbach for publishing it.

In that article Dietrich referred to two kinds of religion. One is religion that thrives on human weakness and failure. Built upon threats of punishment, it teaches humans to turn to a supernatural power as the source of all blessings and promises them a better existence in another world after death. The second religion, in contrast, has faith in people and "looks for no help or consolation from without." It turns human effort from seeking heaven "whence no help comes, to a firm and confident reliance upon themselves, in whom lie the possibilities of all things." Humans do not go to a kingdom beyond this life; they create their kingdom on this earth.

Dietrich maintained that the world would be radically different if the churches had preached the second type of religion instead of the first. He felt the second type needed no argument, for "it is transparently true. It is the universal experience of man through the ages." In this article, Dietrich's humanism was obvious; it was the same kind of humanism he had been preaching for the past four years. The fact that a denominational official, especially a Unitarian, would deplore the publication of this article was an omen of controversy.

In the same year that Dietrich's article appeared, Reese resigned as minister of the Des Moines church to become secretary of the Western Unitarian Conference whose office was in Chicago. In his administrative position Reese suggested that the *Christian Register* carry an article on professor Roy Wood Sellars, who at that time was associate professor of philosophy at the University of Michigan. He had written four books, of which *The Next Step in Religion* (1918) was the most recent. Sidney S. Robins, minister of the Unitarian church in Ann Arbor to which Sellars belonged, wrote the article; it was published under the title "What Is a Humanist? This Will Tell You."[19]

In an interview with Robins, Sellars had said that religion must move in the direction of humanism. This meant, on the negative side, relinquishing those beliefs intertwined with supernaturalism; on the positive side, it meant an increasing insight into the nature of human happiness and how to achieve it. Sellars said the church must give up the idea that it can teach final truth on any subject, for example, immortality. Belief in immortality, said Sellars, is a "speculative point," not a sacred tenet, and it must be discussed freely. Because it is speculative, immortality should move from the foreground of concern to the background. Similarly, the existence of God is a problem of speculation that should not be embodied in religious creed. Both the attitude that atheism is a word of reproach and the attitude of the dogmatic atheist are out of place in humanistic religion—"Men should be able to discuss speculative questions without affecting their religious fellowship." Jesus of the gospels is a creation of the religious and ethical spirit of the times in which he lived. He had some keen insights and some that were not so keen; he therefore can be accepted as only a qualified authority. When religion becomes humanistic, Sellars thought that there would still be a place for the church. He considered Protestant worship too barren and unappealing; he believed that the "aesthetic element" of worship should be developed and that humanistic religion has a place for ritual. He criticized Unitarianism for being overly intellectual; to restore a proper balance, it must add aesthetic and social dimensions. "There must be," he said, "an added stress upon social problems and education for social life." Since, he said, the Bible is no longer considered the inspired word of God to be interpreted by the preacher, the old emphasis on preaching had been undermined. But although the preacher had no unique body of revealed truth to teach, there was still a place for ministers. Their function had become "to lead the thought of the congregation along lines that are helpful to them." The church should provide opportunities for open discussion to consider all sides of any worthwhile subject. It would appear that one of the main functions of the humanistic church would be as a kind of society for continuing adult education.

The Sellars interview drew strong—and opposite—reactions:

A lady in New Jersey writes to continue the paper, with the comment that he had made plain what she has been vaguely thinking for years, and she is grateful beyond words that we published the admirable article. A gentleman in Washington, D. C., as heartily dissents, and says for such a religion he would not give a dime, and we ought not to have given an interview on such a line place in a Unitarian paper. We are in duty bound to teach God![20]

The editorial concluded that Professor Sellars had made a contribution to liberal religion by making some people "intellectually angry" about some important issues.

From the perspective of this study, Sellars's entry into the discussion was important for two reasons: first, it added a little more fuel to the simmering controversy; second, it represented the entry of members of the academic community into the humanist movement. As we shall see, many academics came to identify with this infant movement as it struggled to grow.

The same summer that the interview with Sellars appeared, 1920, Reese spoke at the Unitarian Summer School, held at the Harvard Divinity School. In his address, "The Content of Religious Liberalism," Reese brought to the East the kind of liberal thinking that was going on in many of the churches of the Midwest.[21] Needless to say, the address was most controversial; in fact, it was so well remembered that an editorial in the *Christian Register* referred to it even six years later. According to an editorial in that journal, some of the strong were indignant, but the weak went so far as to weep. During one of the discussions that followed, one participant passionately affirmed that he would rather have his arm severed from his body than to have God taken from his religion.[22]

In his introduction to the Divinity School address, Reese spoke about religious liberalism in historical terms, emphasizing "spiritual freedom," "the supremacy of reason," "the primary worth of character," and "the immediate access of man to spiritual sources." The main body of his address was divided into three parts. Under the heading of "personality," he noted that the spiritual focus had shifted from the supernatural to the natural, from God to humans. With this shift, rather than being concerned about God, now humans could see "personality as the thing of supreme worth." The value of an institution, especially a religious one, therefore, is determined by its contribution to the development of the creative personality.

Next Reese spoke of the "community of interests," emphasizing that human beings are interdependent, "that the fulfillment of the individual self requires orderly, purposeful association with other selves." In this context Reese touched on social ethics, believing that the type of relationship between people is important; thus, whatever stands in the way of good interactions must be changed, not only in nations but also in the world: "The next step to world progress is the proper coordination of economic forces with intellectual, moral, and spiritual forces."

The final section, "cosmic-cooperation," was the most controversial part of Reese's address. As he had done previously in his "Democratic View of Religion," he attacked the "autocratic" view of people's relationship to the deity; he opposed any understanding of God that demanded persons to prostrate themselves before God like serfs before a feudal lord. He said that liberalism must remain open on the question of the existence of God, and then he dropped his explosive statement: "Liberalism is building a religion that would not be shaken even if the very thought of God were to pass away." Reese closed with the thought that as humans learn more about the cosmic process, they can work with, and at times even control, it. "Consciously to become a co-worker with cosmic processes" he said, "is spiritual experience deep and abiding."

Not only had a minister of an important pulpit and a well-respected university professor advocated religious humanism, but now it was being preached by a man who held an important administrative post in the Unitarian denomination itself. The theists were beginning to stir from their theological slumber. It was after the controversy following this summer address that Reese finally embraced the term *humanism* to describe his religious point of view. Unlike Dietrich, he felt "the label was thrust upon us, we did not choose it."[23]

The Humanist-Theist Controversy

In 1921 the humanist-theist controversy finally came out into the open. In planning the program of the Western Unitarian Conference to take place in Chicago that spring, Reese invited Dietrich to give an address. Dietrich accepted. He was then under consideration as the new minister of the Independent Religious Society of Chicago, whose pastor, M. M. Mangasarian, was nearing retirement. Dietrich's address, therefore, served the dual purpose of meeting his obligation to the conference and allowing the pulpit committee to hear him speak. Because the society was a large and liberal group, Dietrich was, not surprisingly, at his liberal best.[24] He spoke on "The Outlook for Religion" and predicted that religion would have no outlook unless it could be brought into harmony with modern thought; this meant relinquishing the idea of a divine being in control of the universe and telling humans they are the masters of their own destiny. In other words, religion had an outlook only if it became humanistic.

After Dietrich spoke, George A. Dodson, professor of philosophy at Washington University, told Reese of his displeasure over Dietrich's address. Dodson—a theist, a philosophical idealist, and a theological liberal—went so far in his complaint to Reese as to say that a man with Dietrich's views should be barred from addressing a Unitarian conference. Reese replied that freedom of thought and expression were the cornerstones of Unitarianism; Dietrich had as much right to express his views at a conference as anyone else.

Dodson, however, did not accept Reese's explanation, and he took the matter further by writing an article, "Clear Thinking or Death," which appeared in the *Christian Register*.[25] Dodson began by saying that the liberal churches were in trouble. He disagreed with those who maintained that the liberal churches stood for nothing but liberty and that the time had arrived for clear thinking and for those of courage to take a stand if the churches were to be saved. Although he recognized that liberty was important, he also assumed a common faith in God and maintained churches were formed for worship and communion with God. Although this common faith was never formally required by Unitarianism, he never expected it to be denied. Now, he said,

A speaker in the Western Conference in May declared in a clear, sincere, and forceful address that theism must be given up, that the thought of God will have to go, and that the long evolution of the idea of God is to end in no idea at all, and that the future belongs to an atheistic humanism. When a protest was made to the Western Secretary, stating that such addresses ought not to be given under circumstances in which they will naturally be regarded as representative, he defended his action, saying that we stand for nothing but liberty.

Dodson had inferred from his discussion with Reese that Reese considered theism inessential in determining candidates for a vacant pulpit, and that Reese approved of men who preached "atheistic humanism." Dodson estimated that perhaps only 2 percent of the members of Unitarian churches would support a program without some belief in God.

Returning to his earlier point that "Unitarian churches do have a common faith, however reluctant they may be to give it statement," he moved on to say that the public would be confused to hear of a religious fellowship preaching both atheism and faith in God. Furthermore, he did not think that theists could enthusiastically preach their faith if their colleagues believed that it was primitive superstition. Nor did he think that laymen would support such a church financially. He concluded by saying that neither outright atheism, nor process philosophy, nor projection theories of God would do, for the time had come to "avow our faith in God, even though the statement of that faith may remind us of a creed." The refusal to take such a position, he maintained, would imply acceptance of humanism and lead to the extinction of the denomination, "which confusion and negation deserve."

From the time Dodson's article appeared in August until the Unitarian National Conference met in Detroit in early October, a large exchange of letters took place in the *Christian Register*. Dietrich had already been invited to speak at the Detroit meeting; when he read Dodson's article, he wrote Palfrey Perkins, secretary of the General Unitarian Conference, offering to withdraw from the program because it was obvious that Dodson as well as others thought his views unrepresentative of Unitarian thinking. Dietrich, one of three speakers asked to address "The Faith That Is in Us," obviously had been invited because of his particular point of view. Although Perkins refused on principle to allow Dietrich to withdraw, the program committee decided to substitute Dr. William L. Sullivan, an outspoken defender of theism, for one of the other speakers. Sullivan joined forces with Dodson, and the two were determined that the Detroit meeting would adopt some kind of statement of faith affirming theism.

Sullivan's background was interesting. He had been a preceptor at the College of the Paulist Fathers in Georgetown and had left the Roman Catholic church because "he refused to sign the anti-modernist oath imposed by Pius X upon all Catholic teachers in 1907."[26] Through the influence of the Reverend Minot Simons, Sullivan came into Unitarianism and moved quickly from the Unitarian Church in Schenectady to All Souls Church in New York City, an influential church in the denomination. Sullivan had a good mind and was an effective speaker, although he was considered conservative by Unitarian standards. He also was more interested in personal piety than in social meliorism as advocated by the humanists.

In mid-August Sullivan came openly to Dodson's defense with an article, "God, No-God, Half-God," published in the *Christian Register*.[27] Sullivan attacked those preachers and college professors who advocated "No-God," some of whom, he said, argued that one who worships God is a "servile person," whereas others argued that one should not bow down to an undemocratic thing, not even God. Next, he attacked the "Half-God" group, that is, those who advocated "the God who blunders and flounders and experimentally struggles." Although Sullivan could appreciate this group's attempt to reconcile religion with modern experience, he believed that they raised more problems than they solved. Finally, he advocated a traditional theism; most of his article is devoted to discrediting the "Half-God" view from his theistic perspective.

With Reese and Dietrich leading the humanist group and with Dodson and Sullivan marshaling the theists, the controversy appeared headed for a solution in Detroit. But before we examine the meeting itself, two further letters to the editor of the *Christian Register*, by Reese and by Dodson, should be mentioned.[28] Reese argued against using a creed to determine who will be accepted as members or ministers of Unitarian churches. Believing that those churches with established creeds were now either trying to readjust them to the new age or trying to abandon them altogether, Reese said that were Unitarians to demand a creed, they would be saddled with "illiberal liberalism." He maintained that people came into Unitarianism wanting a noncreedal religion, something different. Unitarians, therefore, should not be tied by the "dead hand" of the past, for it would open the door to "instituting heresy trials in a liberal fellowship."

Reese judged theism to be "a respectable philosophical hypothesis,—nothing more" and argued that theists cannot agree among themselves what they mean by the term *God*, for the word has been variously interpreted. Furthermore, theism is not necessary to account for the order and purpose in the universe, for "an extra ruler is being found superfluous." Hence "it is out of the question to require men to commit themselves on highly controversial technical metaphysical problems before commending them to the churches or inviting them to address a conference." Reese concluded forcefully by saying that the Unitarian movement would not consent to throttling the human mind: at most, "theism is *philosophically possible, but not religiously necessary.*"

Three weeks after Reese's letter was published and two weeks before the conference began, Dodson's letter appeared in the *Christian Register*. In it he tried to answer the letters written in response to his original article. He acknowledged that the Detroit conference, scheduled for early October, could not legislate the beliefs of all Unitarians. But although the conference could not say what Unitarians *must* believe, it could say what they generally *did* believe. Dodson asked, "Can we not say that while liberty of thought is guaranteed to all, ministers and laymen alike, as a matter of fact, in the use of our freedom the vast majority of us accept the teaching of Jesus that we are the children of God, and that our religion is that of the Twenty-third Psalm, the Lord's Prayer, and the Sermon on the Mount?" Dodson and Sullivan intended to get the conference to agree to some kind of confession of faith that would affirm theism—and by implication repudiate humanism, or at least point to its small minority status within the denomination.

At last the time of the General Conference in Detroit arrived. On Wednesday night, 5 October 1921, three speakers addressed a large and interested audience on "The Faith That Is in Us." First to speak was the Reverend Dilworth Lupton of Cleveland, Ohio, who gave a calm, undogmatic confession of faith in theism. He was followed by Dietrich, then by Sullivan. It was really Dietrich and Sullivan the audience had come to hear.

In his address Dietrich asked whether Unitarians held a common faith. He spoke of faith not in any "mystical sense," but meant the "deepest convictions as to truth and duty"—that is, "if one's faith is clear, his duty is self-evident."[29]

Dietrich observed that one cannot help seeing the pain and suffering, the poverty and misery, and the hatred and strife around the world. He said that Unitarians thought these conditions could be overcome. Dissatisfaction with the present order and a hope that a new one could be brought about was the common faith holding the various types of Unitarians together. This common faith is not unique to Unitarians; the early Christian also had it, in their strong convictions about the coming "kingdom of God." Dietrich said, "It was not the pathetic tale of the life of Jesus, nor the tragic story of his death; no, nor the innocent myth of his triumphant resurrection"; it was this faith in the coming of the kingdom of God that gave the early Christians power, and their faith that the world can be changed can empower Unitarians.

The mainline denominations, said Dietrich, had not been concerned with changing the present social order and creating the "Commonwealth of Man." In fact, having sanctioned the present social order, they had little impulse to create a new one. With the traditional churches refusing to champion social change, Dietrich was convinced that this was the task of Unitarianism. He sounded like an ancient biblical prophet when he proclaimed that the world "does not need an ecclesiastical religion, it does not need more priests and prayers and holy books, it does not need literary essays on academic subjects; but it does need the voice of the prophet going up and down the land, crying 'Prepare ye the way of mankind, and make its way straight.'"

Dietrich thought the power to realize the great ideals of humanity resided in humans themselves: "The kind of world we live in depends not upon some God outside of man, but upon man himself, or, as some of us would put it, upon the God that dwells in humanity. It matters not which way you put it, the responsibility clearly rests upon man...."

In many respects, Dietrich had turned the traditional concept of the "kingdom of God," which would be ushered in by an act of God, into the "Commonwealth of Man," which can be realized only through human effort. He knew that a perfect social order was impossible: "It is not necessary that [we] actually hope to witness its establishment; it is enough that [we] can think of it, that [we] can believe in its coming, that [we] can work for it with [our] hands and. . .brain." Dietrich's humanism was obvious; he placed responsibility for the kind of world we live in, in humans themselves. "If there is ever to be established an era of peace and justice and goodwill," he said, "we insist that it depends upon ourselves—upon what we are and what we do."[30] When Dietrich finished, the audience broke into applause. Both the small group who shared his views and the young social gospelers were moved.

Sullivan, following Dietrich to the podium and considering his predecessor dangerous, was intent upon destroying any effect Dietrich might have on the conference. Sullivan began his offensive by immediately attacking the view that a single Unitarian could not speak for the whole body, for such a position implied that the Unitarian church is "nowhere and stands for nothing." He deemed liberty without content an evasion of public accountability and argued that historically the Unitarian church had stood for something:

> That man is under a law which he has got to obey because of its divineness, and that the oracle of this law which he must obey or be recreant is conscience within his soul; the faculty of the moral judgment and discernment which, like every other began from humble origins but which goes forward toward the ever deepening sense of the divine authority of the law which it progressively discovers.[31]

To substantiate his position, Sullivan outlined briefly the growth of awareness and conscience in the individual: from the infant driven solely by instinct to an awareness of mother, of family, of school, city, nation, of all humanity, and finally of the moral law of the universe. The moral law seeks to lead humans to righteousness, but what is its source? Sullivan maintained, "A law that prescribes right to souls must come from a source that has the right and authority to command souls, therefore itself at least a soul." Sullivan basically offered a moral argument for the existence of God, for he moved from a moral awareness to a cause of that awareness, namely God.

43

Sullivan acknowledged the vehemence of his speech, but justified his attitude because the issue was so critical. He was convinced that when an individual or a nation lost its vision of God, "that loss is chaos and the wreck of worlds." He argued holy law is "austere and awful," but a redeeming love forgives those who disobey it, when there is "adequate contrition." Sullivan believed that his own faith was traditional Unitarianism, that the church stood for something theistic, and that if one had lost this faith, then, in the name of truth, one should move elsewhere.

In addition to presenting his position rationally, Sullivan attacked Dietrich personally. In doing so, he miscalculated, for he lost much of the support he had had from theists when he stepped to the podium. An editor commented: "Following Mr. Dietrich immediately, the contrast, or at least the difference, was the most impressive thing." (Edited versions of both Dietrich's and Sullivan's addresses appeared in the *Christian Register*.)

Obviously there was much support for Sullivan's position, but he hurt his cause by his personal attacks on Dietrich. Dodson and Sullivan had come to the conference prepared with a resolution that the conference should formulate a Unitarian statement of faith, a kind of creed that would at least assert belief in the existence of God. After Sullivan's address, they decided not to submit the resolution; it was obvious they lacked the delegates to win.

From hindsight, what happened in Detroit was decisive, for the opportunity to pass a creedal statement about belief in God would never be greater. The controversy was not over, for at times over the ensuing years, strong feelings erupted. But as the years passed and humanists and theists worked together, they generally found the small Unitarian denomination large enough to embrace both points of view.

Another attempt to bring the humanist-theist controversy into the open began with an article that appeared in the *Christian Register* in November 1928.[32] In this article the Reverend Marion Franklin Ham, minister of the Unitarian church in Reading, Massachusetts, argued that humanism and atheism are synonymous, that science does not support humanism any more than it does theism, and that "religion without God" is a religion without meaning and motive power. Such a Unitarian denomination, he said, would lose its "influence and usefulness as a fellowship of free churches."

Dietrich responded to Ham's article with a letter to the editor. He said that while science may not support humanism, it certainly does not support theism; humanism, in fact, is closer to science because "it refuses to make assumptions for which there is no scientific justification."[33] Dietrich also wondered where Ham had received his assurance of some other realm of knowledge supporting "our faith and hope." Ham had implied that it comes from religious experience; Dietrich asked how, when, or where one heard the "voice of the living God." He confessed that no one had tried harder than he, but he had received no sound, only silence.

Dietrich suggested that Ham equated humanism with atheism because he used the terms to refer to those who did not share his own understanding of God. As for Ham's belief that humanism was having an ill effect on the denomination, Dietrich maintained that one could not place loyalty to an organization above loyalty to truth regardless of the consequences. He denied that "religion without God" has no meaning or motive power, pointing out that Buddhism had started as a religion without God and that it had done very well. (Note that Dietrich used the term "religion without God" in this 1928 letter, written a year before his 1929 sermon by that title.)

Ham refused to accept Dietrich's criticisms. In January 1929 he sent another letter to the editor, which ended the discussion.[34] Ham replied that Dietrich had failed to show that humanism and atheism were not the same; he, Ham, would continue to think them synonymous. Further, he said, theism makes no claims to scientific evidence; it is based on faith. Finally, Ham agreed with Dietrich that one should not choose an organization over truth; since, however, Ham questioned the truth of humanism, he was convinced it would be wrong for the denomination to follow a false path that would destroy it.[35]

Publication of "A Humanist Manifesto" in 1933 rekindled the discussion and brought new voices into the debate.[36] The "Manifesto" was issued at this particular time because the American people were in the midst of a great economic depression and many had given up hope; the election of Franklin D. Roosevelt to the presidency and his "New Deal" policies caused many humanists to feel more optimistic. They pointed out that while humans were in their great need the gods had remained silent; if humans wanted to improve their lot, they must do so themselves.[37] In a sense, the "Manifesto" was an attempt to offer people hope in the midst of despair. After its publication, Unitarians were again discussing humanism and theism; professors from other denominations were discussing humanism with the signers of the document. Even the *Inquirer,* the weekly journal of British Unitarianism, published the "Manifesto," and a short-lived but heated discussion ensued in English Unitarianism.[38] Finally, it was asked why certain prominent humanists had not signed. Professor Max C. Otto of the University of Wisconsin, for example, refused to sign because he thought it would "serve no sufficient purpose," while professor Charles Lyttle of the Meadville Theological School refused because it appeared to him to be simply a new creed and he was opposed in principle to endorsing any creedal statement.[39] Those who did sign began to interpret the document differently. David Rhys Williams, minister of the Unitarian church in Rochester, New York, said that the "Manifesto" was consistent with "faith in an in-dwelling God whose power and presence can be substantiated by the facts of man's mystical experience."[40] In referring to Williams's interpretation, Sellars, who wrote the original draft of the "Manifesto," replied: "...I believe his is a forced reading which is unique with him, and not shared with the other signers."[41]

The Controversy Subsides

In 1934, the year after the publication of the "Manifesto," the American Unitarian Association established a Commission on Appraisal as a result of low morale and a recession in denominational expansion. Frederick May Eliot, minister of the Unitarian church in St. Paul, Minnesota, was made chairman of the study commission; its report, entitled "Unitarians Face a New Age," published in 1936, recommended some sweeping changes. Louis C. Cornish, who had been president of the association since 1927, decided that it was in the best interests of the denomination that he resign so that Eliot might assume the presidency and lead the denomination in carrying out the commission's recommendations.

Some of the theists were reluctant to have Eliot president, however, fearing that under his administration the humanists would have greater influence. Eliot had contributed to *Humanist Sermons,* a book edited by Curtis W. Reese, and although he was a liberal theist of sorts, he was open to the humanist movement within the denomination. The theists nominated the Reverend Charles R. Joy for the presidency. Joy accepted the nomination, for he thought Eliot too liberal and unrepresentative of the views of most Unitarians. The humanist-theist controversy seemed about to precipitate another battle, perhaps with great deal of damage to the denomination. But both factions realized that nothing could be accomplished by a denominational hassle and much could be lost. Representatives of both groups met; Joy was persuaded to withdraw his name, and Eliot was elected president without a contest.[42]

The humanists were solidly behind Eliot's candidacy, so his election signified to them that their views would be respected and represented in the denominational literature, programs, and personnel. The compilation of a new hymnal, *Hymns of the Spirit* (1937), was the joint effort of both humanists and theists, and consequently it contained humanistic as well as theistic hymns, responsive readings, and doxologies. The Beacon course in religious education was rewritten to reflect the educational philosophy of John Dewey, and Beacon Press published books by humanists as well as those of theists.

In 1938 Edwin H. Wilson, a leading humanist and minister of the Third Unitarian Church in Chicago, wrote an article in which he advocated speaking of the humanist-theist controversy in historical terms:

> We should now be able, theists willing, to regard the controversy as history. The lesson of history, however, ought not to be forgotten; it served as an occasion for creative and vitalized thinking. And its greatest significance was the extension to the men who fill Unitarian pulpits of the freedom that had already been granted to the men who sit in Unitarian pews.[43]

A decade later, Walter D. Kring and Raymond A. Sabin wrote an article, "Humanism, Theism and Unitarianism," in which, using some of the categories from Whitehead's *Religion in the Making,* they attempted to shed light on the issues involved between the humanists and theists. For example, Whitehead refers to three different meanings of the word *God:* the Asiatic concept, which emphasizes the impersonal order to which the world conforms; the Semitic concept, which refers to a personal deity who exists as a metaphysical "fact" and who created and orders the world; and pantheism, which considers God the only true reality and the world merely a phase in the being of God. Kring and Sabin believed that the differences between the humanists and theists were like the differences between the Asiatic and Semitic concepts of God; just as the East and West must coexist and make adjustments to each other, so must the humanists and theists. Kring and Sabin acknowledged the right of both humanists and theists to exist in the same religious body, just as Orientals and Occidentals have a right to exist in the same world:

> So long as our differences do not result in bitter and personal controversy, we

47

should rejoice that we have the opportunity in our free fellowship to exchange viewpoints and to have some part in exploring this mysterious and fathomless universe....Unitarians of every variety of belief may unite in their concern for those values open to inspection to all....[44]

In 1954 Charles E. Park's "Why the Humanism-Theism Controversy Is out of Date" was published as a pamphlet by the American Unitarian Association and was widely circulated. Park maintained that both the humanists and the theists have the same evidence. For example, the humanist says: "You cannot know that God exists; therefore, he does not exist." The theist, on the other hand, says: "You cannot know that God does not exist; therefore he exists." Park argued that "both positions have the same support from knowledge—none at all. Belief in God and denial of God are alike matters of faith, not of knowledge."[45]

According to Park, both humanists and theists are speculating; the main difference is that humanists stop sooner than theists. But this degree of speculation is no ground for ill feeling, argued Park: "Would it not be well to remember that our resources are too meager and our energies too scanty to be wasted in needless controversy?"[46] Both can live with their different speculations and be "best of friends."

We have now examined religious humanism within the context of Unitarianism by touching on the highlights of what has been called the humanist-theist controversy. We saw how, as the second decade of this century drew to a close, the humanists began to assert themselves within a small liberal denomination and, as the third decade of the century approached, people outside Unitarianism began to take account of religious humanism, this strange abnormality of "religion without God." Before the fourth decade had arrived the humanists and theists had become sufficiently accustomed to one another to live within Unitarianism without bitter controversy. To some of the more traditional theists the issue was God or no-God, and they were convinced that one could not be religious without belief in God; to some of the more radical humanists the issue centered on the problem of evidence and belief in the supernatural; finding insufficient evidence for the latter they became convinced naturalists. Others saw the issue in terms of the freedom of the ministers in the pulpit to affirm their faith or doubts, just as the people in the pew had been able to do; this implied that one might be called as minister of a Unitarian society without believing in God. It was argued further that because religion was more basic than a belief in God, it was unnecessary to postulate God as its "cause." Still others focused upon the problem of "spiritual freedom"—that is, the freedom of individuals to follow the dictates of their own conscience without being removed from the fellowship of a religious society, and the corresponding freedom of a religious society to "call" a minister whether humanist or theist. This last issue, although not completely divorced from the others, posed the real dilemma for Unitarians, for they could not oust the humanists without destroying the "cornerstone" of their religious fellowship, namely, freedom of speech and the spirit of tolerance. Humanism therefore was able to advance after 1921 because generally the presidents of the denomination (although some held more conservative views) as well as its members believed firmly in spiritual freedom and congregational autonomy.

With religious humanism located within humanism, American Protestant liberalism, and Unitarianism, we are now ready to examine in some detail the thought of three pioneers of religious humanism. We have chosen for our purposes John H. Dietrich, "the father of religious humanism," Curtis W. Reese, "the statesman of religious humanism," and Charles F. Potter, "the rebel of religious humanism." As we shall consider the men in this order, we now turn to the thought of John H. Dietrich.

PART II

★   ★   ★

THREE PIONEERS

OF

RELIGIOUS

HUMANISM

★   ★   ★

CHAPTER 4

John H. Dietrich:
The Father of
Religious Humanism

*"On the subject of the gods, I am not in a position to know whether they exist
or not, or what they look like. Too many things prevent one from knowing:
lack of evidence and the brevity of human life."—Protagoras*

JOHN H. DIETRICH WAS BORN ON 14 JANUARY 1878, ON A FARM near
Chambersburg, Pennsylvania.[1] His family had descended from some
German-Swiss who had emigrated to Franklin County, Pennsylvania, in
1710 from the vicinity of Berne, Switzerland. Dietrich's parents were
simple, uneducated farm people, his father being a fairly successful
sharecropper. His family professed the Reformed faith, which had
originated with Ulrich Zwingli, the Zurich reformer in the sixteenth-
century Protestant Reformation.[2] A rural minister suggested that young
John, who was a good student, become a minister.

In 1893 the Dietrichs moved to the village of Marks, Pennsylvania,
and John entered Mercersburg Academy. He managed to crowd four
years of work into three, while walking eight miles a day to and from the
academy and doing farm chores; yet he graduated as valedictorian of his
class in 1896. In 1900 he graduated from Franklin and Marshall College
in Lancaster, Pennsylvania, and returned to Mercersburg as a teacher;
his tenure there was short lived, however, because of a misunderstanding over a faculty drinking incident.

The following fall he obtained a position as private secretary to the
multimillionaire Jonathan Thorne, of New York. During this time
Dietrich went occasionally with the Thornes to religious services at All

Souls Unitarian Church in New York City. When he had saved enough money to return to school, Dietrich entered the Eastern Theological Seminary of the Reformed Church, which was affiliated with his alma mater, while continuing to work for Thorne during his summer vacations.

Although he was a good student in both college and seminary, Dietrich was not particularly excited by his school work. At seminary he found his professor of church history, who also taught the history of church dogma, the most interesting; however, Dietrich ultimately became disenchanted with him. As the leader of his class, Dietrich was to read a paper he had written on the history of Christian doctrine at the graduation exercises. In this paper Dietrich apparently stated that Jesus had died the death of a martyr, that he was not a God dying for the sins of the world, and that the obligation of the Christian was to emulate his spiritual example. The professor acknowledged the excellence of the paper and his agreement with its point of view, but he suggested it be toned down to avoid upsetting some of the clergymen who would be present at the reading. Although Dietrich agreed to a number of revisions, he lost respect for his favorite professor.

Immediately after his graduation from seminary in 1905, Dietrich became the minister of St. Marks Memorial Church in Pittsburgh, a church that had been built by a man named Bernard Wolff as a memorial to his brother. When Dietrich assumed the ministry, Wolff's wife and daughter were still members of the church and they were of the opinion that it could not survive without their financial support. The first couple of years went smoothly and the church experienced steady growth. Eventually, however, Dietrich decided to devote more time to sermon preparation and less time to member visitation. He also decided that it was time to update the order of service and to select a new hymnal. The Wolffs, displeased with these changes, at first threatened and then carried out the threat to withdraw their financial support. Because new members had come into the church and because the church generally supported its minister, it was able to survive.

In time, however, a number of factors coalesced and their combined effect was that Dietrich left the ministry of the Reformed Church. The first factor was related to the Wolffs' determination to rid St. Mark's of this upstart. A new science building was being built at Franklin and Marshall College, and the Wolffs had promised to contribute a large sum to help with the endowment of the new laboratory, but let it be known that the money would not be provided unless Dietrich resigned his position at St. Mark's. Hence, one of his former professors approached him, seeking his resignation, but to no avail. Second, Dietrich had once invited Rabbi J. Leonard Levy, a liberal and popular Reform rabbi, to speak at St. Mark's. Because such a gesture was unheard of in the Reformed Church at the time, some of the more conservative ministers became convinced that Dietrich was a radical. Third, a certain professional jealousy had developed among the Reformed clergy against Dietrich, who had been too successful. During his relatively short tenure at St. Mark's the membership had doubled and attendance at the Sunday services had tripled; even members of other Reformed churches often came to hear the popular young minister. Finally, there was a genuine concern in the Allegheny Classis of the Reformed Church about Dietrich's unorthodox doctrine. In fact, theologically, he was a theistic Protestant liberal; in his sermons he often compared orthodox doctrines with liberal ideas, so that his congregation could see clearly the issues involved.[3]

In time all these factors came together and a committee was established by the Allegheny Classis to determine whether Dietrich should be tried for heresy. The committee concluded Dietrich did not believe in the infallibility of the Bible, or in the virgin birth and deity of Jesus, or in the traditional understanding of the atonement. He accepted the theory of evolution, and he had revised the worship service to eliminate the Apostles Creed and incorporate secular readings. The committee recommended that Dietrich be indicted for heresy, hoping that he would resign before a trial was actually held.

The heresy trial was set for 10 July 1911. At first Dietrich planned to present a well-prepared defense, but eventually he decided that such a move would accomplish nothing. He refused to defend himself and was "defrocked," despite the continuous support of his board of trustees and the members, generally, at St. Mark's. After his final Sunday as minister, St. Mark's was closed. The next service was not held there until a year later.[4]

The minister of the First Unitarian Church in Pittsburgh, Dr. Walter L. Mason, was much impressed with Dietrich and recommended that he be invited into ministerial fellowship with the American Unitarian Association. Dietrich accepted. Mason even went so far as to invite Dietrich to become his associate with the idea that in time he would take over as senior minister of the church, but Dietrich refused this generous offer because he felt it would be dishonorable to relocate so near his old church.

On 1 September 1911, Dietrich became the minister of the First Unitarian Society of Spokane, Washington. When he arrived he had a congregation of about sixty that met in a run-down frame building. When he left Spokane in 1916, the congregation had grown to more than fifteen hundred and met in the newly completed Clemmer Theater. While at Spokane, on 25 August 1912, Dietrich married Louise Erb of Appleton, Wisconsin, whom he had met on a steamer returning from Europe in 1910.

In 1913 and 1914 Dietrich lectured on comparative religions. As a result, he began to question even his liberal view of Jesus as the greatest spiritual leader of all history. He came to believe that the world owed a great debt to Buddha, Confucius, the Hebrew prophets, and the Greek philosophers. He also accepted the "scientific method" as the most effective means for arriving at truth. He began to refer to prayer as "aspiration" and to use secular readings in his worship service. He saw the church as a kind of continuing education center for adults, and his sermons became well-prepared, hour-long lectures. Crowds came in 1914 to hear him lecture on the countries involved in the First World War. In 1915, he came out strongly for family planning in a sermon entitled "The Right to Be Well Born." His sermon topics and his views caused him to be under constant attack by fundamentalists.

During his Spokane ministry, Dietrich began to refer to his faith as "humanistic." Carleton Winston described his discovery of humanism as follows:

Though long familiar with the humanism of the Renaissance Dietrich came across the word "humanism" in a different connotation through an article by Frederick M. Gould in the London magazine published by the British Ethical Societies. Gould, an ardent advocate of August Comte and his Positivism or what has been loosely termed the religion of humanity, used the word "Humanism" in the sense of the belief and trust in human effort. And it struck a responsive note in Dietrich. The age-honored word, this "humanism" would be a good name for his interpretation of religion in contrast to theism. Then, leaning confidently upon the background of Renaissance humanism, he drew certain elements of meaning from it and fused them with his own more social concept of this term.[5]

Dietrich increasingly moved to a kind of "naturalistic humanism" and away from liberal theism. In doing so, he went beyond the boundaries of conventional Unitarianism.

On 1 November 1916, Dietrich became the minister of the First Unitarian Society of Minneapolis, a church that Professor Charles Zueblin of the University of Chicago and author of *American Municipal Progress* would later describe as "an organization in whose nest had been hatched most of the liberal and reform legislation of the state of Minnesota."[6] Once again Dietrich took a church that, although it had seen better days, was then in decline, and built it into a large, vibrant, and effective institution.[7]

As we have already discussed the meeting of Dietrich and Curtis W. Reese in Des Moines in 1917, and the humanist-theist controversy that erupted into full view in 1921, we shall bypass them here. It is sufficient to say that Dietrich and Reese became the acknowledged leaders of religious humanism. Dietrich led by preaching humanism from his pulpit, whereas Reese led from his administrative position as secretary of the Western Unitarian Conference.

Minneapolis, like many communities, experienced repercussions from the Scopes Trial in 1925. That fall, Dr. William R. Riley, a Baptist minister in Minneapolis and national president of the Christian Fundamentalist Association, tried to get legislation passed to prevent teaching evolution in public schools in the state. Dietrich formed a committee to defeat the legislation; it succeeded largely because a Dr. Staub, a well-liked Lutheran minister, and Dr. Roy Smith, a well-respected Methodist minister, were persuaded to join the committee. However, both Staub and Smith were more concerned with the issue of academic freedom than with the question of evolution *per se,* whereas Dietrich was vitally concerned about both issues.

His congregation continued to swell. In December 1925 the First Unitarian Society had to move to the Garrick Theater, which could accommodate the large crowds. The following year Dietrich began broadcasting his services over the radio. This brought a strong reaction from both Roman Catholic and Protestant clergymen, who were convinced not only that Dietrich's opinions were dangerous to the community, but also that some of their members were staying away from their churches to listen to him.

Over the years, Dietrich's sermons had been published and mailed to those who requested them. In 1927 a collection of sermons, *The Fathers of Evolution,* was published. It contained many of the addresses Dietrich had given to combat the movement to ban the teaching of evolution in the public schools. Also in 1927, the *Humanist Pulpit* was published monthly; it contained individual sermons which were annually published in book form under the same title. Edited versions of Dietrich's sermons also appeared in several journals, and often they were published in anthologies. Along with this literary activity, he wrote two popular pamphlets for the American Unitarian Association. The first, entitled *The Significance of the Unitarian Movement* (1927), had gone through twenty printings by May 1943. The second, called simply *Humanism* (1934), had by 1943 gone through five printings; it was also published posthumously by the American Humanist Association.

Dietrich enjoyed success during his Minneapolis tenure, but also experienced tragedy. His wife, Louise, who had borne him one son in Spokane and another in Minneapolis, died of cancer on 22 February 1931. In time Dietrich overcame his grief, and on 30 January 1933 he married a young widow, Margaret Winston, who was a writer and poet. Later in the same year, he was awarded a Doctor of Divinity degree by the Meadville Theological School.

In 1935 Dietrich announced to his congregation that the time had come for him to resign from his pulpit and to retire from the active ministry. Although he was then only fifty-seven, he felt that many ministers held onto their churches long past their usefulness, with a resultant decline in the effectiveness of the church. He wanted to retire while his church was strong. He helped to secure a successor, who took over more and more of the responsibilities until Dietrich was able to fade completely from the picture. Dietrich was minister of the Unitarian Society of Minneapolis from 1916 to 1936, senior minister from 1936 to 1938, and minister emeritus from 1938 to 1957.

In 1941 Dietrich moved to Berkeley, California, where he continued to read, think, and deliver an occasional address. A friend who visited him just before his death reported that Dietrich, then in his eightieth year, was standing beside his bed teaching himself Italian, and he eagerly discussed the existential humanism of Jean-Paul Sartre even as the final stages of cancer drained the life from his body. The "father" of American religious humanism died on 22 July 1957.

From this brief biographical sketch, we wish to emphasize three points. First, Dietrich's thought evolved through several stages, from a respectable orthodoxy in the Reformed Church to a humanism so radical that it took the Unitarians years to decide whether they were sufficiently liberal to contain it within their ministerial ranks. Dietrich described the development of his thought as follows:

> I started out as an orthodox Christian minister teaching the doctrines which center about the Apostles Creed. I gradually went through that stage known as Modernism, or liberal orthodoxy, during which period I resorted to reading new meanings into the old phrases, trying to make them fit the new knowledge. Then I came out into Unitarianism,

but at first a fairly conservative and theistic Unitarian. And finally I reached the point where my mind was satisfied only by a wholehearted acceptance of Naturalism and what has come to be known as Humanism.[8]

This final stage of Dietrich's thought is the focus of interest in our study. (As his health failed and his end approached, Dietrich began to modify his thought in the general direction of either deism or pantheism; his remarks at this time are not as precise as they might be. However, his significance as a religious thinker is based on his audacity in rethinking doctrines of the western religious tradition from the perspective of naturalistic humanism.)

Second, Dietrich never wrote any books as such. Perhaps he devoted too much time to preparing sermons to have any left for writing books. His addresses were an hour long, and they were presented from carefully thought out, well-written manuscripts. Although such a format clearly precluded extended argument, his subjects covered the spectrum of human concern, from abstract economic theory to practical guidance in male-female relationships. Needless to say, Dietrich was not an expert in all these areas, but as a religious thinker, he saw theological issues clearly. Here we are primarily interested in his religious and theological thought. It also should be remembered that Dietrich attempted to rethink a religious position; in this effort some of his thought was original, but not all of it. Although he had forebears, in many respects he broke new ground by interpreting religion from a naturalistic and humanistic perspective.

Third, Dietrich's main concern was to develop a religion independent of the existence of God.[9] Traditionally, religion in the West, whether orthodox or liberal, has been closely identified with belief in the existence of God: if one believes in God, one is religious; if one does not believe in God, one is not religious. Dietrich and the other religious humanists challenged this view. Dietrich maintained that it is possible to be religious in the best sense of the word without belief in God. In order to understand his position, we shall look at some of the traditional doctrines in western religious thought from Dietrich's perspective of "religion without God," which also went by the more familiar title "religious humanism."

World View

Dietrich was well aware that people at various periods of history held different views of the world.[10] The biblical man thought he lived on a flat, stationary earth. He also thought that the earth was the center of the universe and that he played an important part in the scheme of things as "the crown of creation," having been "created in the image of God." Slightly above the earth was a crescent—the firmament— across which the sun moved each day. Beyond the firmament was heaven, the abode of God and the angels; it would be the final resting place of the saved on earth. Hell, where Satan and his cohorts lived, was located below the earth. In this geocentric cosmology Satan sent his demons to earth to gain possession of humans; God, in turn, dispatched his angels to help humans withstand these demonic powers. The biblical person lived in a constant struggle between the forces of good and evil. Miracles occurred every day and were performed by good and evil persons. (Acute mental disorders, for example, were referred to as demon possession. Nothing was impossible in the biblical world.)

In the sixteenth century Nicolaus Copernicus revolutionized cosmology with his heliocentric theory of the universe. As humans began to probe the implications of this new world view, which stated that the sun was the center of the universe and the earth only one of several planets rotating around it, they realized that such categories as "up" and "down" were relative to one's position in time and space. The precise locations of heaven and hell became ambiguous.[11]

As time passed, scientists began to see that even the heliocentric theory was inadequate to describe the place of humans in the universe. High-power telescopes enabled scientists to see many galaxies comparable to our own. Humans were beginning to sense that they live in an infinite cosmic order, with no discernible center; the earth and its life lie on the outer fringe of a galaxy in a universe of millions of galaxies. To this new view of the universe, humans are peripheral; they are only an ephemeral manifestation in cosmic time.

The vast universe may contain millions of planetary systems similar to ours. If the physics, chemistry, and climate on these other planets are like ours, life also may have emerged, persisted, and evolved there. If so, life on our planet is not unique. Dietrich endorsed these views: "I believe that whenever and wherever the proper chemical elements combine in a favorable environment life arises."[12]

Dietrich further believed that the entire universe and everything in it is composed of matter. Matter neither comes into being nor ceases to exist; it merely changes its form: "I believe in an ever-existent and self-sustaining universe; that everything in the universe today has always been here in one form or another, and that forms which we find at present

reveal a momentary order in an everchanging 'stream of existence.'"
Dietrich speculated that billions of years ago a huge nebula swirling
through space may have exploded; its parts scattered and finally settled
as a result of the pull of gravity. One of these became the earth. As the
surface of the earth cooled, a vapor formed around it, condensed, and fell
as rain, filling in the pockets on the earth. Because of the chemical
composition of the earth, the climate, and the laws of physics, flashes of
lightning caused a chemical reaction to change inorganic to living
matter. From this early form of life more complicated forms have
evolved until, as Darwin postulated, humans evolved. Dietrich described the birth of the earth and how humans arose on it:

> Solar systems are born and die like everything else. I believe that our earth, like the other
> planets in our system, was thrown off from the sun and originally consisted of a mass
> of molten matter, which as it whirled through space gradually cooled and solidified into
> its present form...I expect it slowly to decay, in time to become uninhabitable, and
> eventually to cease to exist....I believe that this natural beginning of life is the starting
> point of that long process of development, known as biological evolution, which has
> resulted in the many kinds of plants and animals, and which has crowned itself with the
> evolution of the human race.

Although Dietrich stood within the "materialist tradition," he was
a materialist in a special sense: namely, he had been greatly influenced
by the theory of evolution. It might therefore be more accurate to use the
term *naturalist,* which he often used himself. Sellars, in fact, used the
term *new naturalism* to describe the world view of religious humanism.
He differentiated the old naturalism or materialism from the new
naturalism as follows:

> Now, the fault in the older naturalism was that it was *reductive,* that is, it was
> fascinated by the inorganic world and it sought to interpret all the rest of nature, animals,
> human society, art, in terms of a very simple, prevalent theory of inorganic processes,
> the impact scheme of mechanics. But...that is to ignore what is characteristic of human
> life, plans, valuations, intentions. It is to make the world homogeneous.
>
> The new naturalism asserts that nature is actually heterogeneous and that
> heterogeneity is intrinsic. Evolution means for it that new kinds of bodies arise with new
> properties; after electrons and protons come atoms, molecules, chemical substances,
> living things, sentient things, self-conscious things. These new kinds of things have
> properties of their own expressive of their organization, and these new properties are
> said to emerge. It is also held that a whole acts differently from its parts and that the laws
> of the parts are not descriptive of the laws of the whole.
>
> It is clear that such a view is able to do justice to human life in a way that the older
> naturalism was not. It is more empirical and takes things as they are....[13]

Although this sketch of Dietrich's world view is incomplete, we
will flesh it out as we examine other aspects of his thought. For the

moment it is sufficient to note that he was aware of the radical difference between the biblical world view and his own. He thought that any religion predicated on divine revelation and presented in a prescientific world view was in for difficult times in the modern world. Obviously, he opted for the modern world view, maintaining "that little universe which is told about in the early chapters of Genesis is forever gone."[14] Explicit in Dietrich's acceptance of naturalism was a monism—that is, there is one basic reality, nature—which ruled out any dualism or supernaturalism: "I believe that what we call matter and spirit are two aspects of the same substance, and that spirit is the functional aspect of different combinations and organizations of matter. In other words, I am a Monist, and not a dualist in my philosophy."[15]

Authority

In the West, the main source of religious authority has been revelation. Corrollaries to belief in divine revelation have been the conviction that the revelation contained in the Bible was accurately recorded; that rational argument can supplement revelation in understanding divine things; and that religious experience, or the teaching and authority of the church, enables humans to know about God and his will for them. For Dietrich, none of these traditional sources of authority was adequate. He believed that the only source for authority, even in religion, was the scientific method. He denied the duality that holds that while science can tell us about the empirical world, only revelation can inform us about the spiritual. Dietrich argued that if the scientific method is the best method for understanding the empirical world, it is also the best method for understanding the religious world: "I believe in the scientific method. I do not believe everything that is taught under the name of science, but I do believe in the supremacy of the scientific method, or if you choose, the experimental method."[16]

Dietrich thought we can separate truth from falsehood, reality from fantasy, only through the scientific method. People who object to the use of the method, he said, either do not understand it or lack sufficient grounds for belief. A person who has sufficient grounds for belief will view the scientific method not as a threat but as an aid in establishing the validity of the belief. Furthermore, Dietrich was opposed to limiting the scientific method to certain areas of life, for he believed it applicable to all problems of separating truth from falsehood. He was aware that the method is more easily applied to some areas than to others, but the difficulty of its application should not preclude the attempt.

Although Dietrich was not a scientist, he outlined what he considered the basic steps in the scientific method.[17] First is *observation,* looking at the alleged facts.This is no simple process, for sight can convey false impressions; to the naked eye, for example, the earth appears flat and the moon looks small and near. To some eyes a fabric appears blue, to others, green. Similarly, reports derived from different senses can conflict. In other words, it simply is not enough to see or feel a thing, for one testimony must be checked by others. Claims to truth must be corroborated, a process that begins with observation.

Second, *verification* involves the repetition of observation. When possible, other people are called in and the testimony of other senses is used. One report is examined in the light of another to eliminate error. Methods of explanation are tried until the most adequate is found. Only then can we claim to know a particular thing as fact.

Third is *deduction.* At this stage a large number of similar facts have been verified. From these we can deduce a relationship defining the facts. If it remains constant, the theory becomes a law expressing that relationship. If no new fact is discovered that the particular theory cannot explain, the hypothesis or "natural law" is thought to be established. Just as science is not a thing, neither is a law a thing. A law "is simply our way of saying that the relations between certain phenomena, so far as we are able to discover, are constant and unchanging."

Dietrich illustrated the scientific method with a simple example, the freezing of water. Long ago someone observed that as the temperature grew colder water turned into a solid. When an instrument to measure temperature was created, it could be observed that when water cooled to 32 degrees above zero it froze. This first step involved simple observation. Numerous observations verified the original one. Finally, it was deduced that the transformation always took place under normal conditions, and a hypothesis was established that at 32 degrees Fahrenheit water turns to ice; since there has been no evidence to the contrary, it has become established as a "natural law."

Dietrich considered the discovery that the world is ruled by natural laws rather than by caprice to be the "supreme discovery of the ages."[18] He developed this idea by pointing out that paganism blamed the capricious actions of various gods for the chaotic appearance of the world. Later the functions of these gods were combined into the work of one god. Even in this early monotheism, however, belief in petitionary prayer and in unusual happenings called miracles persisted. People prayed for such things as a good food supply, health to those who were sick, and peace for those at war. Through prayer, they thought, God would miraculously intervene to accomplish his purposes. Even those who had already begun to understand natural law thought that it had been created by God, who, although usually he let it run its course, could miraculously intervene when things got out of line.

The realization that the universe was governed by laws created a problem, for the traditional understanding of deity and the way the universe behaved did not always coincide. The relationship between certain causes and effects remained constant whether humans prayed or not. If the universe is governed by laws, then miracles do not occur and prayer for divine aid is of no avail.

Some—notably Bergson—held to the rule of causality without relinquishing a notion of deity. In effect, they said that God created the laws of the universe and carried out his divine will through them; therefore, it would be inconsistent if God violated the very laws he had created. Generally, proponents of this point of view opposed any supernatural understanding of God. Dietrich thought such a revisionist point of view compromised an important part of the Christian understanding, namely, God's omnipotence. If God is limited to work through the laws he has created, his options are also limited. He can no longer enter miraculously into the human arena. Dietrich, therefore, thought that those who took this way out were really attempting to provide an explanatory hypothesis for the existence of the universe and that they had radically changed the meaning of the word *God*. He considered it more honest to accept the universe as being ruled by law and to refrain from using the word *God* at all.

Dietrich denied that natural law had been created by any deity, for there was no evidence for it: "There really is no such thing as a law of nature, in the sense that natural laws were once formulated and then natural forces obey them. What we call laws of nature are merely human statements of the way in which we have discovered certain forces act." [19] The universe simply behaves a certain way, and through observation, humans have seen certain causal relationships from which they have drawn hypotheses. If these stand up to constant repetition, they become laws. These laws are the creation of people and enable them to understand and better control the world. Deitrich believed the reign of law to be an established fact:

All the knowledge of the world points to it more and more definitely as true. Law and order reign everywhere. Curses do not bring storms and prayers do not avert them.

Curses do not make people ill, and prayers do not make them well. Curses do not bring on wars, and prayers do not end them. Storms come and go as the result of well-established laws; disease is the result of well-defined laws of the physical body in its relation to environment; and wars are the result of well-known laws of social relationship. Every department of the universe has its own laws and conditions, and events are controlled solely by these. Nothing can be done in disregard of these laws.[20]

If nature is constant, and if the best means of separating truth from error is the scientific method, then, Dietrich thought, it is possible to reconstruct part of the past and to have some inkling about the future of humanity. The scientific method enables us to speak of eclipses and conjunctions of planets that took place five hundred years ago, and it will enable us to predict eclipses that will take place five hundred years hence. The method also will enable humans to reconstruct history and to explore the probability of many religious claims. It is the correct method for arriving at truth in all areas of human concern.

Despite Dietrich's great faith in the scientific method, he acknowledged its fallibility. Human observations may be inaccurate; humans do not always move with faultless reasoning from observation to inferences and deductions. Nor did Dietrich dismiss such other sources of knowledge as instinct, tradition, and intuition, but he stressed that we must judge what we gather from these sources by the scientific method.[21]

The "Bible of Man"

According to Dietrich, all religions above the primitive levels have their bibles. Each religion, including Christianity, views its particular bible as the true word of God and other bibles as "false pretensions" containing the words of humans. Dietrich, who observed that Christians have been inconsistent in their view of biblical inspiration, outlined five different views of inspiration.

The fundamentalist view of verbal inspiration declared every word in the original Greek and Hebrew manuscripts to have been directly inspired by God; every word in the Bible is literally God's word. Some have gone so far as to suggest that even the punctuation was inspired. Since punctuation is important to the meaning of a sentence, God removed much ambiguity by providing it.

Dietrich distinguished "orthodox Christians" from fundamentalists. He referred to their view as "Plenary Inspiration," from the Latin *plenar,* meaning "full or complete." The orthodox do not insist that the very words and punctuation of the Bible are inspired, but maintain that the biblical writers were so divinely controlled as to preclude the possibility of error.

Somewhat more liberal was what Dietrich called the "two spheres theory," which holds that the Bible is a religious book, not a book of science. While it may err in matters of science or historical events, in the religious and moral sphere it is the true and infallible word of God. As Dietrich rather cynically concluded, "Where things in the Bible lend themselves to scientific tests, they are not necessarily true; but where it is impossible to test them, they are the infallible word of God."

Evangelical liberals advance more cautious claims. They do not insist on the infallibility of particular parts of the Bible, saying only that the Bible *contains* the word of God. Dietrich referred to Harry Emerson Fosdick's book, *The Modern Use of the Bible*, as illustrative of this point of view. Its main emphasis is that revelation is limited to the capacity of its recipient; therefore some books in the Bible have greater religious value and authority because their authors were more capable than others of grasping God's revelation. Dietrich saw a serious flaw in this point of view: it becomes impossible to differentiate between the word of God and human misconception; the only standard becomes individual taste, and the word of God is that part of Scripture one likes or approves. Such a view ultimately leads to a separate Bible for each individual.

Finally, there is the view that although the Bible may not be the word of God in any special sense, it differs from all other religious books. Many of these may be inspiring, but the Bible is the most inspiring, even greater than the works of Shakespeare or Goethe. Many Unitarians and men such as Washington Gladden and Lyman Abbott have held this view. According to Dietrich, Gladden could not accept the view of verbal inspiration, nor did he quite want to say that the Bible was simply one book among many, but he never was able to decide how the Bible was different; he could only vaguely suggest that it was more "inspiring."

Dietrich maintained that the fundamentalists have the most consistent view of inspiration—namely, that the Bible is verbally inspired. The only real alternative to this point of view is to say that the Bible is a "purely human production." In one way or another the other positions avoid this critical problem. Dietrich himself viewed the Bible "as a great body of religious and ethical literature very similar to the literature of other ancient peoples. It contains the mythology, the history, the biography, the poetry, the drama of the Hebrew people during a period of several centuries...." Dietrich believed that the Bible should be approached like any other collection of ancient literature. This, of course, means applying to it the methods of literary criticism. Inconsistencies, repetitions, and anachronisms in the Bible, he thought, should suggest that the Bible contains not the infallible word of God, but the fallible words of humans.

If the fundamentalists' view of the Bible is correct, and if the traditional doctrines of Christianity—such as the creation and fall of humankind, the necessity of the death of Christ to save humans, and the doctrines of heaven and hell—are true, they should have been presented far more clearly and consistently than they are. Had he been God, Dietrich imagined he

would have written in such a language that no man could possibly mistake it, and I would have provided such means of preserving it that it would be as clear to the people in the twentieth century as it was to those of the first. And not only that but if I had failed to do this, as God apparently has failed, I should make a new revelation in unmistakable terms, I should make it so clear and so universal that no man who had failed to take advantage of it could blame me either because he had not heard it or because he did not understand it.[22]

Dietrich acknowledged that the Bible, however inspired, has had a great influence on religious, ethical, historical, and even scientific thought.[23] It has provided inspiration, but it has also hindered progress by opposing any ideas that conflicted with its authority. The attempt to pass legislation prohibiting the teaching of evolution in the public schools in several states during the 1920s is one example. Dietrich thought the value of the Bible limited for other reasons: it contains the experiences of only one ethnic group; considering the Bible as normative is to imply that other religious scriptures or religious experiences are not valid. Dietrich was convinced that many Christians were out of touch with much that was worthwhile in modern thought, that the Bible impedes world brotherhood, and that, by limiting religious literature to two religious traditions, Christians are deprived of a rich variety of possible religious experiences.

For all these reasons, Dietrich thought it was time to create a "Bible of Man." It would contain selections from the Jewish and Christian scriptures, but would omit what is not valuable. It would also contain selections from various world cultures and religions, and it would draw no distinctions between sacred and secular literature. Any materials selected would be consistent with modern science. Realizing that people's needs vary, Dietrich suggested two criteria for making the selections. First, they must meet "common and universal wants":

No Bible is fit to be called the Bible of Man that can be enjoyed by only a single tribe or nation, that can be outgrown in a hundred or more years. If it does not meet a response in a world-wide and world-deep experience, if it is not found native to human feeling, then it is not Biblical literature and deserves no place in the Bible of Man.

The second criterion is that selections "shall communicate moral power," not because they were revealed by a deity, but because they have the power to inspire readers. Literary works on any subjects that interest humans may be included, for Dietrich thought that religion without God needs a much larger and broader bible. Any work that inspires people to live life to its fullest and in purity should be included; and this canon can never be "fixed" or closed, for it should extend into the future as long as humanity endures.[24]

The Problem of God

Like most liberals, Dietrich thought that Immanuel Kant had refuted the traditional arguments for the existence of God. He said Kant "was the first man to prove, by means of a relentless logic, that all the so-called proofs of the existence of God are fallacious...."[25] It is just as reasonable to maintain that the universe is eternal as to think it necessary to postulate the existence of God in order to account for its existence. Dietrich more or less applied Occam's razor and refused to postulate the latter:

The origin of the universe is one of those questions on which atheism has wisely been silent, and it insists that all attempts to deal with such a question can only result in a meaningless string of words. He insists that the theist's explanation is no more sensible than his, for assuming the existence of a God who created the universe, you have left the baffling problem of the origin of God. It is just as easy to assume that the universe has always existed. It is merely pushing the explanation back one step farther, and making God a kind of stopgap for our ignorance.[26]

Dietrich's main problem with the existence of God appears to be reconciling the God of traditional theism with the doctrine of divine providence. By the God of theism, he meant a God who is all-powerful, all-loving, and able to enter into personal relationships with people. It is this kind of God to whom people give thanks in Thanksgiving celebrations. But if an individual who has enjoyed a good year gives thanks to God, what does one who has had a bad year do? If we hold God responsible for good fortune, should we not also hold him responsible for misfortune? If Americans live in a land that God has blessed, what of people who live in over-populated, war-torn lands? Consistency,

Dietrich thought, demanded that we should thank God for good fortune and blame him for bad times.[27]

Dietrich continued this line of reasoning by criticizing the idea that God sends his blessings even when humans do not deserve them. If one is good and is therefore rewarded by God, it is reasonable to thank him; but if God bestows and withdraws his blessings without reason, it makes no sense to give thanks for such capricious acts. If God sends both the good and the bad, why should we help the afflicted? Might God have sent an affliction for his own divine purpose? If so, removing the suffering would go against the will of God. Unable to reconcile such a belief in divine providence, Dietrich concluded, "No, my friends, we are not at the mercy either of a just or unjust God; we are in an indifferent universe to which we must accommodate ourselves."

Dietrich also considered the problem of God in relation to atheism, which he examined from two different perspectives. First, he observed that people have different conceptions of God. These mental notions become confused with reality, and a particular idea of God becomes an idol. Anyone who doubts or denies this particular conception is labeled an atheist. This happened to Socrates, who apparently believed in a kind of philosophical monotheism and denied the polytheism of the Homeric religion. Since the Athenians had identified Homer's ideas of the gods with their reality, Socrates' denial of the popular polytheism gained him the label of atheist, a term whose meaning depends on the historical context. Even the early Christians were once called atheists. Polycarp of Smyrna, who in the second century was called an atheist, in turn called the pagans atheists because they did not believe in his Christian conception of God. Socrates' and Polycarp's experiences have been repeated throughout history, as Spinoza pointed out. Whenever the accepted idea of God is questioned, the questioner is designated an atheist. Historically, then, the term has meant rejecting the current idea of deity.[28]

Dietrich's approach to atheism was also philosophical; that is, an atheist is one who denies not only the popular conception of God, but any and every conception of God:

> The contention of this atheist is this—that everyone denies the existence of certain gods, and what everyone does to particular gods, the atheist does to all gods. Everyone insists that certain conceptions of God are inadequate and unworthy, the atheist goes one step farther and insists that every conception of God is inadequate and unworthy.

Since affirming belief in one god means denying belief in another, those within one religion view those outside it as atheists. An orthodox Christian does not hesitate to deny the existence of Jupiter or Allah or Brahman:

> The Christian theist denies every God but his own. The atheist, seeing no more evidence for the existence of the Christian deity than for the existence of the deities discarded by the Christians, seeing further that there are the same contradictions involved in assuming the existence of any one of the world's deities, places the Christian deity on the list as among those gods in whose existence he does not believe.

Since the idea of God is almost universal, and since Dietrich sought to establish a religion independent of any concept of deity, he had to account for belief in God. Rather than God creating humans, Dietrich thought humans had created God. He was aware of the works of men like Max Muller, Herbert Spencer, and Edward Burnett Taylor, who offered various theories for the origin of belief in God by primitive people.[29] Dietrich thought that humans' earliest conception of God was determined by their primitive level of consciousness; as humans developed, their concepts of God likewise developed and changed.

Dietrich attempted to trace the development of the concept of God through its various stages. An early, pre-animistic period was characterized by belief in a vague, but threatening, ubiquitous power. Since primitive people were conscious of their own helplessness in the face of this power, their natural reaction was fear. As people developed and learned to think, the voices of nature seemed to speak to them. People felt that all of nature was alive, and inferred it was permeated by a spirit like theirs. Animism is the second stage in the human pilgrimage in the creation of God.

Primitive people devised methods to influence these spirits. They used magic, offerings and sacrifices, entreaties and prayers, flattery and praise, giving rise to various religious rituals. The spirits that became preeminent were those controlling the most critical circumstances; a tribe living inland, for example, would have no knowledge of the spirits of the mighty seas, and agricultural peoples would be most interested in the spirits of vegetation. In time these spirit-deities assumed the characteristics of the people and were compartmentalized according to their functions, a polytheistic stage best represented by the Greeks and Romans:

> ...the gods were related, and special functions and responsibilities assigned to each, and the importance of the god or goddess determined by the importance of the function....Thus arose the twelve major deities and the countless minor divinities of the pagan world, forming a well-organized pantheon of gods and goddesses.

70

(4) The next stage was dualism; gods were divided into good and bad ones. These gods generally had human characteristics, both good and evil; but dualism saw the gods as exclusively good or bad. The prime example of dualism is Zoroastrianism, whose good god, Ahura Mazda, wars with the bad god, Angra Mainyu. Following dualism, Dietrich (5) said, came henotheism, a stage in which the lesser gods passed away and each tribe worshipped its own distinctive deity, although it also acknowledged the existence of other deities. The early Hebrews, for instance, worshipped Jehovah, but they never doubted the existence of Dagon, the god of the Philistines, or Baal of the Canaanites.

(6) Henotheism was succeeded by monotheism, "the belief not only that men should exclusively worship one god, but that there was no other god to worship. The existence of all gods but one is denied." Dietrich maintained that some of the earlier Hebrews, as well as many within the Christian church, attributed not only good characteristics to God but also some rather wicked ones. In the name of this God men have engaged in all forms of cruelty—for example, butchering and burning heretics, and maintaining that most of God's children will forever burn in hell. Humans have attributed their own traits to God; their love of flattery, for example, is reflected in the praise and glorification of God in many religious services. As humans matured and developed a higher morality, they attributed higher moral characteristics to God.

(7) A final stage in the development of the idea of God is "cosmic theism," which interprets God as the indwelling power in the universe rather than as an individual power controlling it. God is a term to describe the activating principle within the universe, as life is the activating principle within the body. Dietrich thought that the cosmic theists were wrong in trying to define God, for he agreed with Spinoza that "to define God is to deny him." Dietrich went even further: "I believe that even to name him—the name circumscribed as it is with our petty conceptions—is suggestive of irreverence."

Studying how the idea of God evolved led Dietrich to conclude that humans created God. He believed that a study of anthropology and history would bear this out:

…in any period of man's development the gods or God simply represent an idealized and glorified type of man's own character, a projection of his moral ideals, moulded into a definite form as an object of worship; and therefore have only a subjective existence in the mind of man.

Dietrich's position on God may be illuminated by his reaction to the question, Is the universe friendly or unfriendly?[30] Dietrich noted that modernists are convinced that the universe is friendly, not because it can be proven, but on the pragmatic grounds that this belief lends meaning and purpose to human existence. "Futilitarians," on the other hand (men such as Bertrand Russell in "A Free Man's Worship" and Joseph Wood Krutch in *The Modern Temper*), although they agreed with the religious humanists that there is no evidence of the universe being friendly, went further, concluding that if humans have no cosmic support, the universe must be unfriendly. Dietrich found both the Futilitarian and the modernist positions to be unsupported by evidence.

Loss of the belief that the universe works toward realizing human ideals led the Futilitarians to say that without ethical authority outside human consciousness, life is without value, and because death destroys all that humans obtain in this life, it is meaningless. Dietrich thought the Futilitarians' disillusionment would prove to be temporary and that eventually both Krutch and Russell would get over it. The modernists took the converse of the Futilitarians' arguments to give pragmatic arguments for believing in the existence of God and maintaining that the universe is friendly.

Dietrich argued that both positions are wrong. The universe is neither friendly nor unfriendly; rather it is neutral or indifferent to the efforts and desires of humans. He attempted to answer the questions posed by the Futilitarians. First, he argued that if life on this planet has no value, then prolonging life indefinitely will not give it value. Furthermore, permanence is no measure of value: "A rose is not less valuable because its petals fall and wither." Likewise, the fact that human life ends does not render it valueless.

Second, God is not needed to lend value to an ethical code, which has generally been enforced by the community. Values and ethical codes are created by humans to serve their own needs, for example, making communal life possible. Through humankind the universe has reached the ethical stage. Ethics are important, whether they are based on the revelation of a deity or created by humans to serve their own ends.

Third, Dietrich asked, What gives life meaning and purpose? He did not think that meaning lay in hopes of immortality or belief that values are inherent in nature or thinking that life is a part of a cosmic plan. Life gains significance, he said,

from the satisfaction of furthering its immediate interests and objectives regardless of any relation to cosmic plan. If interests wane, you become bored, and as we say life loses its meaning. When interests flourish, it's the drive toward their satisfaction that gives life meaning and worth. A happy, active person does not ask for some external plan to give his life meaning. He creates it.

Dietrich realized, however, that the meaning we give to life is relative. Meaning varies because people and their circumstances differ. Individuals estimate the worth of life by their particular interests and their ability to satisfy them, not by their relationship to some cosmic plan.

The individual is more than a simple beginning and an end, Dietrich felt, for each is a link in the chain of life. Because we have learned from past generations, we have a debt to the future: "To discover the way of life and to create and preserve those things which are of value to the enrichment of life in this indifferent universe—this should be our controlling purpose."

Dietrich refused to accept the label of atheist for several reasons. He associated atheism with a kind of crude materialism that views the universe as a machine, whereas Dietrich, like Sellars, viewed the universe as evolutionary, involving organism, growth, and change. The atheism he objected to tended to see humans as miniature machines responding mechanically in the universe. Dietrich denied that personality could be limited to such a simple mechanical explanation. Although Dietrich assigned personality to humans, he was unwilling to go along with theists like Fosdick and ascribe personality to God, for he had absolutely no evidence for such a God. Further, the traditional atheist's rejection of God appeared to Dietrich to be dogmatic. He was somewhat more cautious, and he remained willing to examine the evidence for any particular claim for the existence of God. He tended to be more open on the question than some atheists.[31]

Perhaps these cautious words of Dietrich best describe his position on the question of God:

I do not use the term, atheist. Atheism, I believe, is properly used as a denial of God; and my attitude towards the idea of God is not that of denial at all; it is that of inquiry. I am entirely open-minded and not dogmatic toward the idea of God. But while I do not call myself an atheist, neither do I call myself a theist. Theism involves a belief in a guiding intelligence which is working out some definite purpose; and as I look out upon the universe I see no evidence that the processes of nature are guided by a supreme intelligence aiming at a fore-planned result. But, mark you, I do not deny such intelligence. I see no evidence of it....though I be not a theist I am not an atheist.[32]

Humans

Dietrich placed great stress on the individual. Although his language sometimes sounds existential, it actually was influenced by evolutionary naturalism, and he used the universe as a metaphor for explaining the importance of the individual. At one time our planet, Earth, was a part of a floating nebula, without individuality. Then it broke off and began a career of its own; all that has happened on this earth depended on its breaking away from the huge, nebulous mass and establishing its own existence.

When inorganic life gave rise to organic life, a new type of individuality was born. Every step in the progress of vegetable life through animal life was made possible by the development of new individuals in the evolutionary process. This same process applies to the mental and social evolution of humans. Every step forward has been the result of some individual thinking in a new way:

...only as we permit this variation of thought can any progress be made; and the more we encourage it, the greater progress we will have. If at any stage of human evolution, every one had been made to conform exactly to the accepted forms of thought, human development would have been stopped at that point and our social world remained the same.[33]

For Dietrich, then, the expression of individuality was most important; to stifle it is to retard human development. As long as we encourage individuality, growth and progress are possible. Unfortunately, Dietrich noted,

modern industrial civilization, with its mechanization and process of standardization, is crushing out all individuality and reducing human life to a common level of mediocrity, while the political and industrial philosophies which have grown out of our industrial civilization deliberately preach the insignificance of the individual.

Dietrich blamed the industrial revolution for beginning the trend toward standardization, for factory assembly lines separated workers from the finished product. As long as workers remained craftsmen, they had complete control over their product and could take pride in their skill. Living in small villages, they could put an individual stamp on their cottages; but when workers followed the machines into large cities, they were forced to move into anonymous apartments equipped with mass-produced furniture. Machines standardized products in order to produce large quantities. By the 1930s Dietrich feared that standardization had extended to the educational system and the mass means of communication. He was concerned about radio and especially newspapers, for increasingly associated presses wrote the news that appeared in papers throughout the United States. He felt that this drive toward standardization, which tended to make the individual an impersonal cog in society, was dangerous, for "a society composed of individuals who are forced into grooves of thought must ever be a stagnant society, for progress comes only through variation."

74

This crushing of individuality, said Dietrich, had also crept into politics and economics. He acknowledged that the depression mandated some agreement in economic matters, but he feared that conformity was being imposed on our private lives. Both communism and fascism appeared to him to subordinate the individual to the group, spiritually as well as materially, because they measured the worth of individuals by the services they rendered the state.

A severe social critic, Dietrich thought that protestations and criticism are not only necessary to new ideas and development, but that they are intrinsically good. He disagreed that people exist for the state, arguing that the state exists for its citizens; it should help them meet their needs and reach their aspirations. Dietrich knew that throughout history a few individuals with consciences had stood against the masses; this gave him hope that such individuals still existed in his day. He hoped people would affirm their faith in individuals who refuse to be coerced into conformity with the mass: "For the still, small voice speaking through the conscience of man, bidding him choose obloquy and ostracism, even death, rather than conform is now and always the hope of the race."

Dietrich viewed people as both individuals and social beings. Humans obviously need the help of others, and "the primary needs of the individual can only be supplied by an immense and highly organized social effort."[34] Yet we are born alone and must die alone. The deepest passions and the most exquisite tastes are personal: "The whole end of human life cannot be other than the production of great personalities; and so the state, the community, the family, and all other social institutions are merely a means to an end, and the end is the individual."

The dilemma, of course, is finding the proper relation of the individual to society. If the social dimension dominates, the individual exists for the state; loss of individuality and personal freedom ends in "featureless uniformity and mechanical routine." If individualism is pushed to the extreme, "mere eccentricity or crankiness" results. Dietrich believed that the First Unitarian Society of Minneapolis had achieved a good balance between the two polarities: "freedom of mind in unity of purpose." His society was organized to protect the freedom of all members to think and to develop their own personalities. Freedom must be the basis of common fellowship; "Let no man or woman who comes here be stranger because of difference in race or color or creed or class, for this place is intended to be a center of inspiration and fellowship for all men and all women."

Having felt the threat of the crowd mentality several times in his ministerial career, Dietrich thought that maintaining individuality was our most urgent problem. He offered some suggestions for doing so. Because the crowd is threatened by differences, we need to develop toleration and respect for differences of opinion and habits. We must resist the tendency to conform: "We need to break away from the crowd, and discover first, and then live out that distinctive quality that makes each one himself and not another."[35] We must reaffirm our faith in the validity of the individual who refuses to be forced into conformity by mass thinking. The person who seeks to be an individual hears "the still small voice speaking through the conscience." Escaping the pressures to conform requires courage, "and the strength for such courage comes from within. The self-reliant man is the strong man. To have faith in ourselves and our own resources, to rely upon ourselves and our own efforts is to develop strength...."

Dietrich believed that human nature could be changed. By nature he meant both "the physical order of the universe," generally referred to as nature, and "the native biological equipment of man," referring specifically to human nature. Just as we can study the natural world and formulate laws consistent with its order, we can formulate laws about human nature.[36]

Human nature is consistent, said Dietrich. Both primitive and modern humans had in common emotions and impulses, expressed in the need to overcome hunger, to release sexual frustration, and for self-preservation. In themselves these basic impulses or instincts are neither bad nor evil; in fact, they are "sound" or "healthy." To repress them cripples the individual.

Given these basic impulses, the environment in which individuals are nourished will determine their character—they can either be channeled in a socially useful direction or create a problem for society. He blamed the structure of contemporary society, especially in America, for making people selfish, competitive, and willing to engage in war to resolve national differences. Society or the environment should be restructured "toward rational and social ends,"

away from society based on the motive of personal gain toward a society based on the idea of service to all; away from a society that is chiefly acquisitive toward a society that is pre-eminently co-operative; in which every individual and each group alike will be judged and respected and rewarded, not by the amount of material wealth they have been able to accumulate, but by the actual service they have rendered to the common good of humanity, of which each is an integral member.

It should be emphasized that Dietrich did not advocate eliminating impulses, for they are the unchangeable part of normal human nature; rather, he wanted these impulses to be redirected. For example, rather than using the impulse to self-preservation to wage war, we should direct it toward eliminating the causes of war. We should wage war on disease and poverty.

Dietrich thought that human nature is good, not sinful. In this sense it needs no change. People do harmful and antisocial things because of stimuli received from their environment. We must change human behavior, not human nature, and we can do this by changing the environment. Because humans are responsible for the kind of world they live in, they can alter it for either good or evil. Dietrich was enough of a realist to know that we still do not understand everything about the workings of the human being, and he was well aware of the complexities of social institutions; even so, he believed humans capable of creating a better world and, consequently, better human beings.

The doctrine of original sin Dietrich considered a "superstition" that should be discarded. He was opposed to the doctrine, first, because he thought it was untrue. The theory of evolution explained how humans had evolved from the lower animals, and their social and cultural development. Therefore, it was not true that humans had been created perfect and fallen from perfection. Second, he objected to the harm this doctrine has caused. A mother who has lost an unbaptised infant suffers agony over the fate of its soul. Sensitive people have agonized about whether they were among the elect. Telling humans they are sinners discourages their own effort. Although Dietrich blamed the doctrine of original sin for causing great misery, he did not deny that some humans do evil things. "Evil in other words, means that man is still in the process of transition from the animal to the ideal man, and just as he has inherited from the animals his physical frame, so also he has inherited their cruel passions."[37] These passions can be channeled in creative directions. Whether evil or good predominates depends "largely upon circumstances," namely, environment.

Because humans fear death, learning to cope with it is an important part of learning how to live. Dietrich suggested a number of reasons for this fear, the most obvious being our powerful instinct of self-preservation. Since humans want and love life, they naturally fear what will end it; the fear of death is only a form of the love for life. But the love of life is primary. Part of our fear of death can be attributed to people dying prematurely. Were humans assured the fulfillment they long for, they might come also to long for death. Dietrich thought humans could lessen their fear of death by emphasizing life's quality rather than its quantity. If we can live well, then whether we live long is unimportant. The fear of death also results from superstition and ignorance; if we abolish ignorance, the fear will vanish. Some associate death with pain, but Dietrich argued that pain is also part of life. Many suffer severely and recover, and for many "the process of death is as painless as the process of falling asleep."[38] Pain belongs to life, not to death, for the dead do not suffer. Richard L. Rubenstein interpreted death as a kind of messiah and so did Dietrich: "Death instead of causing pain is the one universal release from pain."

Some fear death because they are repulsed by what happens to the body. Dietrich considered this a false fear: if one believes in immortality, the body is merely the house the soul has temporarily inhabited; if one denies immortality, the body is simply the refuse of what had been life and can no longer be associated with a living person. Regardless of belief in immortality, the dead body is a thing to be disposed of, "the quicker and more sanitary [the] way the better." (Dietrich advocated cremation.) Finally, we fear death because of superstitions about what happens afterward. In most areas of life, humans have some experience, but with death they have none. As a result, all kinds of beliefs "about the unknown have developed, e. g., judgment halls, heavens, hells, and angels and demons. Even among those who do not accept such superstition there still exists an uncertainty." Dietrich thought the evidence suggests that death "will be absolute unconsciousness, absolute silence, and eternal sleep without dreams. It will be after death as it was before birth."

It goes without saying that Dietrich saw death as a natural phenomenon, not a punishment visited on humans by a vengeful God because of one couple's sin. It is part of the natural order, subject to the laws of nature, for humans are born to die. Seeing death as a part of the whole cosmic scheme should calm our fears and give us poise in encountering it. We should remember that the billions of other humans who have preceded us on this planet have in their own time gone into the silent halls of death. Death is our common destiny.

Dietrich offered some suggestions about how an awareness of death might affect the way one lives. First, since the pain that usually precedes death is the result of not living a sound physical life, we should observe the elementary laws of health. Second, we should make up our minds to die but once—in other words, to avoid suffering more in fearing death than we will when death actually comes. Death should be faced, but not be allowed to become a morbid preoccupation that stifles living. Facing death also can help us discover true values. Values are not diminished because all humans die; they assume greater importance against the background of death. Pettiness loses its appeal, and those things that are truly great come to the forefront. Dietrich said, "...when death comes, achievement stands the burning test which indulgence turns to dross." Dietrich believed

that man, like everything else, is a temporary expression of the forces of the universe, which momentarily rose to the plane of consciousness and then goes back into the state whence he came, having made his contribution, good or bad, to the boundless sweep of being.[39]

Salvation

To better comprehend the meaning of salvation without God, we must first look at the traditional Christian view of salvation. Dietrich said the Christian scheme began with God's creation of the world and humankind, whom Satan tempted to disobedience. Because all humans sin as a consequence of inheriting Adam's nature, they are condemned by God. Sin is an offense against God, and since in Adam all have sinned, justice requires that all humans be punished; and, since sin against God is an infinite sin, justice demands an infinite penalty—namely, eternal suffering in hell. If all humans for all time are condemned to hell, then Satan has succeeded in destroying God's handiwork and won a great victory. God, therefore needing to devise a way to save at least some humans, sent his son, Jesus, into the world to save humankind. Jesus, both God and man, paid the price for infinite sin, and his death on the cross canceled man's debt to God. When humans turn to Christ in faith, therefore, they receive his salvation and they live with God throughout eternity and escape hell.

Although Dietrich acknowledged that the Christian doctrine of atonement has been variously interpreted, he believed his outline contained its kernel. He emphasized that salvation is based not upon knowledge or good character, but upon faith. Since the Christian doctrine of atonement depends on the historical accuracy of the Adam and Eve story, if that is shown to be false, the whole Christian scheme of salvation must collapse. Dietrich argued that if the theory of evolution is true, the story of Adam and Eve cannot be. (Once again we see the importance of the evolutionary model in Dietrich's thought.) If, as evolutionists maintain, the world is billions of years old and humans have been around nearly a million years, the story in Genesis, which describes a world less than six thousand years old and Adam's creation on the sixth day, cannot be true. In the evolutionary view humankind has not fallen from an original state of perfection; it is still evolving, and if humans are to achieve perfection, it must be in the future. Because the story of Adam and Eve inaccurately recounts humankind's early appearance on this planet, the credibility of the traditional doctrine of atonement is compromised:

And with the passing of this Adam and Eve story, of course, there comes the total collapse of the whole Christian dogma of atonement. If the first man never sinned as described in the book of Genesis, then there is no sin for his descendants to inherit; if there is no sin to inherit, then every child is not conceived in sin and born in iniquity, and human nature is not totally depraved; if human nature is not totally depraved, then there is no need of all men and women, by the mere fact of their humanity, being condemned to future punishment, and the whole conception of hell forthwith vanishes, like an ugly dream; and if there is no hell, then of course there is no need of salvation; and if there is no need of salvation, then of course there is no need of atonement; and if there is no need of atonement, then there is no need of God sending into the world his only begotten son that through him the world might be saved.[40]

Dietrich thought he had sufficient grounds for refuting the traditional Christian view of salvation and atonement. His doubts dated from his early days as a minister in the Reformed Church.

The humanist view of salvation differs radically. Without belief in the total depravity of humans, there is no need of a redeemer. Dietrich saw the problem as freeing human nature from the vestiges of its animal past: "if [man] had succeeded in breaking free from all the instincts and passions of the animal, and in placing his whole life under the power of reason and affection—then there would be no sin." Freeing humans from their past might release their latent possibilities. No divine redeemer is necessary to accomplish this; humans must save themselves by developing their innate tendencies:

A man needs to be saved not from the consequences of the sin which Adam committed yesterday, but from the consequences of the sins which he is committing today. He needs to be saved, not from the devil but from himself, not from the terrors of the next world, but from the temptations of this.

To Dietrich being saved meant "to fulfill the best that is in us and not the worst; to climb slowly to the highest and not fall swiftly to the lowest; to rise up and up and ever up from the unworthy things of the past toward the ideal of the perfect, perfect justice, and perfect good will." Like traditional theologians, Dietrich contrasted being saved with being lost, which is "to be imperfect and incomplete, to fall short of the highest possibilities of our natures."

The humanist's view of salvation is much broader than the Christian's, said Dietrich, for humanists are concerned with saving the whole person, not just the soul. By "human," Dietrich meant body, mind, and spirit—different manifestations of a single conscious life called a human being. The body is not something evil that must be mortified in order to exalt the spirit; it is as integral to the person as mind and spirit.

Dietrich spoke of the "solidarity of humanity"—not only is the individual a unit, but humanity as a whole is also a unit. It is impossible to be concerned only with individual salvation, because the health of the individual is bound up with the health of the whole fabric of humanity. Humanity is saved or lost together. People in affluent suburbs cannot be safe if people living in the central city slums are not. Dietrich laid great stress on the environment, for he was convinced that a poor one creates sick people. To have healthy people, we must change the unhealthy environment. "Humanism," said Dietrich, "concerns itself, not so much with the petty wrong doing of the individual, as with the miserable social environment which has made the individual what he is."

How was Dietrich's view of salvation to be effected? Not by faith in the sacrifice of a redeemer, but by knowledge of the actual conditions of life, by people with the character to act on their knowledge. Humans must save themselves from ignorance, for that is a fundamental evil spawning others; education, therefore, is the way to overcome the evil of ignorance. By education, Dietrich did not mean merely imparting facts, although this is necessary, but enabling people to develop their faculties to their utmost capacity. Education also means knowing the laws of the universe and of human nature, and living in accordance with these laws. Humans need character as much as education; it will enable them to live according to the knowledge they have acquired and to stand firm in the face of ignorance and hostility.

Like Socrates, Dietrich thought humans ignorant and short-sighted in not fully understanding the consequences of their actions. If they realized that this universe operates according to laws, that certain causes produce certain effects, they would know that wrong, although perhaps immediately beneficial, ultimately has bad consequences. Once people understand this causal relationship, they might refrain from evil. Implicit in Dietrich's position is the conviction that humans must accept responsibility for their actions. What good exists in the world, humans have created; they also have created most evil. Humans cannot turn to a saviour to assume responsibility and guilt for a bad act; they can overcome evil only by replacing it with good.

The atonement leading to salvation is the work of many people, not a single saviour. Thus there are many saviours: the truth seekers who try to replace ignorance with knowledge; the reformers who attempt to bring about mutual understanding and reconcile alienated elements of society; the inventors and discoverers who study the laws of nature and use them to serve humanity; the martyrs who stand for their ideals in the face of an angry mob. Anyone can become a saviour by devoting a life to enhancing the welfare of humanity.

Dietrich said that being "spiritual" is a characteristic humanism values and seeks to foster.[41] The term has traditionally been interpreted within a dualistic framework, but Dietrich fit it within the context of a monistic naturalism. Dietrich noted that "spiritual" has two distinct meanings: in general usage it describes graces and characteristics we admire; theologians use it to refer to an "unextended substance." "Materialism" also has two distinct meanings: in philosophy it refers to a position that reduces reality to matter and is interested in the "quantitative" differences in things; the popular meaning denotes "the deterioration, the coarsening or vulgarizing, of the mind or taste of a person or civilization." Because the two meanings of the term are frequently confused, some think that spirituality is incompatible with materialism or naturalism. Dietrich argued that "spirituality" in the second sense is compatible with "materialism" in the philosophical sense; by taking this position, he repudiated the doctrine of two realms—the spiritual and the material—and denied that being spiritual describes our relationship to the spiritual realm.

"Life is energy," said Dietrich, and although energy does not explain anything, it does suggest motion and activity. "Spiritual life" is also a form of energy, for it is an inward power that effects change in the outside world. It is difficult to define this power and to show how it works, but the fact that it exists is obvious. For example, a thought, which is generated from within, is expressed outwardly when it is written down. Someone else reading the thought may be affected profoundly. A good deed can have a similar impact. Although it is difficult to explain exactly how this process happens, no one doubts that it does occur. Spiritual life thus can be a form of energy capable of working vast changes in the world.

Dietrich supported his monistic position by denying an absolute gulf between living and unliving matter. Such a gulf is implied in the Genesis account of creation in which God takes the dust of the earth, forms it into man, and breathes life into it. The traditional view is that "unliving" matter could not have produced life. Dietrich, how-ever, believed "that life arose directly by the process of evolution from the material substance of the earth." He saw no absolute difference or unbridgeable chasm between "dead matter" and "living matter." Plants and animals have developed naturally out of the chemical elements of the primeval slime, a process as natural as reptiles developing from fish.

Pointing out that traditionally spiritual life was thought possible because the "spirit" came to individuals from outside, Dietrich main-tained that "spirituality" is a part of the long evolutionary process and that it comes from within. It is a capacity for living that humans have acquired as they developed a mental life:

...the spiritual emerges when there is intelligence of a fairly high order, a sense of right and wrong, an ability to set up standards, a drive for creation in art and in social relations, a wealth of imagination. The spiritual is nothing more nor less than that function of human life which manifests itself in the more refined and delicate attitudes of mind.

It is unnecessary to postulate a supernatural realm to account for human spirituality. Likewise, the dualism between flesh and spirit is not valid, for spirituality is connected with the flesh, and the only spiritual life humans will ever know is in this life, "developed to its highest and noblest possibilities." Our spiritual life is a function of the physical; we need not conversion, but education and internal development.

Although Dietrich often seems a wide-eyed optimist, he in fact was a realist. Humanism, he said,

has no blind faith in the perfectibility of man, but it believes that his present condition can be immeasurably improved. It recognizes the limitations of human nature, but insists upon developing man's native talents to their highest possible point. In fact, it recognizes the varying capacities of different people, and does not expect to develop all to an equal degree of achievement, but insists upon developing each to the utmost of his latent ability.[42]

Perhaps what Dietrich meant by salvation is "developing each to the utmost of his latent ability." It is salvation in this life, not the next; it is accomplished by humans, not by God.

Morality without God

Traditionally, western religion has been predicated on belief in the existence of God, and morality has been predicated on doing his will.

God's will was alleged to be manifest in the record of his revelation contained in scripture. A particular action is "right" because God commanded it, whereas another is "wrong" because God forbade it. Furthermore, God punishes humans who do not follow his will, and rewards those who do, either in this life or in the life to come.

Once one questions the existence of such a God—because of the theory of evolution, higher criticism of the Bible, or a new understanding of the physical universe—one also must question this basis for morality, which is predicated upon a particular understanding of the nature of God. Dietrich attempted to show that it is possible to establish an adequate morality without God:

> [Morality] is not the result of arbitrary commands on the part of a supernatural being, but rather a part of man's mental structure developed as a result of his experience through his long ages of evolution; ... moral action is not action in fear of punishment or in hope of reward, but...action according to principle, pre-eminently social principle; ...it is born out of social instinct—instincts which belong to every normal man....[43]

In challenging the view that morality derives from God, Dietrich noted that he had been unable to find moral guidance in nature or in "what lies behind nature." He argued that the idea of God has not remained constant; as already mentioned, at times some immoral commands have been attributed to God. Humans use their loftiest ideals to create their image of God. Only because humans have some understanding of justice and love can they imagine their absolute forms and attribute these to God. Did humans not possess such high ideals, it would be meaningless to speak of them as existing in God. Dietrich admitted that although humans might believe that justice, goodness, and love lie at the heart of things, they cannot prove it, for there is no perfect type of these virtues for humans to follow, except in their own imaginings.

Relying upon studies by numerous sociologists of primitive cultures, Dietrich asserted that it is possible to have morality without religion and religion without morality. He thought that morality reveals the development of a particular civilization far more than the characteristics of a particular religion. Civilizations at certain levels of development usually hold similar views of morality, although their religious traditions differ. In the religions of ancient Greece and Rome the gods were more interested in proper rites and ceremonies than in the moral condition of the people. The God of the early Hebrews was "guilty of demanding practically every immorality of his people—dishonesty, theft, murder, rape...." Dietrich went so far as to say that "when Christianity was at its highest, the moral life of Europe was at its lowest.

Even today it is the same. Those countries that are under the power and influence of the church to the greatest extent are the countries in which you find the most ignorance and vice."

Rather than morality being dependent upon religion, Dietrich (giving the problem an interesting twist) said morality has made religion as good as it is. Morality reflects a civilization's level of development, and the morality of religions reflects a civilization's moral ideals: "The gods in heaven speak the words of people on earth." The moral precepts in religious scriptures merely describe the development and experiences of people at a particular time. It is dangerous, said Dietrich, to insist that morality be predicated on religion, for if the religion is questioned, then the morality is also, and people become confused about moral norms. Dietrich maintained that wrong is wrong, not because some god forbids it, but *because it is wrong.* Moreover, we tend to confuse "religious morality" with "natural morality." By the former, Dietrich meant the morality that religions have developed in their creeds, ceremonies, and holy days. To say, for example, that it is a sin not to observe Sunday in a particular way, is religious morality. Dietrich thought most religious morality is dangerous because it fails to distinguish between what is important and what is not. Some people, for example, have thought that it is as bad to miss a church service as it is to commit a robbery. In contrast, natural morality develops out of the needs of humans and social life; a good religion will adopt the natural morality and give it added sanction.

Another danger is that religions have become preoccupied with the next life and ignored or dismissed the problems of this life ("Things could not be as they are, were they not for the best"). Such an attitude dulls the moral conscience, for if things are as God wants them, humans have no right to change them. Dietrich concluded that it is important for both morality and progress to develop a view of life in which morality, rather than religion, plays the determining role: "If we leave our social ills to be cured by providence, they will never be cured. Experience has taught us that much. The true trust is not in providence, but in human endeavor. And true religion would be one that is permeated with the spirit of morality." Although Dietrich demonstrated that religion and morality can exist independently, he did think they should be related, for in their separation they are "imperfect and inadequate." So he attempted to suggest the proper relationship between the two.

Morality originates in the customs of a particular community, and it dictates how a particular people conduct themselves. Through "natural selection" good customs tend to survive and bad ones to die out, otherwise the community would be weakened or destroyed. The surviving customs become what a community considers moral and unconsciously absorbs. Today much morality has become almost second nature, and it has little or nothing to do with religion, which was originally concerned with gaining the favor and warding off the enmity of the gods. It personified the powers and forces of nature, to which people responded with reverence and awe. Temples were built, priests ordained, and sacrifices made in order to gain favor with the divine powers. In this early age, religion had little connection with morality.

However, religion without morality is inadequate. As humans began to reason and ask why they should follow certain customs, they began to see that they must do more than sacrifice to the gods and pray for their help; for example, it is ridiculous to pray for health while breaking the rules that promote it. When people realized that health and happiness were not arbitrary gifts from the gods, but the natural results of certain kinds of conduct, they began to focus their attention on the natural order, and it became the object of reverence and awe:

But when men see that the blessings they crave, the welfare they desire, are based on other conditions, that these things are secured only as the result of a certain type of life among men, that there is no such thing as arbitrary action in the universe, but that everywhere in the world there is recognizable unchanging law, then what a change comes into the very heart of religion. The very ends which religion craves lead it to pay attention to the real conditions of life, to study the laws of the physical world upon which life depends—and then instead of praying or sacrificing for peace and happiness, men do the things which make for peace and happiness....

Religion, rather than being separated from morality, will be ethical and its morality will be guided by science. To see the relationship between religion and morality is to perceive, as did Schleiermacher, that all religions are based on common feelings, however different their outward expression. The Roman Catholic kneeling before the blessed virgin, the Buddhist gazing reverently on a statue of the Buddha, the ancient Greek extending his arms to Apollo, the primitive man standing mute before a sacred stone, the rationalist falling silent before the moral laws of the universe—all are expressing a common feeling. Each is attempting to give outward form to inward feelings; religion is not necessarily connected with any particular view of humans or the universe. Dietrich thought that morality can give rise to the religious emotion; and, if this be granted, then morality becomes the expression of the religious emotion of certain people. To paraphrase the words of Paul Tillich, morality becomes a person's ultimate concern, or as Dietrich said:

...I am speaking of that morality which loves the law of life even better than life itself, which is ready to die rather than be untrue—that morality may be the very ideal which a man may seek all his life to follow, it may be the supreme passion to a man—down on his knees he may bow before it just as others bow before Jesus or before Buddha.

This view of the the relationship of religion to morality is important in understanding Dietrich's morality without God.

Morality is not imposed from without, but is based on human experience of what brings about individual and social welfare; specifically, "right action is that action which leads to the preservation and enrichment of both the individual and social life, and wrong action is that which tends to the destruction and impoverishment of life."[44] Because morality has a natural and human origin, as experience brings new understanding, morality can be changed. As Dietrich said, "It should be remembered also that moral standards are evolutionary, and change from time to time, and often completely reverse themselves."[45] In espousing a religion without God, Dietrich did not advocate discontinuing morality, but finding new foundations for it.

Dietrich sought to ground morality in the natural rather than the supernatural, and he believed this could be accomplished through human experience. In the process of living together, humans have discovered what contributes to social life and what does not; hence, they have come to a recognition of "right" and "wrong" in their relations with others. Right is simply a word used to express the truth discovered through human experience, "that certain kinds of thinking, certain ways of feeling, certain methods of conduct, are helpful to man while others are harmful."[46] Although Dietrich did not use the terms, he was aware that one cannot derive an "ought" from an "is":

Both humanist and Christian are resting their teaching of morals upon an intellectual proposition to which assent is either implied or expressed. And that lies at the basis of all ethical teaching...the authoritative character of the moral law exists for such as accept it, and for no others.[47]

Right and wrong mean nothing in themselves, but "are summary expressions for a lot of experience as to how different courses of conduct work among people."[48] Obviously, Dietrich did not mean that all areas of right and wrong have been decided; such judgments are subject to change. As to the question What is life for? Dietrich replied, "Life is to live." The end and aim of life is life itself, to live abundantly.

Like the advocates of the social gospel Dietrich stressed the social dimension; when the social context changes, morality must change. Among the rapid changes taking place since the Industrial Revolution in the mid-eighteenth century was a mass movement of people from rural to urban areas. Because the old moral system dealt primarily with rural people whose relationships were basically individual, Dietrich thought we needed a new ethical point of view to take into account that "we all live our lives in a vast network of social relations where the old moral laws do not seem to apply." Although many of the principles learned from the past may be retained, the individualistic "forms" must be discarded and the principles translated into the new social situation. For example "we will cease to condemn only the man who beats a child, while we honor the man who kills thousands of children by means of child labor...." The old ethical system is inadequate for dealing with the complicated social relations of the twentieth century.

Dietrich advocated making morality the supreme concern of human life, even enthroning it as the object of worship. He thought that morality is the true religion, hence the religion the world needs. He distinguished true religion from false by the kind of people it produces, and he was confident that those who followed his path would be better human beings than those who followed other paths. Humanism, a religion without God, could withstand his test for judging a religion.

While traditional morality has been predicated on a supernatural theism, Dietrich sought to ground morality in the natural world. The main concern of the individual is to live the abundant life, and society should be structured to make this possible. Once morality is placed on the religious altar as a people's ultimate concern, religion and morality are properly related. Humans attempt to accomplish this moral agenda by realizing that they live in a universe that is totally indifferent to human morality, for "the universe seems to know no good and no bad. It makes no distinction and protects the death-dealing germs as well as the health-giving."[49] Dietrich was aware that like all other moral or ethical systems, the humanist view cannot be proved; but clearly he thought it best squared with the facts as he saw them.

Immortality

Dietrich considered the doctrine of immortality important, for Christians believe this life is a preparation for the next. Roman Catholics tie the doctrine to membership in the church and participation in the sacraments; Protestants emphasize the inward experience of receiving God's grace; liberals stress the development of character as the prerequisite for the afterlife. Immortality, said Dietrich, is the great underlying thought of Christianity; and if it be true, the world ought to consecrate itself—its time, its money, its power—in delivering men from this immanent danger. [But]...if it be not true, then it ought to be brushed completely to one side, so that we fix our attention on the true end and aim of life, on what ought to be the goal of human endeavor.[50]

Because Dietrich took immortality seriously, he asked, "Has man a soul?" As always, Dietrich depended on the scientific method to distinguish truth from falsehood; in fact, he considered use of the scientific method one of the salient differences between the humanist and the liberal. Humanists, said Dietrich, must use it to question all their own presuppositions.

The western religious tradition, said Dietrich, has maintained a dualism, holding that both matter and spirit are real. Humans contain both, for when God created man's body from the dust of the earth and breathed into his nostrils, he became a living being with a soul. When man dies, his body returns to the dust of the earth from which it was originally created, whereas the soul, having come directly from God, is immortal. The primary purpose of religion, then, is to save the soul to ensure that it will remain eternally with God. Both Socrates and St. Paul held similar views. Paul maintained that the soul must "put on" a spiritual body once it has shed its earthly one. Socrates thought that man was "saved" by cultivating his mind or soul, whereas Paul was convinced that salvation came through faith in Jesus as the Christ. But both held there were two realities, the soul and the body, and both believed that the soul was the most important aspect of man.[51]

Dietrich found no general agreement about the relationship of the soul to the body. Some think the soul enters the body at conception, others say at birth, and still others think at the "age of accountability" when one reaches awareness of the difference between right and wrong. Some have located the soul in a small pocket in the prefrontal lobe of the brain, where at death there is a small empty space. But over the ages there has been a widespread belief that a soul inhabits the human body and that when the body dies, the soul goes to a spiritual realm beyond the physical.

It is impossible, said Dietrich, to ascertain the origins of this belief. It might have originated in primitive people's thinking about the relationship of a shadow or reflection to their bodies. Just as the shadow likeness that appears in sunshine vanishes in shade, our souls may leave us at death. Dreams also may have influenced an elementary belief in a soul. Since dreams seemed almost as real to primitive people as the experiences they had while awake, they may have thought their souls were having the dream experiences. Dietrich thought the belief in the existence of the soul went far back in history; once the idea arose, religions began to develop doctrines of improving the soul so that humans might obtain salvation.

Dietrich applied the theories of several sciences to belief in the existence of the soul. He pointed out that anthropologists can show that the human mind has developed just as the physical organism has evolved from lower to higher forms. The central nervous system became more sophisticated as the body developed; thus a correlation exists between the evolution of the body and the mind. Anthropologists tend to view humans as sophisticated animals, implying that humans differ from other animals, not in kind, but in degree. If this is so, and if humans have a soul, animals also must have souls. If we insist that only humans have souls, at what stage in their long evolution did the soul arise? Dietrich concluded that the anthropological evidence suggests "that the whole theory in regard to the possession of a soul by man is a figment of the imagination."

A biological perspective reveals that living organisms have the same chemical elements as inorganic matter; the differences between them are of complexity and organization. The human living organism is composed of billions of cells, organized in a particular pattern and operating according to certain chemical, physical, and mechanical laws. These laws are as consistent as the laws that operate in all of nature:

[A human being] is composed of electrons organized into atoms, atoms organized into molecules, molecules organized into cells, cells organized into organs, and organs organized into the body; and all the possibilities of this body are due to the highly organized condition of these component material parts.

His biological analysis of humans and their functions revealed no evidence that the soul exists.

Dietrich also considered humans from a psychological point of view. He argued that the soul, mind, or "inner life" of humans is only one of the body's numerous functions, though it may be "infinitely superior" in character and results. The mind (or soul or consciousness) depends upon the physical collection of cells that make up the brain, and there is no evidence that consciousness can survive its destruction.

By equating the soul with the mind, and the mind with the brain, an organ in the body, Dietrich espoused a view apparently based on the works of Wundt, Fechner, and Watson. He saw support for this theory in the fact that changes in physical states produce corresponding changes in mental states. For example, the condition and growth of the brain correspond to those of the body; a newborn child has an infant consciousness, a well-educated middle-aged woman may be at the height of her intellectual powers, and an old woman may be senile. Were the mind capable of physical survival beyond death, one would not expect to find such correlations between body and mind states. A similar correlation can be seen when a severe blow on the head produces unconsciousness. A blood clot pressing on a certain part of the brain can alter one's mental, moral, and spiritual life; once the clot is dissolved and the pressure removed, a normal mental state is restored. Once again, the evidence led Dietrich to conclude that the mind is a function of the body; when the body is destroyed, so are the mind and consciousness. There is no evidence for the existence of a soul within or without the body.

Although Dietrich repudiated the doctrine of a soul as a spiritual substance that can exist apart from the human body, he accepted the notion of the soul as an individual's personality. With this naturalistic understanding of the soul as personality, the task of religion without God is not to save the soul for some future life, but rather to help it grow and mature so it can enjoy the present life. But Dietrich was not content to leave the question of immortality here. He was especially concerned to contrast the humanist and Christian positions and to demonstrate that the former better corresponds to the human condition. First he raised the problem of rewards and punishment, heaven and hell, which Christianity has taught not as a possible theory, but as revelation.

The primary flaw in promoting a belief in personal immortality, apart from its questionable speculative nature, is that humans who make the afterlife their ultimate concern tend to neglect this life and allow "ignorance, disease, poverty and misery" to wreak havoc. Humanists, because they can know nothing of another life and do not care to speculate about it, devote their energies to this world: "Instead of trying to get ready to emigrate into some unknown world we should do our best to make life in this world so beautiful, so exalted, so free, so attractive, as to make the people in the next world, if there is such a world, long to come and live with us." [52] Dietrich added that if there *is* another life, the people who make the best of this life will certainly attain it; if there is not, they will not have wasted a lifetime trying to attain something that does not exist.

Although Dietrich was not interested in speculating about personal immortality, he did assert there is something immortal in humans. He therefore attempted to give a limited view of "immortality" consistent

91

with naturalism and the scientific method—an immortality of influence:

...every man leaves behind him that which enters into the construction of civilization. The individual as a conscious person may perish but he continues to live in the race as an influence, just as the whole past history of the race lives in him. The human race is the immortal being. Man is immortal, if not men.

He also said, "The race is an organism and the individual men and women are the cells that discharge their momentary function and are then dismissed." It should be emphasized that Dietrich's understanding of immortality was not limited to the heroes of the race, but included common people. Every parent passes on not only the gift of life, but also values. If the human race is to improve, it will be through average people passing human values on to their offspring. Dietrich's humanistic interpretation of immortality included "the voices of the dead." John Milton, for example, has more influence today than he did during his own lifetime, and Dietrich argued that the West might be radically different had Napoleon never lived. Dietrich observed that the dead are everywhere and

the world is full of their spirit. They speak to us from the houses of learning, from the pulpits of churches, from the books of the philosophers, from the paintings of the masters, from the stones of the sculptors, from the songs of the musicians...they speak to us through our minds and bodies. Even in ourselves we find reproduced the characteristics of our ancestors. It is impossible for man to sever himself from the immortal power of those who have died.

The point is obvious: humans are indebted to their forebears, both great and not so great. Even the shape of a person's features, the color of skin, eyes, and hair are determined by ancestors. Every person, then, is immortal, not by going to another world, but by leaving the impress of personality on this world. Every life, good or bad, helps determine the humanity of the future. Some enhance it, others retard it.

Unlike the Christian, the humanist has no hope of reunion with close friends after death, but this does not mean that the deceased no longer influence the living. The dead live on in the memory of survivors, and their good qualities serve as an example. In this sense the dead do not leave their friends completely. Sometimes they become teachers of the living in a way that might have been impossible when they were alive.

Dietrich cautioned that the humanist view of immortality is not a "substitute" for those who hope for personal immortality in the afterlife. But it has the virtue of certainty, which the theist's view lacks. The humanist view leads us to do our best for humanity, whereas the theist view can lead us to neglect this world in order to secure eternal b~~...~~ the next. Dietrich did acknowledge there is no inconsistency in embracing both his and the Christian view. But he cautioned, "We make a mistake in perpetually turning our thoughts to a life beyond the grave. Rather let us work here, and be strong."

Dietrich's reaction to the traditional Christian view of immortality was "complete agnosticism," by which he meant that he neither affirmed nor denied the doctrine. But his religion without God did not promote immortality. Perhaps this statement best captures Dietrich's thinking on the subject:

> I believe that each individual human life ends with death; I may be mistaken, and I have the highest respect for people's belief in immortality.... As I weigh the evidence pro and con and try to face the facts, I invariably come back to the same conclusion; and not in despair as some may think but in perfect satisfaction. I do not feel that it is necessary to live forever in order to make life worthwhile. It is possible that one can appreciate it all the more because of its brevity.[53]

The Church

By and large, Dietrich thought, the liberal church in the twentieth century had been ineffective. (By the liberal church, he referred to the Unitarian denomination, although he admitted that Unitarians had no monopoly on liberalism.) He suggested two fundamental causes for this ineffectiveness. First, the Unitarian church had lost the "liberal spirit" but retained the liberal doctrine. When Channing, Parker, and Emerson originally broke away from traditional Christianity, they possessed not only a liberal theology but also a liberal spirit. Since the days of these early pioneers in liberal religion, Unitarianism had kept their doctrines but forfeited their spirit. Eventually, when the traditional denominations caught up with liberal theology, Unitarianism became only one more Protestant denomination. Second, Unitarianism originally was representative of the ruling class. Since then a social revolution has shifted power from the upper classes to an "undistinguished mob." Unless Unitarianism can recapture the liberal spirit and gear its message to transcend class and racial boundaries, its future will be bleak.[54]

According to Dietrich, Unitarianism could deal effectively with these problems by discarding the shell of Christianity and adopting "a naturalistic and humanistic philosophy in religion." Its emphasis should be on humans taking matters into their own hands rather than turning to a personal deity for aid, for there is no help from heaven. Because this is what the modern world actually believes, Unitarianism should try to develop a religion in accord with such a point of view. Dietrich meant to retain the truths contained in Christianity, not because they are Christian but because they are true. He also wanted to include truths from other religions and nonreligious traditions. Just as no one scientist is the norm for all science, so no one religious tradition can be the norm for all religions.

Dietrich asserted that what people need is not a theological doctrine about the unity of God as advocated by the early Unitarians; they need a human doctrine stressing the unity of all people. Believing that many of the movements in modern society have alienated people from each other, Dietrich thought there must be a common ground where all people can meet as equals; the liberal church should fulfill this need by holding out a vision of human unity to a torn world. He saw Unitarianism as a fellowship of churches, each free to teach its own doctrine and follow its own policies, rather than as a separate denomination. The common glue holding such a fellowship together would not be adherence to a common creed or belief in the unity of God, but an emphasis on the unity of humanity. It would be a church embracing all nations, religions, classes, interests, and purposes.

Dietrich thought churches should be opened every day of the week. In addition to regular worship services, they should offer dramatic performances, study classes, and meeting places to discuss social and community problems. To encourage the free flow of ideas, there should be freedom both of the pulpit and the pew. Ministers should have absolute freedom to speak on any subject, and those who sit in the pews should be free to judge their presentations. Dietrich did not seek disciples but encouraged people to think and to reach their own conclusions. He said, "I seek not so much to persuade you to my way of thinking as to stir you up and stimulate you in your attempt to solve the vital questions of life for yourself."[55]

Once again, Dietrich stressed the many forces in society that separate and alienate people and lead to conflict. If world community is to be achieved, the church must do its part by bringing together people of all points of view and backgrounds. Even the theist and atheist must be brought together to worship. Dietrich often chided his Unitarian colleagues for having given up on the poor and ignorant and going after the well-educated and influential.

A religious society has not only a mission to its own members, but a responsibility to the larger community. Dietrich believed that to improve the lot of the individual, we must change our social structures. The church should not become a one-reform society, such as a prohibition society, but it should encourage individuals to work for the social reform movements they are qualified to help. A major function of the church is to examine human problems from an ethical perspective, although Dietrich realized that when we compare human problems to an ideal, they often appear incapable of solution. The liberal church should constantly remind people that they are their own saviours, for no God will intervene into the human arena and save them. "And so the thing above all else that we are trying to do is to get humanity to stop dreaming about other worlds and outside help and settle down to its job of building an ideal world here by its own effort."

Acknowledging worship is a problem for a religion without God, Dietrich believed it has a legitimate place in a humanist church. He interpreted worship, like other aspects of religion, from a naturalistic and evolutionary perspective, noting that worship also has passed through several developmental stages. Although these stages were not necessarily similar in every culture, they did give Dietrich a context for forming his own interpretation of worship.[56]

An early stage of worship relied on magic. When nature appeared hostile, people developed magic to eliminate or reduce their fear of it. Magic controlled the natural forces of the universe and made them conform to human wishes. The modern clergyman has his ancestry in the primitive magician; in such rites as ordination, where a power is passed on via the pronouncements of a formula and the laying on of hands, magic lingers.

A second stage, superstition, viewed the forces of nature not simply as malevolent, but as benevolent too. Rather than subduing the natural powers through magic, superstition personified and propitiated them. If the gods were sufficiently pleased and flattered, they would shower humans with benefits. Worship then became propitiation of the gods.

At a third stage in its development, worship centered on a single God who was viewed as wholly good and all-powerful. Dietrich maintained that only at this stage did worship truly become worship: "with all cause for fear and all sense of obligation removed, people had but one emotion toward God—and that is reverence." The reverence Dietrich referred to is a kind of admiration or devotion expressed in service to others and in emulating what we admire. The highest form of worship is to aspire to be like God. The worshipper is not drawn to God because he exists, but because he possesses characteristics humans esteem. The qualities that humans worship in God are the very qualities they value in themselves. It is not God's omnipotence and infinitude that draw people to him, but his justice and love.

Here Dietrich gave his naturalistic turn to the exposition, for if humans revere the qualities rather than the being that embodies them, then those qualities can be appreciated even if they are merely human. Justice and love, for instance, are the same whether they are found in God or embodied in people. Worship, in the highest sense—namely, paying reverence to valuable qualities—is not dependent upon belief in the existence of God. Worship is an attitude involving mind and emotion; it is directed toward certain worthy qualities, not necessarily the being in which they reside. Thus it is possible for humanists to worship without belief in God.

Worship was important to Dietrich, for he saw a correlation between the values we admire and our nobility. Admiring and aspiring to embody great values changes character. As we strive to attain values, we are transformed, we resemble what we value. Dietrich believed that worship or aspiration is necessary for growth, for "if there is no capacity to admire that which is above and beyond you, there is no hope of progress."

Humanists may believe in worship without necessarily believing in God, but they tend to be hesitant about public or collective worship. The problem is that most collective worship expresses values as creeds derived from antiquity and often unrepresentative of a worshipper's views. However difficult public worship is for radical religious non-conformists, Dietrich felt it was beneficial for expressing a sense of unity among humanists. He tried in his own church to invest worship with meaning; he included modern readings, aspirations, music, and an hour-long lecture or sermon. The aspiration, which replaced both prayer and creed, was an attempt to express the ideals of the group. Every week a new aspiration had to be written, to prevent its developing into a fixed creed. Dietrich considered music important even in a humanist service of worship, but thought the words of the hymns should be updated to express the concerns of the congregation. But however much he valued worship, Dietrich acknowledged,

The important thing in worship is not that we go to church, not that we read the Bible, not that we pray, not that we sing hymns—the important thing is that we be so uplifted and moved to admiration of the highest and finest things in life, that we are not satisfied until we have made them a part of ourselves.

Perhaps these words best capture Dietrich's understanding of the church: "The church is a social organization whose task is the development of the noblest living, both individual and social, in the presence of religious experience."[57]

Religion without God

When we first examined Dietrich's address "Religion without God," given in December 1929, we saw only the tip of a theological iceberg. Now we can better understand the implications of the term. It applies to a type of humanism that Dietrich had started preaching in 1915 and continued to preach until he retired from the active ministry in 1938. Although Dietrich's theology was not predicated on belief in God or in personal immortality, it lends itself to a systematic exposition of the themes that have traditionally demanded the attention of western theological thinkers. His world view was naturalistic; his method for determining the validity of a statement was scientific; his understanding of morality was humanistic; his salvation focused on this world and was attained by human effort; his church was a social institution created by people for the purpose of improving themselves and the world.

Dietrich thought that religion, like human evolution, had passed through numerous stages. Christianity, a product of religious evolution, had served its purpose; it was time to move on to the next stage, which would be something similar to his own understanding of humanism. Dietrich said Christianity "entered as a place in the evolution of the world religion, and having fulfilled its mission it must yield before the promise of something better."[58] He was convinced that religious humanism, a religion without God, was that something better.

CHAPTER 5

Curtis W. Reese: The Statesman of Religious Humanism

"We value the life of the spirit. We put a high estimate upon the function of intelligence. We believe in worthy standards of conduct. And we intend that the quest of these shall be an organized quest." —Max Otto

CURTIS WILLIFORD REESE WAS BORN ON 3 SEPTEMBER 1887 on a farm in the Blue Ridge Mountains in Madison County, North Carolina.[1] The Reeses were devout Southern Baptists, and many of them had been ministers. Reese once said, "One of my paternal great-grandfathers was a Baptist preacher, one of my paternal grandfathers and two of my paternal uncles were Baptist preachers, my father is a Baptist deacon, two of my brothers are Baptist preachers, and a sister married a Baptist preacher."[2]

With so many clergymen in the family, it is understandable that when Reese earned his first dollar he gave it to the Baptist church to help pay the minister's salary. It also is not surprising that Reese "accepted Christ as his personal saviour" at the age of nine. He had been taught that if he reached the age of accountability without becoming a Christian and were to die, he would spend eternity in hell. Believing himself capable of making such an important decision, the nine-year-old boy stood before the congregation and confessed that he was a lost sinner and trusted Christ to save him. Although it was mid-winter, he and other converts were baptized in an outdoor creek.

Later Reese thought that God had given him the "call" and he decided to enter the ministry. He was graduated from the Baptist College at Mar's Hill, North Carolina, in May 1908 and ordained to the Baptist ministry. He went to Alabama where his brother, T. O. Reese, was the minister of the First Baptist Church in Geneva and where he was able to supply a small rural church at Bellwood. He departed in September to enter the Southern Baptist Theological Seminary in Louisville, Kentucky. There he supported himself by pastoring two half-time churches, one at Gratz and the other at Pleasant Home. At the latter church, Mount Pleasant, he met Fay Rowlett Walker, whom he married on 7 February 1913.

During his seminary studies Reese began to have doubts about his religious faith. Since he believed the Bible was divinely inspired, it came as a shock to encounter "higher criticism," even in a conservative Southern Baptist context. Reese's friend Ralph E. Bailey, who also later made the transition from the Baptist ministry to the Unitarian, remarked, "In 1908, he and I were students at the Baptist seminary in Louisville, where I soon shocked him to his knees by my heresy. Much of his time was devoted, I think, to prayer that I be corrected in my outspoken apostasy from Baptist truth."[3]

In Louisville Reese first came into contact with Unitarianism. He took some Baptist tracts over to the Unitarian church and picked up some of the Unitarian materials. One pamphlet especially appealed to him; entitled "Salvation by Character," it may have contributed to Reese's later decision to become a Unitarian.

After graduating from seminary in 1910, Reese took a job as state evangelist in the Illinois State Baptist Association, which was composed of approximately five hundred churches that had split off from the Illinois Baptist State Convention. This position allowed him time for further study, so he enrolled for courses at Ewing College at Ewing, Illinois, a now-defunct Baptist school. In 1911 he received a Ph.B. degree from Ewing. Reese said of this period, "During the year as State Evangelist, my heresies, which had begun even during my seminary days, due to the impact of Higher Criticism, began to grow apace." In 1911 Reese became the pastor of the First Baptist Church in Tiffin, Ohio; he thought it a "liberal" Northern Baptist church, but still he felt cramped: "I preached twice each Sunday, but following the evening service my conscience bothered me. I could and did say what I believed, but I did not feel free to say what I did not believe." Finding the Northern Baptists too conservative, Reese decided he must transfer into a more liberal ministry. He considered the Unitarians, the Universalists, and the Christians; finally he decided to more closely examine the Unitarians because of a work that he had read by Francis G. Peabody, a Unitarian who was a strong advocate of the social gospel.

Reese arranged a meeting with the minister of the Unitarian church in Toledo. At this meeting Reese presented a brief statement of his faith which consisted of the following: "(1) a Universal Father, God, (2) a Universal Brotherhood, mankind, (3) a Universal right, freedom, (4) a Universal motive, love, and (5) a Universal aim, progress." Reese was assured that his faith was consistent with Unitarianism. When he returned to Tiffin he gave the matter serious thought, and he decided to transfer from the Baptist to the Unitarian church. After conferring with the secretary of the Western Unitarian Conference, Reese was recommended for the ministry of the Unitarian church in Alton, Illinois, which accepted the recommendation. Reese began his career as a Unitarian minister in 1913.

Reese did not lightly make this move from the Baptist faith to the Unitarian. It caused him great personal turmoil as well as creating a rift with his family:

My mother said very sincerely that she would rather have seen me dead. This is understandable, for had she heard of my death she would have had the satisfaction of knowing that I was flying around with angels in heaven. But now she was sure that if and when I died, I would burn in hellfire and brimstone forever and ever.

Reese was close to one of his sisters and had been proud when she named her son "Curtis Williford." When he became a Unitarian, his nephew was renamed "Bruner Truett" for two well-known and solid Southern Baptist ministers. Eventually the family became reconciled to Reese's decision; his sister even attended a Unitarian fellowship for a while and might have become a member had her husband not been a Baptist deacon.

Although Reese was in Alton for only two years, he had a number of significant experiences. He became a strong anti-vice crusader, mobilizing the clergy in an active campaign to rid the city of "gaming houses" and "brothels." He raised money to hire a private detective to gather substantial evidence about vice, and as a result the crusaders backed a successful mayoral candidate on a "clean-up ticket." So zealous was Reese in his efforts that the underworld had him shot at several times, and once it was necessary for him to hide in a parishioner's attic. Another time he was attacked at a railroad depot, but only slightly injured. The widespread newspaper coverage these episodes received provided fuel for the election campaign. On election night, while Reese and his wife escaped to a parishioner's home, a mob gathered in front of his home and lit several fires.

Two other experiences merit mention. One summer Reese returned to Gratz, Kentucky, where he had been a pastor while in seminary. He rented an auditorium and conducted a week of lectures on Unitarianism. People came to hear Reese for various reasons, some because they had never before heard of a Baptist becoming a Unitarian; descendants of the old village doctor came because their father had been a Unitarian and they wanted to learn about this faith. In contrast to his days as a Baptist minister, Reese took no offering and tried to convert no one; his lectures were simply to enlighten.

Reese agreed to run a three-week summer camp at Lithia Springs, Illinois, and guaranteed that all expenses would be covered by income. Because it rained nearly the whole time, attendance dropped and the budget ran into the red. To honor his commitment, Reese paid the expenses out of his own pocket. This sort of integrity helped to elect him secretary of the Western Unitarian Conference four years later.

Despite an increasing membership in Alton, Reese left in 1915 to become the minister of the Unitarian church in Des Moines, Iowa. There he again became involved in a number of social issues. Concerned about the morality and welfare of the servicemen at nearby Fort Hood, he opened his church on weekends so that soldiers from the base could meet young women in a properly chaperoned setting. He found the problems typical of most military situations: illegitimacy, prostitution, venereal disease, and the lack of morality among large numbers of men away from home and thrust together in one community.[4]

It did not take long for Reese to be moved by the poor housing conditions. Rather than fight the politicians as he had done in Alton, he brought the conditions to the attention of the mayor, who suggested that Reese speak to the governor. Reese succeeded in interesting Governor W. L. Harding in seeking a solution to the problem; the Iowa Housing Bill resulted and, largely thanks to Reese's intense lobbying, it passed without a negative vote. This is alleged to be the first state housing bill to be passed in the United States. Reese, the "father" of the bill, was appointed the first Housing Commissioner of the State of Iowa. The idea underlying this comprehensive bill was to ensure that "no housing shall be permitted which impairs the health of the occupants or endangers the health of the community."[5]

Reese gained much publicity following passage of the bill. In effect, he was asked to run for mayor of Des Moines and promised the backing of organized labor, and he also was offered a lucrative position as a stock and bond salesman. Reese declined both offers to become secretary of the Western Unitarian Conference in 1919. His new base of operation was Chicago, and his primary responsibility was to help churches secure the "right," most capable minister for their pulpits. Although this administrative position was potentially controversial, Reese was able to retain the respect of both the conservatives and the radicals.

During this period Reese was elected to the board of directors of the Meadville Theological School, then located at Meadville, Pennsylvania. For some time attempts to relocate the school in a more advantageous city had failed. Now there was talk of moving the school to Ithaca, New York, to be affiliated with Cornell University; Case Western Reserve University in Cleveland also was interested in having the school become a part of it. Reese, however, wanted to relocate the school in Chicago and he secured a pledge of $100,000 from Morton D. Hull, a wealthy businessman and an active Unitarian, to do so. At its next meeting, in February 1926, the board of directors voted to bring Meadville to Chicago. Reese also negotiated with Shailer Matthews, dean of the Divinity School at the University of Chicago, "an associated relationship" between Meadville and the university, as well as negotiating the purchase of the President's House and Channing House. At about the same time that Reese was active in the relocation of Meadville, he secured another significant sum from Hull to build a new Unitarian church in Hyde Park on the edge of the University of Chicago campus. It is little wonder that when the honorary degrees were awarded in 1927 Reese became the youngest recipient of the Doctor of Divinity Degree from the Meadville Theological School.

In November 1928 Reese embarked on a trip around the world. He stopped in India to represent the American Unitarian Association at the centennial celebration of Brahmo Samaj, a kind of "Hindu Unitarianism" started by Ram Mohun Roy in the early part of the nineteenth century.[6] Reese attended the main meetings held from 22-30 January 1929 in Calcutta, where he was in great demand as a speaker. He gave nine addresses to various groups, and at the University of Calcutta he received a standing ovation for saying, "No race or nation, whatever its color or culture, is good enough or wise enough to rule another race or nation—and that means both England in India, and America in the Philippines."[7] Reese said of this occasion, "By the instant response

103

from the large audience, I realized as I had not before, what a mighty movement is stirring underneath the surface of Indian life." It was "a trip from Chicago westward by way of San Francisco, Honolulu, Japan, China, the Philippines, India, Egypt, Italy, Southern France and New York, back to Chicago"—all "in the period from November 4 to March 19...."[8] Reese spoke in several countries en route to India.

In addition to his position as secretary to the Western Unitarian Conference, Reese was appointed president of Lombard College, a Universalist school located in Galesburg, Illinois. His appointment apparently was an attempt to bring the Unitarians to the aid of the Universalists in saving the school from financial collapse. The college, founded in 1851 as a coeducational institution, was the second school in the United States to admit women on an equal footing with men. Carl Sandburg is perhaps its most distinguished alumnus.[9] Reese was president for only a little over a year; the depression worsened its financial situation and in 1933 the school became a part of the Meadville Theological School.

In January 1930 Reese resigned as Western Conference secretary to accept the position of dean at the Abraham Lincoln Centre in Chicago, which had been founded in 1905 by the Unitarian minister Jenkin Lloyd Jones. Reese lived in an apartment in the Centre designed by the famous architect Frank Lloyd Wright. The programs for the Centre were many and varied; a Friday morning forum provided a platform for outstanding speakers of all varieties of opinion. The Centre published a journal, *Unity*, of which John Haynes Holmes was editor for many years; Reese was an associate editor. Both Jones and Holmes were dedicated pacifists, and pacifism was the official policy of the journal. When, during the Second World War, Reese abandoned his pacifism and convinced the journal's directors to support him, a rift developed between Holmes and Reese. As a result, Holmes relinquished his editorship of the journal and Reese took over. The Centre offered counseling and ran a clinic for "optional parenthood."[10] It sponsored "study classes, social service, a boys' and girls' camp, a public library, domestic science classes, instruction in music with glee clubs and an orchestra, various special activities for boys and girls, and dramatics."[11] Non-Jews, Jews, and blacks were on the staff, and in the early days Reese maintained a 50 percent balance of whites and blacks in all programs; later, as the neighborhood changed, the percentage of blacks increased.

Reese served on an astonishing number of committees devoted to social service. They ranged from a Juvenile Court Committee, to the board of directors of the Religious Education Association, and to the presidency of the Humanist Press Association. Occasionally he taught courses at George Williams College and at the Central Young Men's Christian Association College in Chicago, with emphasis in the area of "Principles and Methods of Adult Education."[12]

In his connection with *Unity* over a period of nearly forty years as contributing editor, managing editor, and editor, Reese wrote numerous articles that ranged from a sophisticated level of scholarship to simple editorials. His articles also appeared in several other liberal journals. In 1926 his first book, *Humanism,* was published; it was followed in 1931 by *Humanist Religion* and in 1945 by *The Meaning of Humanism.* He also edited *Humanist Sermons* (1927) and *Friedrich Nietzsche* (1931), which contained the lectures of the late George Burman Foster, professor of comparative religion at the University of Chicago. Reese's autobiography, "My Life Among the Unitarians," was submitted to Beacon Press but never published. Generally, Reese's books are short, contain insights, but are somewhat thin in the development of arguments; however, they do document his interest in the movement of religious humanism and add greatly to an understanding of it.

After retiring as dean of the Abraham Lincoln Centre in 1957, Reese and his wife moved to Kissimmee, Florida. On 22 May 1959 he was presented the Weatherly-Holmes Award for service to liberal religion by the American Unitarian Association. On 5 June 1961, while attending a board of directors' meeting of the Meadville Theological School and its commencement exercises, Reese died of a coronary. With his passing another pioneer of religious humanism faded from the religious scene.

This brief biography suggests a number of significant aspects of Reese. Theologically, he moved from a Southern Baptist fundamentalism to a vague type of Protestant liberalism and finally to a nontheistic humanism. Unlike so many who reacted strongly against their earlier religious training, Reese always remained appreciative of the Baptists. He especially admired their doctrine of separation of church and state, their belief that the individual has direct access to God without going through a cleric or a religious institution, and their belief in a democratic form of church government. Other aspects of Baptist doctrine, however, Reese found unaccceptable. Influenced by biblical criticism, he could not accept the Bible as the infallible word of God, the virgin birth of Jesus, or the belief that humans were redeemed by the death of Jesus; nor could he accept the belief that lost souls would suffer in hell fire, for he simply could not reconcile such a view with a just and loving God. Reese apparently moved from theism to humanism without a strong inner struggle. Once he began interpreting religion from a humanistic perspective, the question of the existence of God appeared irrelevant. The real struggle for Reese was the move from fundamentalism to liberalism. (This does not mean that others remained calm in the face of his humanism, for they did not, as the humanist-theist controversy attested.) Reese made little attempt to knock the old theology; he tended to avoid such issues. Yet, it might well be, as Reese opined in his autobiography, that his humanism kept him from the presidencies of Meadville Theological School and of the American Unitarian Association.

It should be stressed that Reese spent the major part of his professional career as dean of the Abraham Lincoln Centre—from the spring of 1923 until February 1957, when he was forced to retire as the result of a severe coronary. This Centre had distinguished members on its board of trustees, among them Paul Douglas, who later became a United States Senator from Illinois, and S. O. Levinson, who developed a plan for "outlawing all war."[13] The Centre was so well known that both the House and the Senate of the State of Illinois, on separate occasions, passed resolutions commending it for its fine service to the state. Reese worked and wrote about the world from the context of a kind of settlement house and social and cultural centre, rather than from an academic or ecclesiastical vantage point.

The main sources for understanding Reese's thought are his four short books and the many essays he wrote for *Unity,* the *Christian Register, Open Court,* and the *Humanist.* Reese's articles were often published in more than one place; for example, his well-known Harvard Summer School address was published in both *Unity* and the *Christian Register* as well as being included as a chapter in *Religious Humanism* and as a part of a chapter in "My Life Among the Unitarians." This was true of many other articles, which appeared with minor changes or none; hence his work contains a great deal of redundancy.

At the time of Reese's retirement Ernest W. Kuebler delivered an address to the Western Unitarian Conference meeting in Ann Arbor, Michigan, entitled "Curtis W. Reese—Liberal Statesman."[14] In this address Kuebler said that over the years he had attended meetings chaired by Reese that appeared to be paralyzed, but Reese always was able to bring the group around to some positive action. Kubler thought the term that best described Reese was "liberal statesman," and he pointed out seven areas in which Reese's statesmanship was obvious: in his running of the Abraham Lincoln Centre; in his working out an acceptance of "A Humanist Manifesto" by men with independent minds and diverse backgrounds, as well as in his contribution to the humanist movement generally; in the Adult Education movement; in his influence in the Western Unitarian Conference; in his sermons and addresses; in influencing the Meadville Theological School to become a part of the Federated Theological Faculty of the University of Chicago; and in helping prepare the way for the merger of the Unitarians with the Universalists. Reese was one of the founders of the American Humanist Association, its president for fourteen years, and was acknowledged as a "humanist pioneer" in 1956. We can only follow Kuebler's lead and refer to him as "the statesman of religious humanism." As we did with Dietrich, we shall concentrate on Reese's thought after it reached the humanistic stage, and look at how he understood and interpreted religious thought.

World View

Reese was aware of humans' uncertainty about their relationship to the cosmos. He saw that, generally, the human race is in an appalling state, for it always has been plagued by poverty, ignorance, disease, and war. He was also aware of the "old mechanical naturalism," which saw the law of entropy as running inexorably to destruction. This mechanical view held that the human being is not the final cause of the universe; "his existence is an accident, his story a brief and transitory episode in the life of one of the meanest of the planets." Sometime in our distant future

...the energies of our system will decay, the glory of the sun will be dimmed, and the earth, tideless and inert, will no longer tolerate the race which has for a moment disturbed its solitude. Man will go down into the pit, and all his thoughts will perish. The uneasy consciousness, which in this obscure corner has for a brief space broken the contended silence of the universe, will be at rest.[15]

In considering these predictions of doom, Reese found that we cannot be sure that humans are the favorite of the cosmos, nor can it not be said dogmatically that both good and evil are finally doomed.

Reese made three assumptions. First, he regarded the universe "as the given" and was not particularly interested in speculating about either its beginning or end. He was not interested in an "uncaused cause" although he acknowledged that his position left much to be desired.[16] Second, Reese was aware that the old views of the universe were being challenged. Awareness of the vastness of the universe had caused

107

humankind's sense of being at home in it to vanish: "Our sun is a star; and the universe contains millions more, many of which may have their own planetary systems. The nearest star to our earth is four light years; i. e., twenty-four trillion miles away...."[17]

Third, Reese also stressed the fact that life has evolved on this planet for at least a thousand million years. He speculated that as the earth whirled through space it picked up stray matter and eventually the germ of life arose. Since then, species of various degrees of complexity and intelligence have arisen, and the evolutionary process has passed through numerous stages: the growth of the earth itself, a time when vegetation existed only in the water and the only animals were the "skulless creatures of the sea," a period when ferns appeared on land and fish in the sea, a period in which pines and reptiles appeared, the time when mammals appeared, the period of prolonged infancy, the stage of leafed forests, of birds and animals, and finally, the period in which humans appeared and began to assume "responsibility in the creative process." Humans are the highest achievement of the evolutionary process, heirs of the past and parents of the future. Reese's world view is in this context, and in order to better understand his position, we must examine his criticisms of both materialism and theism.

According to Reese, the materialism that originated with Democritus and resurfaced in the seventeenth century denied a purpose in nature and was suspicious of everything that cannot be explained in terms of the locomotion of matter. Reese argued that we now know that even the atom can be broken down into smaller parts, which sometimes behave unpredictably. Even if we concede that everything is composed of matter, we still do not know exactly what matter is; therefore, any idea of a "block universe" is inadequate.

Reese cautioned against confusing mechanism with materialism even though the "old form" of materialism tended to be mechanistic. Generally, mechanism encouraged experimentation and searched for real differences in order to understand how various organisms worked. And, of course, modern mechanism is not to be confused with the old mechanism, for the old machine theory has been replaced by chemical and biological processes, which do not act like parts of a machine. In other words, said Reese, even mechanism is adapting to the model of organism.[18]

Reese further maintained that it is incorrect to equate naturalism with materialism. The "old naturalism" had not accepted evolutionary theory, it had no room for novelty, and it did not take mind seriously as a variant of matter; hence it was locked into a restricted view of science which, rather than bringing "brain up to mind," brought "mind down to brain." Reese thought that the strong point of the old naturalism was its avoidance of an unnecessary dualism and its explaining the universe in terms of efficient cause without "calling into service the doctrine of final ends as consciously held in the purposes of God." Believing that the "organic" model best explained the facts, Reese maintained that materialism as expressed in the old mechanicalism and old naturalism is inadequate to working out even a humanistic religious view of life.[19]

Reese used the term *theism* in two senses, one broad and the other narrow. The first included such points of view as animism, vitalism, deism, absolutism, and theism proper. Here we shall focus on the narrow or "proper" sense of theism, which Reese correctly interpreted as the attempt to bring into balance two beliefs about God, his transcendence and his immanence. Reese defined theism as:

...the hypothesis that the ultimate ground of the universe is Intelligent Will fulfilling a moral purpose, in the course of which he either consciously and specifically influences human fortunes, or so orders the cosmic situation as to make possible the realization of moral ends by human beings.[20]

Although Reese acknowledged that the theistic view of the universe is satisfying psychologically, he thought it could not be defended rationally and therefore its claim to truth is questionable.

Reese objected to the theistic view for several reasons. First, he thought terms like *moral* and *intelligent will*, which make sense in the human realm, cannot be applied to the universe as a whole; to do so is to misuse language. Second, he noted that only the good qualities of people are projected onto a personal God; could we not use the same process to infer a personal devil? Third, the term *moral* has no cosmic significance, for "the universe seems to be either above or below good and evil." Fourth, if there is a cosmic goal, as theism maintains, a mechanistic view would seem better suited to reaching a predetermined end; this would not require supernatural intervention in human affairs. Fifth, given the vastness of the universe, divine concern for human welfare seems most improbable; there also is no evidence for divine influence on human fortune. "For these reasons," said Reese, "the theistic hypothesis seems to me to be an unsatisfactory way of finding purpose in the universe."

Finding both "materialism" and "theism" incapable of providing a world view adequate for modern people, Reese turned to humanism. He defined it as "a philosophy of life that interprets man within the setting

109

of the organic conception of the nature of reality." The key word is "organic," for organisms function for some purpose. The organic model suggests "evolutionary processes, purpose capacities, creative levels, plastic categories, diversity, uniqueness, mutual support, and the like." The organism contains the past that lives in the present and is the link with the future. Although each organic level has certain physical, chemical, and psychological properties, "the whole is greater than the sum of its parts," and the parts function differently in isolation than in the total setting. Reese believed, then, that the organic model provides "an empirical teleology." Furthermore, he maintained that a cumulative and creative synthesis takes place at each stage of organic development, and that the idea of "the future is purposive in the present."

Humans, although continuous with nature, have developed "mental levels." Consequently they are conscious of their purpose, namely, to enhance human life. "Human purposes are grounded in experimental experience, conditioned by the knowledge of relations, aim to attain goals that are judged valuable, and are directed by intelligence." By learning how the creative process works, humans can participate in it. Reese believed that "the object of human purpose is the arrival at ends that are adjudged valuable in the human setting."

Reese repudiated both materialism and theism, maintaining that humanism provides the best answer for humankind's present situation. The rest of this chapter will be devoted to a more detailed explanation of Reese's humanistic world view:

Religious humanism, centering largely in the Unitarian church and the liberal Jewish group, with increasing numbers in other fellowships, aims at an interpretation of religion in naturalistic terms. While abandoning the supernatural, this movement expands the natural, and commits man to the causes and ideals that seem to him to have significance in his personal and social quest.[21]

Authority of the Evidence

Reese described philosophy as an attempt to express "the unique nature and experience of the philosopher."[22] Because the experience of each individual is unique, philosophy is pluralistic rather than monistic. Humanists are egocentric because they can view life only through the narrow windows of their own being. So when humanists attempt to give a world view, they realize that it is "basically personal and improvable." Reese explained that his view of humanism was a private one, and his humanist theology was confessional inasmuch as he presented his view

110

of the nature of reality with little supporting argument.

Reese saw life as multiple and evolving. Life is multiple because it involves a complex of both the personal and the "other-than personal." Unlike Fosdick, he maintained that the "personal" cannot be separated and held to be "more worthful" than impersonal processes. Because Reese maintained that creative evolution is at work within the universe, he denied that we could "sew up the universe," say that its golden age was at the beginning, or claim that the "creative" impulse originates outside the universe.

Traditionally, said Reese, humans have claimed to arrive at truth in four ways: through revelation, intuition, speculation, and the scientific method. He critically examined the first three methods and found them inadequate. The claim to truth through revelation appears in various religions, in different forms, and in different times and places, he said. Knowledge of the divine may have come through oracles (for example, Socrates and the oracle at Delphi), through religious institutions (such as Roman Catholicism), through individuals (the Pope or the pre-Second World War Emperor of Japan), through books (the Koran or Bible), or through "great souls" (Jesus or Buddha).[23]

It was obvious to Reese that revelation cannot be accepted as a source of truth, for "supernatural revelation is itself a product of the human mind"; humans determine what revelation is. Also, the revelations of one religion may contradict those of another. In Theravadin Buddhism, for example, the way to "enlightenment" is through the Eightfold Path, whereas St. Paul considered "salvation" to be the free gift of God manifest in Jesus Christ. For revelation to be a legitimate way of arriving at truth, we must have ways of distinguishing false claims from true ones. Although various religious traditions have attempted to establish norms, they appear arbitrary, and there is no norm to determine which religion contains the "true" revelation. Reese maintained that "modern people no longer take seriously the claims of supernatural revelations."

Intuition also is invalid for arriving at truth, Reese found, for conflicting claims are made from intuition just as they are from revelation. While people may "intuit" certain truths, their validity must be checked by experience. Consequently, the truth derives not from intuition, but from the test of experience. At most, intuition provides the possibility of truth. And since the elements of intuition are human, its insights "are to be trusted only when based upon human experience and checked by the verified findings of human science." Reese concluded that he could place "no reliance on either revelation or intuition."[24]

Humans speculate because they have highly developed minds. If speculation is to be trustworthy, it must be "premised upon the facts blasted from the quarry of reality by the power of human investigation."[25] Hence there is both true and false speculation. Reese viewed both theology and philosophy as products of human speculation, to be evaluated as such. The more closely they conform to truth that has already been established by human investigation, the better. Reese believed that both theologies and philosophies should be subordinated to human life—that is, they should serve humans rather than the reverse. Even speculation should be subject to checks—namely, does it correlate with human investigation, and does it aid humans? But even when speculation meets these criteria, it is still merely speculation.

The scientific method is the only way to establish truth, said Reese, and the scientific method was his "source of authority." However, he cautioned that he did not want "to be understood as regarding the scientific method as absolute."[26] He meant that the scientific method is concerned with understanding reality, and this understanding is conditioned by many factors, including human nature.[27] Because humans are what they are, they understand reality as they do. Although this limits understanding, humans still have a long way to go before they exhaust their potential.

Understanding also is conditioned by human interests, for humans seek knowledge in the direction of their interests and needs:

Interests may be physical, as the desire for food; or emotional, as the desire for love; or aesthetic, as the desire for beauty; or speculative, as the desire for consistent theories; or they may all be subsumed in a larger generalization, as the desire for organic satisfaction. But in all cases the recognition of human interest is fundamentally the effort to understand ourselves and the world.[28]

Understanding of reality is conditioned by experience. Through experience human nature itself is changed; as humans expand and their interests broaden, they often discover that their earlier understanding of reality was inadequate. As they discard old understandings, they hope for new and better ones. More and more, humans are coming to realize that experience and observation are the most reliable sources for information about reality.

Although Reese cautioned that the scientific method cannot always separate truth from falsehood, he thought it was the best method for arbitrating conflicting claims to truth. He wished to extend the method beyond the limited domains of the hard sciences to include all areas of human concern. Reese often spoke of the "authority of evidence," believing that the scientific method was applicable to all practical concerns, including jurisprudence. In this context he frequently quoted Thomas Huxley: "The deepest sin against the human mind is to believe things without evidence."[29]

In applying "the authority of the evidence" to religion, Reese concluded that many religious beliefs are based on "uncriticized desire, ecstatic experience, and false logic." Although the tenets of many creeds refer "to things unknown if not unknowable," they derive rules of conduct from them. Reese, finding no evidence about the nature and purpose of "ultimate reality," thought a moral code based on notions of ultimate reality "a house of straw on shifting sand."

Traditional authoritarian systems of religion cannot survive the test of the authority of the evidence, thought Reese, "but it is better to have fewer beliefs than to have so many that are not true." Reese advocated a religion based on a reasonable interpretation of the evidence. No area of belief should be exempt from the requirement of evidence: "Though the evidence slay him, yet will he follow it...."

Reese tried to establish how truth based on evidence relates to "the supremacy of intelligence." Evidence is the means for arriving at truth; intelligence guides humans toward the goals revealed by truth. Reese advocated questioning precedent and maintaining a skeptical attitude toward one's own bias, intuition, or pure reason. Every traditional basis for human conduct should be subjected to the critical eye of intelligence:

Intelligence applied to any given problem involves, (1) the collation of all pertinent facts, (2) fair weighing and ordering of the facts, (3) definite understanding of a goal that is both desirable and possible in view of the facts, and (4) the technical skill to enlist and direct all available forces in the achievement of the desired goal. This is human engineering.

Too rarely, thought Reese, has human intelligence been applied to the "problem of conquering the world and of living an abundant life."

In summary, Reese did not find revelation, intuition, or mere speculation legitimate means for discovering truth. He found the scientific method, despite its limitations, the only sure way, for "while science may give us inadequate knowledge, it gives all we have and we must make the most of it."[30]

Humans

Reese viewed humans as an organic part of nature, a result of the evolutionary process. But because humans possess self-consciousness and insight, they are not a fixed part of nature but highly plastic and flexible, with potential for development. Humans are creators; they dream and can follow their dreams. They can cooperate with the natural processes of the universe and, within certain limits, guide and control them. The universe is unconcerned with good or ill, but it provides the conditions under which humans can grow and develop by taking the intelligent initiative.[31]

Because humans have self-consciousness, they tend to separate themselves from the other forms of nature, even other animals. Reese objected to such a tendency because it perpetuates a dualism of the spiritual versus the physical. He believed the mental and physical overlap, interpenetrate, fuse—are "basically one." To speak of the "material" and "spiritual," the biological and mental, is a practical distinction that should not imply a dualism.[32] Reese was concerned with the total person: appetites, passions, hungers, thirsts, desires, and aspirations, all of which create the texture of life. He was not interested in some fixed, absolute standard impossible of human attainment; he wanted to realize "the fullness of the inherent and the unique needs of individual man in his social setting." Reese's gospel sought to satisfy the whole of human life; nothing was taboo. It sought the fulfillment of the spiritual as well as the physical, including our sexual nature. It entered into the thick of the battle to gain a full life for all humankind: "Issues shift, needs change, men grow old and pass away; but always there remains the human struggle to wring a satisfactory life from environing situations that are none too friendly."

Like many of his generation, Reese was interested in bettering human nature. The church had struggled with this problem for centuries by "breaking man's will," attempting to turn people from their own stubborn wills and persuading them to surrender to the will of God. The rules of society have operated in a similar way. He thought that both the church and the state had been wrong: we should not break people's wills, but redirect them; we should channel basic human impulses in a useful direction. He had faith that people could change their natures by directing their impulses to achieve desired ends. The kind of rechanneling Reese sought was the "democratization of human nature"—the gradual organization of instincts or impulses in "harmony with community interests."[33] He said, "Original human nature is a bundle of unorganized impulses. It has become what it is by a gradual process of reorganization. To democratize human nature is to reorganize impulses in harmony with community interest. This is not reversal but development of primitive impulses."[34]

Implicit in the "democratization of human nature" is a conviction that the individual is sacred; therefore, to violate the personality of an individual is a serious offense. The more the human race progresses, the more it becomes aware of the value of the individual. And if the individual is sacred, so is society. Reese understood the difficulty of trying to define "society" precisely, but he did say that it involves a system of psychical relations in which our lives are interrelated and our ideal is to create human community. Just as the rights of the individual are inviolable, so are those of society. People therefore must organize their impulses so that they will neither stifle their own selfhood nor violate the selfhood of another.

Individuals can, taking into account their own impulses and the sacredness of society, become what they wish to be. Will is the principal agent of change in human nature. Reese maintained, "Human nature is the most plastic part of the living world. Within very large margins human beings may not only do what they will but also become what they will."[35] The real problem is determining the direction in which to channel our impulses. Because our impulses are general, they may be steered in a variety of directions, but they must never violate the sacredness of human personality. For Reese, "original human nature is neither depraved nor divine; it is simply unorganized and undirected. Its remaking, its regeneration if you prefer, consists in organization and direction toward worthy ends." Once intelligence determines what those "worthy ends" are, the "will" must be persuaded to seek them.

Certain social arrangements are inconsistent with this understanding of humans. Reese specifically attacked what he referred to as "individualism" and "socialism." Individualism stresses social and economic laws that protect private interests, and it implies that social arrangements should be allowed to arise by chance. This laissez-faire policy of objecting to the social whole interfering with its parts at best encourages "good-natured rivalry"; at worst, it breeds anarchy.

Reese defined socialism as "the dogma of the relentless operation of economic determinism, of class conflict, and of cataclysmic events."[36] He said its weakness is advocating a tyranny of the many over the few; the position is doctrinaire, forcing facts into a priori theories instead of inferring theories from the facts. Its belief that it is the only method of social salvation is a kind of "political fundamentalism."

Believing that both individualism and socialism are political blind

115

alleys, Reese advocated a doctrine of "mutualism" that embraces the strong points of both. It recognizes both the needs of the individual and the mutual assistance society can provide. In practice, mutualism takes the form of "experimental democracy." Rather than being doctrinaire, experimental democracy is mobile in its willingness to attempt a plan of action and to change it if the plan fails.

Reese apparently was trying to promote a society where good people can live. He defined a good person as "one who inquires diligently into the meaning of facts, who is concrete in his devotion to worthy causes, and who translates purpose into action."[37] Because Reese considered ethics and human nature as inseparable, we will now look at his ethics.

Ethics

Reese disagreed with both what he called "the old view of ethics" and the "idealistic" view. He criticized the old view for being autocratic, for being based on an arbitrary will considered superior because it was supernatural. The old view separated ethical action from natural inclination. He thought morality proceeds from humans' reasonable nature. The new view of ethics has shifted from the absolute to the finite and concrete. In the past, religion dealt with the relation of individuals to God, and ethics dealt with the relation of persons to persons; but now, said Reese, "Godward action is found in manward action."[38] He viewed ethics not as a quest for absolute standards of right and wrong but as a search for values "for the promotion of the common welfare." Something is good insofar as it enhances human life. People do not follow ideals to approach an ideal standard; they follow them to promote human welfare. Accordingly, humanistic ethics is experimental, for it lays no claim to finality. Its statements are tentative, and its programs are subject to change if experiment indicates that another action will be more beneficial to human life. Present-day morality, in short, is based on present-day knowledge.

For Reese the responsibility for morality resides in humans, for they initiate morality and experiment in ethics. One aim of humanistic ethics is to develop individual freedom. Moral living is possible only to people who have the freedom to initiate behavior and who operate in a universe where nothing is ultimate and fixed. Without autonomy, individuals have no capacity for living a moral life, because to be moral, an action must be performed by free will. Actions we are forced to perform cannot

116

be considered moral: "The moral life begins with freedom to choose or not to choose a line of action; and no moral significance can be attached to any action in the absence of this freedom." Not only must one be free, one also must have knowledge of right and wrong to act morally; since knowledge is always approximate and tentative, however, ethics is always in a state of flux. Assuming responsibility for our actions adds another dimension to freedom, for the individual "must direct his action toward ends designated by the unbiased judgments of a free mind and the unselfish aims of a noble soul." To act from passion or prejudice causes suffering.

Reese, who stood within the naturalistic tradition, based his ethics upon humans in a natural setting rather than in an "idealistic" cosmic or transcendental setting. He did not deny the continuity of humans with the cosmos, but emphasized that cosmic events appear to have little concern or connection with human behavior and do not validate it.[39] The main weakness, according to Reese, of an idealistic theory of values is its moving from a specific, human context to a general, cosmic one. There is no valid way, for example, to move from the statement "I love my wife" to the conclusion "therefore the universe loves me." Human values have no cosmic significance; a value is what humans esteem. Without a human being, the evaluator, value does not exist.

Reese, however, did not maintain that value judgments are purely personal, for they arise out of a social setting and are conditioned by human needs: "a value is not a value unless it satisfies; it cannot satisfy unless it meets needs; and needs grow out of nature, social experience and the interplay of self and the world. The process of valuation is not arbitrary." Just as values do not simply reflect personal taste, conscience alone is an insufficient guide for morality, for the conscience may be misinformed. Values should be compared with their rationale. Individuals must know themselves and the world, but even sufficient knowledge will not eliminate differences of opinion. Reese found both the old and the idealistic views of ethics unacceptable, but he thought that one can make moral choices that are more than merely personal whims.

Reese held human life to be of "supreme worth." He did not believe its value derives from our creation by a Supreme Being, but that life is inherently good. Like Kant and Felix Adler, Reese considered humans ends in themselves. This view led Reese to take verbal swats at both traditional Christianity and Marxism—Christianity for holding that people were created to glorify God, and Marxism for holding that people are an instrument for establishing the socialist order. Both views render

117

humans secondary, and Reese considered them primary; everything else is important only as it contributes to human welfare.[40]

Morality, which grows out of the human situation, should create a means for aiding, not obstructing, human development. The economic, political, and social orders are "means to the ends of human life, not human life means to their ends." Social institutions should be evaluated by their contributions to human welfare, and should be constantly reexamined and revised according to their success in meeting human needs. Likewise, personal relationships must never be means to an end: no one should be used by another or by an institution to further its own selfish purposes: "the good of each must become the concern of all."

Reese thought that humans can change the world, that they can succeed where traditional religion has failed. Although it has provided solace for those in distress, the church has done little to set or achieve social goals. Humanism, in contrast, believes that individuals can control and direct themselves, alter their environment, and find ways to realize their ideals.[41] Human progress can come about only when humans assume responsibility:

[Humans are] capable of so ordering human relations that life shall be preserved, not destroyed; that justice shall be established, not denied; that love shall be the rule, not the exception. It but remains for religion to place responsibility at the heart of its gospel. When this is done, science and democracy and religion will have formed an alliance of wisdom, vision and power.

Human progress depends on competent leadership; without it, the masses will follow demogogues and charlatans. Reese felt that much of the leadership of his generation was incompetent although it was often magnetic, for a striking presence can often mask a lack of ability. We must therefore learn to distinguish between spurious and genuine leadership; we must examine the basic issues and comprehend the motives of those who aspire to leadership—enough, at least, to separate the experts from the fakers. Expertise is as important in the social as in the physical sciences. Just as we need experts to construct bridges, we need them to enact and administer our law. When we choose experts over incompetents, "then will begin the manhood of humanity."

Reese drew several implications from his overall view of humanism: (1) social values must be available to people regardless of their race, nation, or other distinguishing characteristics.[42] (2) All social arrangements must be evaluated by their contribution to a satisfactory life for all people. Both laissez-faire capitalism and dialectical communism are inadequate; in their place Reese advocated "experimental democracy," which has a built-in means for its own improvement and may be modified as needed. (3) Our major concern and primary responsibility is building values in the social order. Because humans create both the social order and the values it espouses, people can make their society what they want it to be. (4) The social order should be structured to sustain and enhance all aspects of life. Believing that traditional religion had neglected them, Reese empasized meeting people's physical needs. (5) Since humanists are concerned with the well-being of all people, they must create a world order embracing all humanity. He felt a small minority cannot progress very far without improving the lot of the majority; people rise or fall together.

Reese envisioned a "commonwealth of man." The indispensable requirements for building such a commonwealth are universal education, social guarantees, and world organization. Because only educated people can establish and build the commonwealth of humanity, Reese emphasized raising educational standards, universalizing educational opportunities, and finding ways to determine and develop human potential.[43] Individuals obviously cannot achieve the commonwealth alone; they must work together to eliminate as much as possible the terrors of accident and unemployment, of improvidence and sickness, of old age and death. Almsgiving and philanthropy alone are not adequate; some form of social insurance should be implemented. How such a program should be administered is a matter of expediency, but it must be done. As to world organization, Reese said, "Manifestly the world must be managed co-operatively, the peoples and the nations are intertwined and are forever inseparable. No nation or people can prosper permanently at the cost of any other nation or people. All the world goes up or down together." Prophets of the past have spoken of a world order; any religion that fails to proclaim this gospel is neither an heir of these prophets nor the parent of the future.

Whereas Dietrich tended to be stoical in facing life's difficulties, Reese was optimistic; in October 1929 he proclaimed: "Theoretically, we are wedded to the idea of progress....We believe in the progress of mankind onward and upward forever. It is valid gospel, and we must apply it as never before."[44] Reese envisioned the ideal man living in his "commonwealth of man":

Humanistic liberalism understands spirituality to be man at his best, sane in mind, healthy in body, dynamic in personality; honestly facing the hardest facts, conquering and not fleeing from his gravest troubles; committed to the most worthwhile causes, loyal to the best ideals; ever hoping, striving, and achieving. To know one's self as inherently worthful, actually to find fullest expression in the widest human service and consciously to become a co-worker with cosmic processes, is spiritual experience deep and abiding.[45]

Although Reese's theory of ethics is not always clear, one thing is certain: one can be moral without any apparent belief in God. Humans have evolved from an eternal cosmos, and they can control it to create a true "commonwealth of man." Not only can humans do this, they *will*. (Reese, in fact, thought they were already doing so.) Reese's ethics was "natural rather than transcendental, human rather than cosmic, experimental rather than final."[46]

Religion

Reese's view of religion was humanistic. He did not see religion as a person's response to "the determiner of destiny" or to "superhuman sources of fortune" or as "man's conduct facing Godward." He denied that religion is necessarily tied to any theistic interpretation of cosmic existence. He interpreted religion

...as a human effort to find satisfactory models of living, in the course of which many personal, social, planetary, and cosmological theories may be postulated, tested, and abandoned; the abiding thing being the urge to newer and newer efforts to reach ever receding goals.[47]

Religion, then, is related to the best that humans think and do—their sacred memories, noble sentiments, and lofty ideals:

Without religion and the institutions of religion the world could not have reached its present heights; without them the heights beyond are unattainable. Amid the struggles and achievements of mankind religion has constantly evolved new motives and goals. Being of the very texture of spiritual urge, religion requires growth in its content and change in its expression.[48]

Reese thought that religion constantly undergoes reformation. Examples of this process are Christianity's arrival on the stage of history out of Judaism, the sixteenth-century Protestant Reformation out of Roman Catholicism. Humanism represents yet another reformation, which, if it is to succeed, must cast aside some old religious conceptions. It must first discard the old world view, founded on people's wishes rather than on scientific fact. (As we have already seen, Reese found both the materialistic and theistic world views inadequate.) Second, it must set aside the old method of metaphysics, which attempts to harmonize the old with the new; if the old cannot stand the test of evidence, it must be relinquished altogether. Third, trust in the old doctrines because our ancestors believed them must be replaced with "the creative imagination" that focuses on the future, not the past. Hence, animistic, metaphysical, and naive faith must go if the humanist reformation is to occur.

Reese saw not only obstacles to the humanist reformation, but also factors that made religious reform "inevitable and imminent." Science, for example, had made great strides in helping humans understand their world, and technology was providing ways of controlling it. Also, "biblical criticism has destroyed many of the dogmas of orthodoxy and remade much of the Bible." Philosophy, which claimed to have absolute standards—as in Plato's "ideas" and Aristotle's "forms"—was being replaced by "experimental experience" as the test of truth. Social thinking had shifted toward democracy, hence "castes and stratifications are doomed."

Reese thought that as religion discarded the old, unnecessary, doctrinal baggage, it was changing for the better. Religious leaders were beginning to take an interest in worldly affairs, and he hoped the creative endeavor to change the world would become the focus of the religious consciousness: "the building of human souls for worthy habitation in a world of hard facts, and the constant remaking of the actual world about us and the ideal world beyond us." Reese thought that creeds and ceremonies, which were primary in the old religious vision, would be replaced by "purposeful service, free fellowship, and brave living." Humanistic religion, furthermore, instead of emphasizing the attitude of acceptance, demonstration, and agreement, which were important to the old religion, would urge exploration, discovery, and construction.

In *Humanistic Religion* Reese recapitulated his religious position:

In summary, the trend in modern religious developments is away from the transcendent, the authoritative, the dogmatic, and toward the human, the experimental, the tentative; away from the abnormal, the formal, the ritualistic; and toward the normal, the informal, the usual; away from the extraordinary mystic expression, the exalted mood, the otherworldly; and toward the ethical, the social and the worldly; away from religion conceived as one of man's concerns, and toward religion conceived as man's one concern.[49]

Although Reese did not use the phrase "religion without God," the word *God* is absent from his understanding of religion. His religious position is, in fact, a "religion without God."

The Church

In the midst of the economic depression of the early thirties, a time Reese spoke of as a period of revolution, he chided the church for being more interested in a future life than the present one. It appeared to him that the main revolutionary movements of his day either ignored or criticized the church. If the church were to become relevant to the revolutionary world, he maintained that it must become radical. For Reese, this meant becoming humanistic. The church must focus on "the human centre, where every race is at home, where every opinion may be examined purely on its merits, and where the corporate sympathy definitely faces a new world order."[50]

The radical church will be led by humanist ministers, who must be wide open to human experience, not retreat from the world. They must follow the truth, yielding to no influences in presenting their message, but always retaining an open mind. Such leaders must free themselves of inhibiting professionalism, disdain stereotyped methods, and become vital forces in the creative movements of the day.[51]

Humanist ministers should exemplify in their own lives the ethical ideals and excellence for which their religion and the ministerial profession stand. As family and church members and as citizens, they must be above reproach.[52] They also must be diligent, alert, and competent in administering their churches, which are subject to the same laws governing the success or failure of any social organization. Church administration is both an art and a science, and ministers must be masters in this field. They must serve the personal needs of their parishioners and have a broad, sympathetic understanding based on wide experience with all sorts and conditions of people. To make intelligent referrals, they must be acquainted with the resources in their community. They must have a certain art in counseling and observe the strictest confidentiality. Furthermore, they should represent the church and its high ideals in the remainder of the community. They should be informed and active in civic affairs, able to think straight on national and world issues. They must be able to separate the ideal from the possible. Finally, they must preach as evangels from "the world of imponderables," meaning the world of justice, mercy, and love. They must condemn injustice, brutality, and hate. Preaching, thought Reese, is the most important function of the humanist minister; it "is proclamation of profound convictions."

The humanist address or sermon must be both inspirational and informative. It should correct error, synthesize the truth, and enlarge academic instruction. Every area of thought should be possible subject matter for addresses, which "must clarify public opinion and create public conscience."[53] The address must have "the approval of the preacher's whole being," meaning that it should be without reservation. In a sense, the message should be the minister's life put into words.

The humanist church also must develop humanist rituals. "The readings, hymns, prayers, and benedictions of the new service must embody contemporary values, interpret emerging goals, satisfy the intellect and stir the deepest emotions." The ritual should cover all the areas of human concern—education, politics, science, and art. Reese also referred to the "humanistic pew." The pew will be composed of laypersons who can separate the essential from the nonessential and who can see beyond their everyday concerns to a vision of utopia. It will be a pew "that recognizes and respects honest thought, frank utterance, and brave conduct." The traditional Christian church can recover a position of power only by becoming humanist, by admitting that the old dogmas are dead. Now that thinking people no longer accept the doctrine of an afterlife in a supernatural world, the church is free to decide what it wishes to become.

Reese mentioned three aspects of what he called the church with a humanistic purpose. First, the church should create "humanistic sympathy" by opposing autocratic forms of religion, remaining willing to experiment, and fostering democratic movements. Second, the church should be a "mobilizing agent of humanistic thought" and articulate the humanistic point of view to regain its intellectual leadership in the world. Rather than being theistic, religious thought will be humanistic. Third, the church should direct "sympathy and thought into humanistic conduct." It should actively fight racial discrimination, poverty, ignorance, and disease. Reese, writing in 1926, specifically mentioned such goals as social insurance, optional parenthood, priority of personal over property rights, women's rights, and a world federation of peoples. In other words, the church should direct its concern "toward the goal of a free society in which free persons voluntarily and intelligently cooperate for the common good—where the needs of each shall become the concern of all."[54]

Religion without God

Was Reese's religion a religion without God? In his theological writings he did not use the concept of God to account for the existence of the universe, for humans, for ethics, for the church, or for religion. He ignored the subject of immortality, except in a few passing references

("As to immortality, the Humanist shifts the emphasis from longevity to quality. But Humanism encourages research in the realm of the spirit."[55]) Reese never used the phrase employed by Dietrich, "religion without God."

During the heat of the humanist-theist controversy Reese objected to the theists referring to humanists as atheists:

The radical Unitarian Humanist is inclined to say, "Very well, if Humanism be Atheistic, so be it." But in point of fact, there is not the slightest ground for calling Humanists Atheistic.[56]

The Unitarian discussion might be summed up as "Theism or no Theism," but not as "God or no God," since most of the Humanists hold some one of the several non-Theistic theories of God.[57]

Significantly, Reese did not declare himself among those who held to a nontheistic view of God. After 1920, the nearest that Reese came to affirming belief in a God was a statement in his book *Humanism*:

...the liberal recognizes and zealously proclaims the fact that purposive and powerful cosmic processes are operative, and that increasingly man is able to cooperate with them and in a measure control them. What these processes be styled is of but little importance. Some call them cosmic processes, others call them God.[58]

Neither did Reese identify himself with those who called the cosmic processes God, even in his latest works, *The Meaning of Humanism,* published in 1945, and his autobiography, "My Life Among the Unitarians," written in 1961 and never published. After his controver-sial address at the Harvard Summer School in 1920, Reese frequently repeated a statement from that address: "Liberalism is building a religion that would not be shaken even if the thought of God were outgrown."[59] This was as close as Reese ever came to stating a position.

I conclude that Reese had no theistic notion of God. Considering his apparent disavowal of personal immortality and his ignoring even a naturalistic doctrine of God, it seems likely that he did not believe in God at all. Professor Elmo A. Robinson, who was introduced to religious humanism through Reese, wrote:

[Religious humanism] first came forcibly to my attention in the summer of 1921, when Curtis Reese was urging upon a group of ministers attending the University of Chicago the proposition that theism is philosophically possible but not religiously necessary. By this he meant that it is possible to be religious without believing in God and immortality.[60]

Reese was a pioneer of religious humanism. His type of humanism was undoubtedly a religion without God.

CHAPTER 6

Charles Francis Potter: The Rebel of Religious Humanism

"Man is nothing else but what he purposes, he exists only in so far as he realizes himself, he is therefore nothing else but the sum of his actions, nothing else but what his life is."—Jean-Paul Sartre

CHARLES FRANCIS POTTER WAS BORN ON 28 OCTOBER 1885 IN Marlboro, Massachusetts. His family was simple and hard-working (his father was employed in a shoe factory); it was also religious, and was active in the First Baptist Church. From a very early age, the church and the school were Potter's two main interests. He was an excellent student and almost from the beginning was interested in religious questions. The church provided him with a number of opportunities to exhibit his quick mind, and its Sunday School and youth programs gave him opportunities for public speaking.[1]

At the age of fourteen, because of a lack of money, he dropped out of school to work in the office of the shoe factory. At the same time, he became a Sunday School teacher; the boys in his class asked many of the questions that he himself had asked. Because he had not yet discovered adequate answers, he determined to receive a college and theological school education.

By taking a job in his spare time with the local paper, the *Daily Enterprise*, he was able to return to high school. At the age of seventeen, he had succeeded in getting some fiction published in a magazine, and the Baptists had licensed him to preach. He entered Bucknell University in the fall of 1903, with only two and a half years of high school behind him and only twenty dollars in his pocket.

He was able to survive the first year by doing odd jobs and speaking in small rural churches on Sundays. In his sophomore year he transferred to Brown University so that he could be nearer his home. Although he did excellent work at Brown, he returned reluctantly to Bucknell for his junior year because the Pennsylvania school was much less expensive. At Brown, however, Potter was taken under the wing of Dr. William Herbert Perry Faunce, who was then president. It seems that one of the ministers of the Marlboro church was a Brown graduate and had written a letter to Faunce on Potter's behalf. Faunce took an interest in Potter and was obviously a liberalizing influence on him, for it was through Faunce that Potter was made aware of the works of the liberal German theologian Adolf Harnack, the author of the well-known text *What Is Christianity?* Potter named one of his sons after Faunce, and when he decided to transfer from the Baptist to the Unitarian church, he discussed his proposed move with Faunce.

Potter was graduated from Bucknell *summa cum laude* in June 1907. That fall he entered the Newton Theological Institute, chosen because it was near his home. At the end of his first year, at the age of twenty-two, he became the minister of the Calvin Baptist Church in Dover, New Hampshire. He married Clara Cook and was ordained into the Baptist ministry. After two years at Dover, Potter became the minister of the Mattapan Baptist Church in order to be nearer his theological school so that he could complete his final two years. In Dover, Potter had begun to question the foundations of the Christian faith; returning to the Institute would provide him with an opportunity to seek some answers. He was thoroughly grounded in Greek, took the basic course in Hebrew, and was exposed to "Higher Criticism." With a growing family and strong intellectual doubts about the validity of many of the tenets he had accepted as a child, Potter resigned his ministry in January 1914. He could no longer believe in the church's teachings about messianic prophecy and the second coming of Christ; nor could he believe in saving grace and salvation through the blood of Jesus, as did his Baptist colleagues. Since he had begun to preach more about ethical concerns, he decided to become a Unitarian.

His first position as a Unitarian was in a mission church in Edmonton, Alberta. Under his leadership the first Unitarian church in that city was built.[2] During this period (1914-16), Potter first heard of a John H.

Dietrich, who was preaching "humanism" in Spokane:

There was an interesting man in the Edmonton church named Turner. He was a school official and spent half his time in Edmonton and the other half in Spokane, Washington: I never knew how or why. What did interest me was a remark he made after hearing me preach a few times: "In Spokane there's a minister in the Unitarian church named Dietrich, another maverick like you. Neither of you is really what is commonly called a Unitarian or even a Christian. He calls himself a Humanist: you say you're a Personalist. But as far as I can determine, you both are preaching the same line of thought."[3]

Potter then told about how he first heard of Curtis W. Reese:

There was at this time in the Des Moines, Iowa, Unitarian Church a young man who had been ordained as a Baptist minister in 1908, the same year as I, and had become a Unitarian at the same time I did. Dr. Lewis G. Wilson, then secretary of the American Unitarian Association, thought the Des Moines minister, Rev. Curtis W. Reese, and I should get acquainted on the basis of our parallel experiences. The resulting correspondence revealed that Reese was another "maverick" preaching the same general line as Dietrich and I were, with perhaps more of a social emphasis. He sometimes referred to his faith as the Religion of Democracy.[4]

About his own position at this time, Potter said, "My 'theology' was...a sort of experimental, non-supernatural Personalism. It was loosely monistic, but not very well integrated."

Potter left Edmonton in May 1916 to return to his hometown. He became minister of the Marlboro Unitarian Church. In 1918 he moved to the Wellesley Hills Unitarian Church, where he remained only a year. In 1919 he became the minister of the West Side Unitarian Church in New York City, where he remained until 1925. In these six years, Potter took a small nucleus of a church, enlarged its membership, relocated it in a modern building, and made it an effective influence in the New York community.

During Potter's tenure at West Side Unitarian Church the fundamentalists renewed their attack on the modernists. The battle line often was drawn on the theory of evolution. The fundamentalists thought that evolution repudiated the Genesis account of the special creation of humans, thus throwing into question the infallibility of the Bible. Dr. John Roach Straton, pastor of the Calvary Baptist Church, was the unchallenged leader of the fundamentalist cause in New York City. In early December 1923, he had brought together such well-known fundamentalists as Dr. Thomas T. Shields of Toronto, Dr. J. Frank Norris of Fort Worth, and William Jennings Bryan to launch a campaign against the modernists. As Potter read newspapers accounts of the meetings and reports of personal attacks on modernists, especially liberal Baptists and

Unitarians who were personal acquaintances, he decided to retaliate. The outcome was the famous Straton-Potter debates.

Originally five debates were scheduled between Straton and Potter. The first debate was held on the evening of 20 December 1923 in the Calvary Baptist Church before an overflow crowd of twenty-five hundred. The subject was "Resolved, That the Bible is the Infallible Word of God."[5] Straton, of course, took the affirmative. Potter, debating the negative, was declared the winner. The next three debates were held in Carnegie Hall before a packed house. The second debate, on 28 January 1924, was "Resolved, That the Earth and Man Came from Evolution."[6] Although the judges awarded the debate to Straton, a radio station poll found Potter the victor by a margin of 57 to 43 percent. The third debate, on 22 March, was "Resolved, That the Miraculous Virgin Birth of Jesus Christ Is a Fact and that It Is Essential Christian Doctrine."[7] Potter won this debate on a split decision. Straton was victorious in the fourth debate, held on 28 April; its subject: "Resolved, That Jesus Christ was Entirely Man instead of Incarnate Deity."[8]

Potter was unable to get Straton to schedule a fifth debate on "Resolved, That Jesus Christ will Return in Bodily Presence to this Earth and Establish the Reign of Universal Peace and Righteousness." Straton obviously saw the difficulty of winning a debate on such a subject, but there were perhaps two other reasons that he never scheduled the debate. Several of his advisors had tried to persuade him to cancel the debates because with each one it appeared to them that Potter was winning the uncommitted to Unitarianism. Straton had entered the debates hoping through them to win Potter back into the Baptist fold, even to hire him as his assistant; when he saw that Potter's backsliding was irreversible, he gave up on him and saw no further purpose for the debates.

In 1925 the Scopes Trial was held in Dayton, Tennessee. Potter attended as "a librarian and Bible expert for the defense."[9] In many respects the Scopes Trial was a recapitulation of the second Straton-Potter debate on evolution. Only this time the central characters were Clarence Darrow and William Jennings Bryan, and the stakes were higher. Bryan had collaborated with Straton in the debates, and most of their arguments were similar; Bryan even used the same phrases—for example, "I am not so much interested in the Age of the Rocks as I am in the Rock of Ages." Darrow had Potter work up a list of historical and other inaccuracies in the Bible, but was able to make use of only a few of them. Potter was convinced that the people in Dayton who instigated the Scopes Trial got the idea from reading newspaper accounts of the Potter-Straton debates.[10]

Two months before the Scopes Trial, Potter resigned from the ministry of West Side Unitarian Church. That fall he became the executive secretary of Antioch College in Yellow Springs, Ohio. His main responsibility was fund raising, although he taught a course in comparative religions.[11] During the debates with Straton, Potter had described his religion as being deistic with a small mixture of pantheism; by the time of his resignation he was rapidly moving toward a nontheistic humanism, finding even Unitarianism too confining. After being in the limelight for some time, it appeared to Potter that he needed to "cool his heels," as his wife expressed it. He had also begun to wonder whether education was not properly replacing religion, so the offer from Antioch appeared to be just what he needed.

Apparently Potter was less successful in raising money for Antioch than he expected to be. He left Antioch in January 1927 to head the Bureau of Lectures of the National Association of Book Publishers. This position provided him an opportunity to encourage the building and expansion of libraries and culture generally. In a short time, however, at the urging of friends, Potter accepted a call to become the minister of the Universalist Church of the Divine Paternity in New York. The church was old, with a prestigious tradition, but Potter proved too radical for its congregation. He resigned in March 1929, resolved to organize a humanist society in New York.

Six months after leaving the ministry of Divine Paternity, on 29 September 1929, Potter held a service to organize the First Humanist Society of New York.[12] This first meeting was held in Steinway Hall, which seated about 250. When the time for the service arrived, the hall was packed; hundreds had to be turned away. Potter explained his understanding of humanism, which he saw as "a new faith for a new age." After the service 206 people signed cards expressing interest in the movement, and 106 signed on as charter members of the society. Two weeks later the society met in Chalif Hall because it had a larger auditorium. Potter conducted his first humanist wedding on 2 November 1929, his first humanist funeral on 3 March 1931, and his first humanist recognition service on 3 June 1934. The recognition service corresponds to the baptismal service in Christian churches; a rosebud was used to symbolize new life and its celebration.[13]

Although Potter was in great demand as a lecturer and magazine writer, he managed to publish five books during the 1930s, and many others in the ensuing years. Apart from the debates and articles, his first published book was *The Story of Religion* (1929), which contained the biographies of the founders of the great world religions and was the companion volume to Will Durant's *The Story of Philosophy*. *Humanism: A New Religion,* published in 1930, provided a kind of theological manual for humanism. Generally he received good reviews for this work, and the American Library Association included it among the best fifty books on religion for that year. *Humanizing Religion* (1933) contained fourteen of Potter's addresses to the Humanist Society. *Is That in the Bible?* was also published in 1933. Subtitled "A Classified Collection of the Odd, Amusing, Unusual, and Surprising Items of Human Interest in the Bible," the book originated in the questions Potter had prepared for Darrow to use in his encounter with Bryan at the Scopes Trial, and the manuscript had been completed in 1926. This work was followed by *Technique of Happiness* (1935), a kind of "power of positive thinking" that preceded Norman Vincent Peale and grew out of an advice column Potter had written for *True Story*. Although the articles were well received and the reviews were favorable, the book never sold. Next to appear was *Beyond the Senses* (1939), which deals with extrasensory perception. Many of his humanist acquaintances were skeptical about this new interest; although Potter remained a humanist and monist, he still thought there was some empirical basis for extrasensory perception that currently was not understood.

Next to appear was *The Creative Personality* (1950). In this book Potter picked up on one of the themes of *Humanism: A New Religion,* the need for the fullest possible development of human personality. In 1951 Potter's autobiography, *The Preacher and I*, was published. It was followed by *The Faith Men Live By,*which combines chapters on the world's major religions and on various denominations, including "The Liberal Churches and Religious Societies." In this chapter Potter gave a brief statement about humanism. This book apparently sold well; the paperback edition was published in April and had gone through its fourth printing by June.

Although Potter became a humanist, he retained an abiding interest in Jesus. *The Lost Years of Jesus* (1958), which originally appeared in paperback and sold more than 200,000 copies, came out in hard cover after his death. In this work Potter interpreted for the layman the scholarship centering around the Dead Sea Scrolls and the Nag-Hammadi discoveries. He attributed both literary finds to the Essenes, who he believed provide the link between Judaism and Christianity. On the basis of the great similarities between some of the teachings of Jesus and the Dead Sea Scrolls, Potter thought that Jesus might well have been a member of the Essene community during the "silent years." Finally, he believed that the scholarship on the Dead Sea Scrolls supported his belief that Jesus was a historical person only, who had been elevated to divine status by the church. Another book on Jesus, *Did Jesus Write This Book?* was published posthumously in 1965. The title refers to a discovery in 1892 by some British scholars in Serbia of a work sometimes called "The Book of the Secrets of Enoch." Because the original work dates from the time of Jesus, and because it bears similarities to the teachings of Jesus in the gospels, Potter suggested that Jesus might well have been its author.

From the time that Potter founded the First Humanist Society of New York until his death, he made a precarious living by lecturing and writing. He wrote on many nonreligious subjects and published in many popular magazines, such as *Reader's Digest,* the *Saturday Evening Post,* and *Esquire.* He always remained a strong advocate of what were considered liberal causes. He was a founder (in 1938) and director of the Euthanasia Society of America.[14] He also was an active advocate of birth control, the abolition of capital punishment, "civilized divorce laws," and women's rights. He worked to promote books, for he believed that reading good books would raise the cultural level of America and thus strengthen democracy. He appeared before committees in both the Senate and the House to urge lower postal rates for books.

Exactly when Potter became a humanist is unclear. When he left the ministry of West Side Unitarian Church, he apparently was struggling with the question of humanism. Shortly after moving to Antioch College, he wrote an article for the student publication, *Blaze,* entitled "Humanism-Theism," in which he discussed the differences in the two positions, and clearly supported the former. It is evident that Potter had been reading the works of John H. Dietrich, whom he quoted extensively in that brief article.[15]

The last few years of Potter's life were plagued with suffering. In the late fifties he developed cancer of the stomach, and he underwent surgery in 1960; shortly thereafter he was a passenger in an automobile that was involved in an accident and was seriously injured. Finally, cancer got the better of him, and he died in a New York hospital on 4 October 1962. With his passing a colorful, vivacious advocate of religious humanism passed from the scene.[16]

Several things about Potter's life should be emphasized. He grew up under the influence of Baptist fundamentalism and later became a liberal. He transferred to the Unitarian church, but eventually found even it too confining. Ultimately he became a humanist, trying to chart his own unique course in religion. In explaining the evolution of Potter's thought, Harry Elmer Barnes said, "Dr. Potter passed through a drastic intellectual evolution before he espoused Humanism: Baptist, conservative Unitarian, radical Unitarian, misplaced Universalist, and all-out Humanist."[17] It is this final stage in Potter's thought that interests us.

The main sources for understanding the humanist stage of Potter's thought are his books, of which the most important are *Humanism: A New Religion, Humanizing Religion,* and *The Creative Personality.* The concept of personality played an important part in Potter's thought from the early days when he became a Unitarian; at first he interpreted it within a theistic context, but later within a humanistic one. The central thesis in *The Creative Personality* is present in germinal form in *Humanism: A New Religion.*

Because Potter did not come completely to the humanistic point of view until about 1926, perhaps some justification is needed for including him in a study of "pioneers." In fact, a case could be made for including Roy Wood Sellars or A. Eustace Haydon instead. However, since both Dietrich and Reese were clergymen, Potter's having been a clergyman has a certain advantage. Both Sellars and Haydon were clearly identified as university professors; either might be passed off as an eccentric who had proposed a "religion without God."A well-educated, duly ordained clergyman who advocated such a radical point of view while pursuing his vocation in a religious institution cannot be so easily dismissed. In other words, both Potter's affirmation of religion and his denial that it needed to be predicated upon God were exemplified by his vocation as much as by his words.

Potter pioneered in attempting to go beyond Unitarianism and to organize humanism under its own religious structure. As Wallace P. Rusterholtz said, "To Potter, credit is chiefly due for divorcing Humanism from Unitarianism."[18] As a result of Potter's efforts, the First Humanist Assembly was held in October 1934, under the auspices of the First Humanist Society of New York. Such notables as John H. Randall, Jr., who spoke on "The Task Before Humanists," and John Dewey, who led a discussion on "The Social Objectives of Humanism," were in attendance. The term *religious humanism* was used to describe the assembly.[19] Furthermore, Potter contributed literature to the humanist movement, most notably *Humanism: A New Religion* and *Humanizing*

Religion. His location in New York City and his talent for gaining headlines undoubtedly attracted more publicity to the movement than any other single individual could have garnered. Potter was also one of the original signers of "A Humanist Manifesto." But above all, Potter was a social activist and a living example of humanist principles put into practice:

> Dr. Potter's unique contribution was to write the best popular statement of the Humanist position and to take Humanism beyond enlightened doctrine into diversified and effective social action in behalf of human betterment....Dr. Potter has been primarily the dynamic man of action in propagating and practicing Humanism.[20]

We have designated Potter "the rebel of religious humanism" for two reasons. First, Potter was always interested in what lay beyond the senses. This curiosity led him in the direction of extrasensory perception and, at times, spiritualism, subjects that were anathema to most humanists. Second, as already noted, there was a conflict within the humanist movement over whether the humanists should work within the established denominational structures, trying to humanize them, or organize their own societies, even their own denomination. Potter rebelled against both Dietrich and Reese, who chose to work within the established denominations, especially the liberal ones. Although Potter was not a systematic theologian, his thought lends itself to systematic exposition. We shall explore it topically, as we did the thought of Dietrich and Reese, beginning with his world view.

World View

Potter was aware that world views are relative. He did not expect someone of the twentieth century to hold views similar to those of the first century. The New Testament attributed sicknesses to demon possession; today we know that disease is caused by germs. Potter maintained that biblical stories (creation, for example), like stories of the South Sea Islands, are only myths. Moreover, the biblical view tends to be dualistic: the world of nature versus a supernatural realm. To the first-century person, the universe was small and cozy; God in heaven watched over people below. Because these old world views obviously are untrue, and because they are based on alledgedly divine revelation, Potter thought it is impossible to "reconcile an ancient religion with...modern life."[21]

Potter, then, believed that the old world view has become a liability; it is possible to piece together in his works what he believed to be a more accurate view of the world. First, Potter knew that humans live in an infinite cosmic order:

The knowledge that there is a universe countless millions of light-years in diameter, containing a great many super-galaxies of galaxies of solar systems, the stars of which contain somewhat less than a hundred chemical elements in various combinations, and that, on one planet at least, one or more of the chemical combinations became alive and from it or them various biological forms have evolved of which he man is one....[22]

The universe envisioned by Potter is far vaster than the ancient Hebrews conceived it to be.

Second, Potter maintained that the universe is composed of matter; because matter is indestructible, there could not have been a time when the universe did not exist.[23] Therefore it is foolish to speculate about the creation of the universe, for it is equally reasonable (or unreasonable) to speculate about the creation of God as about the creation of matter. The universe and the world may have had different forms, but matter is the basic stuff of the universe and needs no creator to account for it: "When man wakes to the fact that he is cousin to all life and all matter, he finds in monism a thrilling philosophy...."[24]

Third, Potter had a naturalistic view of the universe and denied the traditional dualism of the natural and the supernatural. He reasoned that since inorganic matter is made up of certain chemicals, organic life is simply the result of a different chemical reaction; and since humans are a product of the evolutionary process, they are a product of nature; and since the human mind is merely a function of the brain, it is composed of matter.[25] Such a naturalistic interpretation of the universe requires no appeal to the supernatural: "The torturing dualisms of man versus nature, mind versus matter, subject versus object, and divine versus human will dissolve in the new interpretation. Monism will bring us peace at last."[26] _Like Dietrich –_

Like so many liberals of his generation, Potter used the evolutionary model to explain how humans arose in the world and their place in it. He used the term *saltations* to refer to the great "jumps ahead in evolution."[27] After periods of very little evolutionary action, significant developments can be discerned. These saltations or genetic mutations Potter also referred to as crises.

Potter's scheme encompassed four major saltations or crises. The first was the change from nonliving to living matter: "Long, long millions of years ago, then there came a point in the process of evolution when gradually changing combinations of chemical elements on the surface of this planet began to live and move and have being." Although it is not clear how this metamorphosis occurred, it was a pivotal point in the evolutionary process.[28]

The second crisis occurred millions of years later, after life had evolved through many forms and developed a primitive consciousness, such as is found in lower forms of animals.

The third crisis of the evolutionary process arrived when consciousness became self-consciousness, when the thinking animal realized that it was thinking. This capacity for self-recognition differentiates humans from other animals; therefore the third crisis marked their advent. The fourth crisis is much more speculative, for it is predicated upon the belief that a new saltation is imminent, that human evolution is on the verge of another leap ahead. Potter recognized there are many varieties of humans; some are hardly self-conscious, others have more highly developed personalities. Among the latter group Potter expected the new crisis, a stage he defined as cosmic consciousness:

> that state of mind into which an individual may enter during which he is conscious of the cosmos. In this state of mind, he becomes intellectually and emotionally aware of the universe as definitely and closely related to himself. He recognizes himself as an integral part of the universe, and even in spirit identifies himself with it. He partakes of its creative nature. He becomes cosmically and creatively conscious.[29]

Clearly, Potter's evolutionary scheme of four saltations or crises—"life," "consciousness," "self-consciousness," and finally "cosmic consciousness"—was naturalistic, not theistic.

Authority

Generally speaking, Potter thought that science should be the source of authority in religious humanism. But he never addressed the subject of science in a detailed or systematic way, although he dropped the word often enough in his writings. He was able to believe in certain forms of extrasensory perception although he gave science the final say in determining truth from falsehood. Having made these general statements about Potter's position, we shall attempt to be more specific.

Potter disagreed with the ways religious thinkers have traditionally sought to establish the truth of their statements. Perhaps with tongue in cheek, he remarked that in ancient Israel the will of God was sometimes determined by casting "the Urim and Thurmim," a sort of ecclesiastical game of dice. Later certain books were thought to reveal the will of God; since the message was not always clear to everyone, priests were needed to interpret the scriptures. Such beliefs have developed about the Bible, the Koran, and the Vedas; yet the will of God revealed in each of these is often contradictory. Potter advocated casting aside claims to revelation in favor of "science."[30] He specifically stated that science involves discovery, embarking on quests with an open mind. Tested experience must be the criterion for truth, and an opinion or belief must be relinquished if it is proved false.

In dealing with the problem of knowing, Potter explained and apparently approved what he believed to be Spinoza's position: we derive knowledge of the world from our five senses, from reasoning about sensory experience (the level at which most science operates), and from "intuition." Potter was well aware that intuition is problematic, for theologians have used or misused it to substantiate all sorts of contradictory religious claims. Yet Potter believed that intuition may well be the "highest" form of knowledge, involving the realization of the whole cosmic order. It appears to be a quickened form of reasoning. Yet, he insisted intuition must be interpreted within a naturalistic framework; what is known through intuition might go beyond the immediate, but it must be consistent with what is known in the other ways. [31]

Potter wished to affirm the validity of science and yet to caution against its limitations. He placed great value on the careful acquisition of facts and the ability to think, for "it takes a scientific training in accuracy and careful observation to enable a person to determine when faith degenerates into credulity."[32] The study of nature and the formulation of natural laws will enable people to use cosmic energy for higher purposes.[33] Yet, because science is not infallible, it must not be used to create a mechanistic and deterministic world view "worse than the old Calvinism."[34] As science has extended our fields of knowledge, belief in supernatural explanations has diminished accordingly. Science may not be perfect, but it has developed a better way of checking error than anything previously known.[35]

God

Theism, said Potter, originates in the unknown. The existence and the attributes of God are founded on a superstition, and "to start with God is to beg the whole question."[36] Potter thought that primitive people created gods to help them adjust to their environment, but that the time had come for people to assume responsibility for their own destiny: "man, who in the infancy of the race created gods to help him, can in the maturing of the race develop a social system, a method of controlling

yet I think people can be responsible for own destiny
I believe in the Divine

136

society, a commonwealth of mankind, without celestial assistance."[37]

People today realize that the word *God* is vague. In contrast to the Old Testament's anthropomorphic God, who walks in the garden in the cool of the day and tires after laboring for six days to create the universe, is the modern view of God as the cosmic force itself. Potter found both views untenable; the conception of God as an impersonal cosmic force is not a valid alternative to the Old Testament view of God as good. Goodness, said Potter, exists only in humans; logically, then, to define God as an impersonal cosmic force is to deny his goodness.[38]

Defining God as an impersonal force also implies the absence of a supernatural realm; the moderns, said Potter, have thus redefined God in naturalistic terms. On that score both Potter and Fulton J. Sheen agree: namely, to remove the supernatural element from religion is to abandon the God of Moses and Jesus, as well as the God of the popes and Luther. Potter said, "The retreat of the supernatural before the advance of science is making it necessary for the modernist to give up the supernatural and radically redefine the word, God."[39]

Because they could no longer define God as a power outside the natural process that consciously created humans to work his divine purpose, said Potter, the modernists redefined God as "the force for good in the world," "the power making for righteousness," or "the principle of concretion." Such attempts at redefinition merely reveal the inadequacy of the modernist conception of God. The difficulty centered on the question, Is cosmic energy personal and conscious? Cosmic energy obviously exists, and it allows evolution to proceed, but Potter saw no evidence that it is directed by a conscious force.

Thus Potter saw no reason to believe that cosmic energy has personality or consciousness. Only as human consciousness continues to evolve will the universe be conscious of itself. Elementary forms of life possess only a potential consciousness; so far as we know, consciousness and personality exist in an advanced form only in humans; therefore, they are responsible for directing evolution in the future. Given Potter's view that humans represent the highest known form of consciousness, it would appear that Potter's theology contains no God.

Humankind

Potter saw humans not as the result of special creation, but as the product of the evolutionary process: "You are an original knot in the bundle of the fibres of life: the fibres stretch back to the dawn of life itself, and you

137

are a part and a result of forces primeval and powerful. Your heredity has given you a rich heritage for weal or woe."[40] Before humans appeared on the stage of history, the evolutionary process had been largely random. In humans the process became self-conscious, and for the first time the possibility of consciously directing the evolutionary process became a real option. Chance yielded to conscious creative control.[41]

As a product of evolution, humans manifest cosmic energy in conscious form. They can improve their own lives and also the world. Cosmic energy must be allowed a creative outlet: "These impulses toward a larger life are the divine part in us and the refusal to gratify them is the worst heresy."[42]

Potter repudiated the view that humans are by nature sinners who deserve eternal damnation. Few people are as bad as advocates of the doctrine of the fall would have us believe. Obviously people are not perfect either, for "true self appraisal reveals one's limitations as well as one's possibilities."[43] Life gives cause for pessimism and cynicism, but also ample evidence of human "perfectibility." We should not evaluate humans by immature and incomplete personalities; nor should we judge "the leaders of the spear-head of progress" as typical. Most of us fall somewhere in between.

Although we cannot know what humans will become, they obviously have not yet achieved their highest potential. Potter, like Jean-Paul Sartre, thought we make ourselves into the kind of human beings we wish to be: "Draw a picture, an outline, of the man you would like to be, the man you ought to be. Or the woman. Then set about painting it with the best materials and skill you have or can get."[44] The world would be improved if we all possessed the virtues of the few great people. Studying their lives can help us to grow, for "there is a projective power in man whereby he can extend his personality beyond the limits of his former self and thus obtain a larger selfhood."[45]

Self-improvement was Potter's answer to the traditional doctrine of salvation:

It is a psychological impossibility for any man or god to "save" another man. A man is never built up in personality and character unless he does it himself. For character is achieved by choosing the right path when one could choose the easier wrong path, and no one can do the choosing but man himself. Human personality is not only self-perfectible; it is perfectible by no other agency than the self.[46]

Potter, in short, saw humans as a product of the evolutionary process. Because they are far from perfect the process must continue. Potter's chief concern was the improvement of people, both for their own sakes and for the evolutionary process: "The future still holds the advent of the great man."[47]

Creative Personality

"Creative personality" best describes the kind of salvation that religious humanism should seek. Potter preferred to avoid the term *salvation*:

When a person has his life unified, when there is meaning in it, when he sees himself and his relation to the universe, then he is "saved," as it used to be termed in theological circles. But some of us do not like that word; it has too many implications, some of them rather sanguinary.

For Potter the key word was *personality;* it was a leitmotif in his thought from his early, liberal theistic period.[48] Yet he realized that personality is difficult to define precisely. He agreed with Kant that humans should be treated as ends in themselves, never as means only. From this Potter inferred that self-consciousness and self-determination are two crucial aspects of human personality. Humans are "both the source and end of thought and conduct" and personality is "that unity of qualities and powers which we call the self."[49]

Potter saw personality as self-recognition, self-direction, and self-giving. These terms are related not only to the self, but also to the environment. Self-recognition implies an awareness of that which is not the self. Self-direction implies a phenomenal world through which the self can express itself. Self-giving implies a recipient of the gift, an other. Potter contended that all well-rounded personalities possess these three attributes; the creative personality has achieved a proper balance among them.

Both the individual and the race have experienced moments of self-recognition. That moment comes to a child when it first uses the personal pronoun, *I*. Implicit in the *I* is an awareness of the difference between subject and object. Far back in the evolutionary process, this distinction did not exist; when intelligence developed to the point of making this distinction, consciousness dawned: "Self-recognition, the knowledge that one is a self, a being able to act on his environment intelligently and to know that he is acting on it and is distinct from it— this is the first and distinguishing mark of personality." Self-recognition is the most fundamental aspect of human personality, and it is a lifelong process. Lack of self-understanding cramps our lives and shrinks our horizons. When we forget (or do not learn) that humans are capable of adapting, we become fearful of new situations. Raised to a high level,

139

self-recognition is the "divine" spark that exists in some people. The more we develop it, the more we are able to shape our own destiny.

Shaping one's own destiny is a function of the second aspect of personality, self-direction. The more we control our environment, the greater our self-direction. Primitive people, for example, had to go around the mountain; we can bore through or fly over it. As we learn to accomplish what we choose, the will becomes "the very core and essence of personality." People who leave their mark on history have attained a high degree of self-direction. Self-recognition leads to self-control, which in turn leads to self-direction; and, as each increases, personality grows.

"Self-giving" is the third aspect of personality. Whereas self-recognition is based on intellect and self-direction on will, self-giving relates to our affections or emotions; it reveals our human need to express ourselves to others:

It is true that one cannot share his immediate ego with even his closest friend, much as he or the friend may wish it. Yet, he finds himself growing the more he enters into other life. He increases his personality by giving himself away in creative activities or in love for others.

Each personality is linked to others; for one individual to grow, others must grow also. Potter was convinced that our personality grows to the extent that we embrace a social outlook:

His self-recognition and his self-direction are called into the service of self-giving, and his self-giving reveals to him a deeper knowledge of himself and a wider field for self-direction. Thought, will, and feeling interblend and fuse in the higher operations of a developed personality.[50]

Potter saw intelligent self-giving as the highest aim of the mature or creative personality. Not all the benefits of giving accrue to the other, for the giver also receives. By contributing to the public good, one creates a better community in which to live; community esteem, one's self-respect, and one's friends increase. Self-giving can be a form of self-expression, an impulse for the creative arts. Such self-expression expands the human personality. But the goal of the creative personality can be elusive:

Of the three elements of personality, then, we have found the primary one, the one prerequisite to all the others, to be self-recognition. Until a consciousness of self, including self-grasp and self-estimate arises, there is no man. The second element, the central power, progressive and yet unifying, is self-determination, with its branches, self-direction and self-development. The third and culminating one is self-communication, including self-expression and self-giving. It depends upon the other two, but intensifies and fuses them both. Rarely are the three equally developed. Only unusual souls attain to personalities that are coordinately evolved and well-balanced and integrated. No person has yet lived who may be said to have been completely cognizant of himself, always self-determining, forever self-giving.[51]

Cosmic Consciousness

At this stage in human development, the creative personality is the goal of religious humanism. But it is not the ultimate goal. Potter thought a higher stage, characterized by "cosmic consciousness," was imminent. The possessor of this ultimate consciousness Potter called the great "Next-Man" or "Superman." Clues to the Superman's characteristics may be found in some of the great figures in history. Potter thought that "religious geniuses" who claimed mystical experiences or theophanies possessed this kind of cosmic consciousness. He noted that although the theological language used to interpret such experiences differs, the experiences themselves are similar. For example, Jesus described his baptismal experience in theistic language, whereas Buddha interpreted his experience under the Bo-tree in naturalistic language. What is important is the experience or the level of consciousness, not the particular explanation.

Such experiences are often described as accompanied by a bright light—symbolic, of course, of a new insight. Some refer to being in contact with the deity, with resultant feelings of peace and oneness with the universe. Disorganized personalities become organized; a lack of direction changes to purpose. Potter listed nine characteristics of cosmic consciousness: (1) a visual sensation as a bright light; (2) an auditory sensation as of a voice or music; (3) a sudden sense of mental clarity; (4) a consciousness of the immensity and unity of the universe; (5) a conviction that even material things are alive; (6) a feeling of self-expansion to include all things; (7) a disappearance of guilt, doubt, and confusion; (8) an influx of great exaltation and joy of spirit; and (9) an assurance that immortality has already begun.[52]

Potter thought the level of consciousness experienced by such men as Jesus and Buddha "will characterize the men of the next stage of evolution." We should study these experiences carefully; as long as they are interpreted naturalistically, the term *mystical experience* is acceptable. Such experiences need not be accounted for by the supernatural intervention of God. When the mystical experience is fully understood, cosmic consciousness may well be attained without any mystical experience.

In Potter's epistemology reason replaced instinct as humans evolved; when the Next-Man appears, intuition may replace reason. Instinct and reason will still have a place; neither is an infallible source of truth, and intuition will not be infallible either. In attempting to describe cosmic consciousness, Potter said, "The most significant point about the experience is that the person who awakes to the immensity, unity, and vibrant life of the universe has an overpowering feeling that he is related to it all even to the extent of identity. There is a sense of self-expansion to include all things. Matter has become alive and conscious in him."

Jesus

Potter devoted more study to Jesus and esteemed him more highly than did either Dietrich or Reese. The influence of Harnack's *What Is Christianity?* which Potter read while a student at Brown University, is evident. Potter argued that the thought of Jesus differed considerably from that of Paul. If the gospels accurately record what Jesus taught, then Jesus and Paul are far apart in theology; in comparing the teachings in the Sermon on the Mount with those of Romans, for example, Potter found many humanistic elements in Jesus' teachings. If "Jesus" refers to the historical man from Nazareth, and if "Christ" designates the saviour of Pauline Christianity, Potter concluded that Christ was a theist and Jesus was a humanist.[53]

Potter did not approve of worshipping Jesus; that is to deify him and to imply a supernatural realm. Nor did Potter see Jesus "as a unique, sinless, perfect leader, adequate as a guide in all the problems of today."[54] Despite the many problems surrounding the synoptic gospels, Potter was willing to assume that Jesus lived and to grant that his basic teachings are contained in the gospels; but Potter could not endorse these teachings, as the modernists did, as contemporary guides: "if Jesus cursed the fig tree because it had no figs on it when he was hungry, he would be apt to curse a red traffic light when he was in a hurry to get somewhere. It is the same principle; blaming an inanimate object for something it cannot help." Potter accused the modernists of picking and choosing what they will accept from the Bible. If the modernists reject the cursing of the fig tree as inauthentic, why should they accept the Sermon on the Mount? Jesus also believed in demon possession; he is reported to have transferred the demons from a man to a herd of swine,

but it myth!.
according to Potter
earlier —

which consequently went wild and plunged over a cliff to their deaths. We obviously cannot accept Jesus' teachings about mental illness; can we then say that we should follow the teachings of Jesus?

Potter saw Jesus' uniqueness not in his deification by the early church, but in his "remarkably developed personality."[55] Jesus had developed his self-recognition to the point of possessing assurance and authority. So great was his self-direction, that stories sprang up about his ability to go where he willed—on the surface of a lake and through closed doors. His self-giving was so pronounced that virtue seemed to emanate from him. His personality was so well developed that he impressed everyone who met him. His impact changed lives. Little wonder that people thought he possessed supernatural powers. After his death, stories about his life continued to grow. Because his followers felt that such a personality could not be destroyed, they pictured him as risen from the grave and seated in heaven at the right hand of the Almighty.

Potter acknowledged that Jesus' central belief—that "God was his Heavenly Father"—was theistic. Yet because Jesus' view of God was so intimate, so humanized and personal, one can appropriate Jesus' values without endorsing a theistic interpretation of his religious experience. We can disagree with Jesus' understanding of mental illness and still believe that Jesus had a therapeutic effect. "Humanists recognize that in Jesus himself lay the power which he and his followers attributed to God. The power was human and natural, not magic and supernatural." Potter evaluated Jesus very highly because of his creative personality and because of his cosmic consciousness, but he offered a naturalistic rather than a supernaturalistic explanation for Jesus' uniqueness:

The Humanist attitude toward Jesus is that Jesus was an unusual personality, and in his self-development, self-direction, self-giving, a marvelous person whom we admire....

...since the development of personality is the aim of Humanism and since Jesus developed his and sought to help others in that way, we honor him and study his life as best we may from the fragmentary documents for a suggestion of the method of self-development which he employed.[56]

Ethics

Although Potter never worked out a systematic ethical system as such, his writings imply an ethics based on naturalism. Humans must work out their ethical system without recourse to the supernatural.

Potter referred to *Technique of Happiness* as the "science of applied Hedonics"; the end of ethical behavior is happiness, not in some "kingdom of God," but here and now. The way to happiness is to develop the creative personality, for "a completely happy person is that man or woman with a completely integrated personality."[57] We can attain the creative personality by developing and harmonizing the three aspects of personality: self-recognition, self-direction, and self-expression. "For a human character, a well-developed creative personality is the very goal, the richest fruit, the highest product of the whole long process of evolution on this planet."[58] To obtain happiness, humans must train their desires. Potter suggested four ways to accomplish this. First is *selection;* one selects for training those desires that will best contribute to attaining our ideal. Second, *concentration* involves focusing on those things that will lead to our goal. Third is *contemplation* of such things as the good, the true, and the beautiful; contemplation of beauty arouses a desire for more beauty and incorporates it in our character. *Action* results from the first three: "That is the eternal creative impulse of the universe which takes you in your susceptible moments and translates into action the feelings and impulses which you have."[59]

What is good and bad must be determined by humans; simply stated, whatever limits and cramps the human personality is bad, and whatever contributes to the development of the creative personality is good.[60] People who are considered evil either have not evolved fully or the aspects of their personalities are out of harmony: "people who are hindering the progress of civilization are those in whom some part of their personality has shot off at a tangent. They have been pulled out on one side. They have become so abnormal that they are really monsters."[61] As people take responsibility for their evolution, they will attempt to develop and improve the best qualities of their forebears, and eschew their bad qualities.

Potter insisted that humans are responsible for the future of evolution. He used the term *evolution* to describe the process up to the development of humans, *advolution* to describe the process since. Evolution suggests that matter underwent many experiments, some of which resulted in dead ends; there is no evidence of purpose. Human control of the evolutionary process injects purpose into the process. Advolution, in short, is purposeful (teleological); evolution is not.[62]

Humans can now plan their future on this planet. This requires accepting social responsibility and subordinating personal liberty to social progress. Because we must also maintain individual freedoms, working out the relationship of the individual to society is an important challenge to human advancement. As we expand our focus to a cosmic consciousness, we will need experts in eugenics, economics, culture, and even the development of values. The overall go improving personality and enabling society to evolve creatively.

As for economics, Potter was critical of both capitalism and communism. He thought that capitalism encourages self-interest; he found capitalism consistent with the old theism, which was concerned with saving individual souls at the expense of general well-being. Although he considered communism a correct protest against these wrong beliefs, he thought communism had so regimented and standard-ized the individual that it prevents the proper development of human personality.[63] Potter thought the old, theistic view could be supplanted only by humanism. Humanism will replace competition with some form of collectivism; group interest will replace self-interest, and wealth will be equitably distributed. Potter believed, "For an ideal to strive toward, the Humanist looks to a completed personality in an ideal social state."[64]

The Church

Potter advocated that free religious societies replace churches, which have gradually lost importance as their former roles have been taken over by other agencies. Churches were once actively engaged in education and social welfare, now the province of the state. Yet Potter thought that religious institutions would not disappear altogether, for they still have a role—"inspiration and preservation of high ideals."[65] Potter believed that "when churches disappear, their various other functions taken over by different institutions, certain new religious societies, such as this Humanist Society, for instance, will furnish a gathering of the kind people want, where they can go to think about things most excellent."[66]

Potter viewed the religious society as a kind of cultural agency that would help direct the cultural growth of the community. At the same time, it would lift people "toward the plane of cosmic consciousness."[67] Members of the Humanist Society of New York were expected not only to participate in the "worship service" but also to join one of the committees doing practical work to improve humanity; they were expected to make a commitment to both personal and social improve-ment.

Although their nature was changed, Potter thought prayer and worship have a place in the humanist service. Prayer is no longer a petition to a deity but a meditative exploration of oneself. Potter himself held to this "new" understanding of prayer, which he considered psychological rather than theological, humanistic rather than theistic.[68] He saw prayer as access to personal power: "By meditation, quiet thought, high resolve, combined with an analysis of the problem facing him, he has risen from his knees a stronger person. He has called on his own resources."

Potter's interpretation of prayer also is consistent with his naturalistic understanding of the universe; he maintained that we often underestimate our conscious and subconscious power. Through mediation we reach a store of racial and personal experience that enables us to address problems. A simple person, unaware of this unconscious storehouse, may attribute such help to supernatural forces; "God gets the credit for what man had done for himself."[69] Potter concluded that worship need not involve the adoration of a personal God: "The values resident in worship are beauty, repose of spirit, fine music, common concentration on a high ideal, the hearing of tried and true words of scripture and of an inspiring address, and association with similarly minded people."[70]

Immortality

Like most individuals, Potter was interested in the problem of immortality, although he thought death was not always an evil; "Death is a most merciful surgeon, and when he comes to cut the thread of life, he brings ether with him. The horrors of death exist most in the minds of the theologians. It is the ones who are left behind who suffer."[71] Since death is inevitable, Potter stressed "the importance of living the good life here and now, rather than worrying much about what is to come afterward."[72]

Although Potter concentrated on the interim between the cradle and the grave, he was interested in the various theories that have been advanced about an afterlife. He maintained that Christianity has at least two theories, the first of a physical resurrection that involves "the reassembling of the chemical elements of his decayed body and its transference to a heavenly city" (seen in the biblical stories of Jesus' empty tomb and of doubting Thomas touching his resurrected body) and the second, found in the thought of Paul, who spoke of a spiritual body. (Potter wondered if Paul's "thorn in the flesh" might account for his desire to be rid of his body in death.) Both the physical and spiritual views hold that humans will spend eternity with God—if, that is, they are saved. The two Christian views are not the only theories of the afterlife. In India, for instance, humans are thought to be absorbed into

God to the extent that they have lost their personal identity; the mystical trance of *samadhi* gave believers a preview of the life to come.[73]

Potter also enumerated several naturalistic theories of the afterlife. The indestructibility of matter suggests that humans are never completely destroyed, merely changed into another material form. Another theory, that the germ plasm is what is immortal, holds that we live on in our children, for we pass on not only a body, but also mental and moral characteristics (this leaves a problem for those without offspring). The immortality of influence suggests that we survive through our impact on others; thus Plato is immortal, for he continues to influence the lives of those who study him. Institutional immortality is the reward of those who create great institutions that persist long after they are dead. Many modernists, including Fosdick, believe that human personality is the most valuable thing we know; this highest expression of the evolutionary process must live on, or the universe is meaningless.

Potter said we do not know when and how belief in immortality originated. Despite attempts to trace such beliefs to dreams or to animism, "The cause of both origin and persistence of immortality beliefs lies in an urge within man of which he cannot be rid. It is the evolutionary urge itself, the upthrust of the life-force, which, once it becomes self-conscious in man, 'cries like a captain for eternity.'"

Consciousness enables humans to master their environment by inventing tools, domesticating animals, and harnessing natural forces. Potter argued that immortality is less a hope of personal survival than the life force trying to overcome all limitations. Various theories of personal immortality are merely attempts to extend personality beyond its limits.

In this context Potter was struck by Jesus' impact on his disciples and his influence on the Christian church. In Potter's view, Jesus possessed the most remarkable personality in history. Potter was concerned not with divinity but with manliness, with Jesus' "exposition of the possibilities of human nature." Just before and immediately after Jesus' death, his disciples fled fearfully to their villages, but eventually they dared to revisit the places where Jesus had taught. There they found others who remembered him; they concluded that Jesus was not dead: "It was a strange psychological fact that they were sure Jesus was with them." The disciples described what they thought had happened, and their stories expanded considerably before they were written down.

What was it about Jesus that made such an impact on his disciples? Potter thought it was Jesus' creative personality and his state of "cosmic consciousness, which has also been noticed in other men, but not such an extent. In him the 'growing tip of the racelife' burst into flower long enough for men to catch its fragrance and the human race has never been the same since." In other words, Jesus revealed what a man might be:

> The Now-Men found among them a Next-Man, and the wonder of him exhausted their vocabularies. Men possessed only of self-consciousness tried with that equipment to appraise a man equipped with cosmic consciousness and failed. They only knew that whatever it was that he had, which they knew they did not have, they wanted it badly. To be immortal would be to be like him, of that they were sure.[74]

One of Potter's definitions of immortality was "oneness with the all of life,"[75] for which Christianity's symbol is the ever-living Christ. Potter interpreted this naturalistically; Jesus "lives in the lives of men made better by the memory of him. And every great soul that ever lived has a similar immortality." Immortality is based not on the length but on the quality of life; if we work to realize our dreams, they will live on. Creative personality, cosmic consciousness, personal immmortality—Potter interpreted them all within a naturalistic framework:

> Now, Humanists do not deny the possibility of the future existence of human personality beyond death. They do not deny it; they say it may be; but it has never been proved. It may be proved sometime but has not been proved yet, and to assert the resurrection of Jesus proves immortality is to indulge in wishful thinking. The continuance of the personality after death is a problem for science, not for revelation from the skies, concerning which we are rather suspicious.[76]

Potter was not alarmed by the prospect of the extinction of individuality at death; he found life itself worthwhile. He needed neither the hope of heaven nor the fear of hell to persuade him to be good.

Religion without God

Potter thought religion and gods were created by people, and "religion itself is but a means to an end, the improvement of man. It fails if it does not further that purpose."[77] Specifically, he thought the purpose of religion is the improvement of human personality: "when humanists dare come forth and maintain openly that the improvement of human personality, individually and socially, is a sufficiently challenging task, a sufficiently worthwhile object to make religion out of, then the world is bound to listen. . . . This is our religion."[77] Obviously Potter thought religion can exist without God. "To the average Westerner, a Christian of Europe or America, for instance, religion without God is almost inconceivable. But in the East, religion without God is no novelty."[79]

Potter could find no evidence that personality exists apart from humans; his religious humanism, like Dietrich's and Reese's, was a religion without God.

Potter referred to four types of atheism—agnostic, negative, dogmatic, and moral—and found differences within each type. "Agnostic atheists" do not know whether there is a God and suspend judgment; they may not care whether God exists or they may constantly seek evidence. They are undogmatic. Agnostic atheists live without any significant understanding of God, but remain willing to examine the evidence. Their minds are not made up, in contrast to the "negative atheist," who does not believe in God.

The "dogmatic atheist" declares categorically, "There is no God." Whereas the negative atheist maintains we have insufficient evidence for belief in the existence of God, the dogmatic is sure that God does not exist. Even though this position is as difficult to substantiate as the theist's, dogmatic atheists often become overtly antitheistic.

"Moral atheists" are opposed not only to the idea of God, but equally to all that the idea of God has traditionally meant. Potter agreed with Feuerbach's view of the moral atheist: "he alone is the true atheist to whom the predicates of the Divine Being,—for example, love, wisdom, justice,—are nothing; not he to whom merely the subject of these predicates is nothing." [80]

It is moral atheism that gives the term its negative connotations; in popular usage it has come to describe a person who not only does not believe in God, but is wicked. Good and God have become popularly joined, so that to abjure God is to abjure good. To be sure, some atheists are immoral, just as some theists are, but it is impossible and nonsensical to impute immorality to atheism. [81]

Potter himself did not identify with the fourth group, for he and other religious humanists were most concerned with morality and emphasized that truth, beauty, and goodness are to be "sought after with earnestness and patience." Nor was Potter a dogmatic atheist. He might be described as a negative atheist if that means denying God as a supernatural, personal, deity. Generally speaking, however, agnostic atheism best describes his position; the concept of God played no important part in his religion, though he remained willing to examine any new evidence.

In other words, Potter opted for atheism, but he was tolerant toward other positions and open to change should new evidence demand it. He saw this position as neither a virtue nor a vice. "When man gets to the point where he realizes that God was man's own creation for a temporary purpose, he needs God no longer. The idea of God has served its purpose and may be laid aside."

CHAPTER 7

Critics of Religious Humanism

"What urges you on and arouses your ardour, you wisest of men, do you call it 'will to truth'?... But it must bend and accommodate itself to you!... That is your entire will, you wisest men; it is will to power; and that is so even when you talk of good and evil and of the assessment of values."—Friedrich Nietzsche

THE RELIGIOUS DEVELOPMENT OF JOHN H. DIETRICH, Curtis W. Reese, and Charles F. Potter was remarkably similar. They were all born into Protestant fundamentalism, then they became Protestant liberals, next Unitarians, and finally humanists. Dietrich came into Unitarianism from the Reformed church while Reese and Potter came from the Baptist. Perhaps because the Reformed church lays greater stress on systematic theology than does the Baptist church, Dietrich approached theology more systematically than the others. In fact, Wallace Rusterholtz referred to Dietrich as "the systematic theologian of Humanism."

Although the pioneers of religious humanism had a great deal in common, they also had some differences. Three are most obvious. All agreed that the "scientific method" was the best and only way of determining the truth and repudiated other methods for obtaining alleged religious truth, such as revelation and speculation. Even in this, however, they had subtle but distinct differences. Dietrich interpreted the scientific method in a very limited empirical sense: truth was empirical truth and obtained through sense experience. Reese tended to be more cautious in his faith in the scientific method. He injected a pragmatic element: namely, that truth occurs in the context of some human purpose. Of the three, Potter tended to be most "liberal" in interpreting the "scientific method," even including "intuition" as a part of it. Although neither Dietrich nor Reese denied that one may "intuit" some truth, they thought such intuitions must be confirmed by the scientific method. Potter, however, was to say something more—that intuition is the highest form of truth; it cannot conflict with the truth that has been established by the scientific method, but it may go beyond it. Despite these differences, all three interpreted the scientific method within a naturalistic framework.

A second area of difference centered around the nature of a religious humanist society or church. The three pioneers agreed that all religious institutions were created by people, rather than gods, to serve human needs. But on two basic points Dietrich and Reese disagreed with Potter. The first had to do with the composition of a local religious society. Potter thought it should be homogeneous, whereas Dietrich and Reese thought it should be pluralistic. In other words, Potter thought it should be comprised of like-minded people, a somewhat exclusive organization, but Dietrich and Reese maintained it should be composed of people with various educational, professional, racial, economic, and theological backgrounds and points of view. They saw it as a democratic microcosm, an inclusive institution; Potter's view was more elitist

They also disagreed about the relationship of religious humanism to the established denominations. As noted earlier, Potter conceived of humanism as an entirely new religion, competing with the established religions; he advocated creating humanist societies somewhat along the lines of a denominational institutional structure. Dietrich and Reese, on the other hand, thought the best strategy was to work within the established structures, especially the liberal denominations such as the American Unitarian Association and the Universalist Church of America. At times critics called Dietrich's and Reese's view a "cuckoo" theory, referring to the bird that does not build its own nest but takes over one built by another bird. As a result, Dietrich and Reese had much more concern for the problems of ecumenicity.

A third difference concerned the pioneers' view of Jesus. Dietrich often spoke about Jesus in his sermons, but his main concern was to use "higher criticism" to explode some myth about Jesus (that he was born of a virgin, for example, or raised bodily from the grave). Generally speaking, Dietrich thought that not enough material in the New Testament was sufficiently authentic to establish a positive assessment of Jesus. Thinking that most of the materials in the gospels was the creation of the early church, he used historical criticism to repudiate it. Consequently Jesus played an unimportant part in his religious thought. In fact, Dietrich did not consider himself a Christian, not even a liberal one.

Reese rarely mentioned Jesus at all, which is curious, since Jesus plays such a central role in Baptist thought and worship. Reese considered Jesus at most one among the various founders of world religions, like Buddha and Zoroaster; like them, Jesus should be evaluated by the relevance of his teachings for the modern world.

Unlike Dietrich and Reese, Potter remained interested in Jesus throughout his life. He thought that if there were any credibility in the gospel records, Jesus was more of a humanist than the Christ created by the early church. However, the uniqueness of Jesus, according to Potter, was his highly developed personality, not his alleged deity or the uniqueness and superiority of his teachings; Jesus was unique because he expressed the highest form of humanity ever evolved. Jesus should be studied to learn how he achieved this "cosmic consciousness." Thus Potter provided a naturalistic interpretation of Jesus, though he remained a naturalistic, nontheistic Christian. In his interpretation of Jesus, however, Potter came nearer the Christian fold than either Dietrich or Reese.

During the humanist-theist controversy in Unitarianism, many theists criticized a "religion without God." Most of these critics focused on one of three arguments. First, since religion has traditionally been related to some concept of God, the humanists were wrong to apply the term to their position. Second, since morality traditionally has been predicated in some way on the existence of God, people who do not believe in God cannot be moral over an extended period of time. And third, since human existence gains meaning from belief God and in personal immortality, the denial of these doctrines is tantamount to denying that life has meaning.

The humanist-theist controversy did not remain confined to the Unitarian denomination. It spread out into the theological world generally. In this chapter we shall review some of the criticisms of religious humanism by those who were, with few exceptions, outside the pale of Unitarianism. The battle was fiercest between the humanists and the liberals or modernists; therefore we shall consider criticisms by liberals, neo-liberals, and ex-liberals who were influenced by neo-orthodoxy. These opponents of "religion without God" provide valuable insights into the nature of religious humanism.

Willard L. Sperry

In 1929 Willard L. Sperry, the dean of Harvard Divinity School, gave the Ayer lectures at Colgate Rochester Divinity School; he entitled them *Signs of These Times*.[1] A section of one lecture was devoted to "Humanism." Sperry identified three primary causes for its rise: (1) Nietzsche's vision of the "death of God"; (2) the attempt to make religion consistent with the modern world—religious humanism "represents nothing but a mildly laudable desire to move with the times"; and (3) the theological problem of suffering, exacerbated by the First World War. The humanists could not reconcile the vast amount of suffering in the world with the good traditionally thought to result from it. Sperry said, "Modern humanism implies a certain healthy impatience and indignation with too easy cures for the pain in the world during our generation."

After thus explaining how humanism arose, Sperry launched his criticisms of it. First, he thought that because the humanists viewed themselves as the highest form of consciousness in the universe, they would exploit the rest of the universe to achieve their ends. Theistic religion has tried to help humans overcome their urge to exploit; humanism, because it is anthropocentric, will increase it. Believing that humanism therefore had built into its system the seeds of its own destruction, Sperry argued that the exploitation of the universe cannot be overcome in religious humanism. "The positive ethics of the religion of humanity promises therefore to be self-defeating." Sperry also thought that humanists would be unable to maintain their agnosticism toward mystery; they must inevitably become indifferent, move to faith, or become anti-religious. In other words, agnosticism must yield to some recognition of the nature of mystery, for "to be a man is to go on record about the nature of the mysterious universe around us."

A closely allied criticism was that limiting religion to humans will stifle important human activity. Bold minds will continue to ask crucial and difficult questions about the universe and to hazard working answers, whereas tired minds will stop. Sperry thought that humanism would eventually become too enervated to pose these questions and supply tentative answers.

Sperry believed minds that grapple with the mystery of the universe will ultimately come "to believe in the unborrowed reality of our neighbor the universe." He apparently meant that only those who struggle with the mystery come to know the otherness of the divine. As long as humans have a desire to know their "neighbor the universe" (or the divine), religion will live; "when that endeavor dies the strongest incitement to religion dies with it." Further, Sperry believed that the capacity of the human will to do good is linked to the desire to know the divine. Because humanists maintained what Sperry considered to be an indifference to the "environing mystery," they would never know the divine; the loss of the divine and therefore of religion itself would extinguish the human desire to do good. Their indifference to the "environing mystery" thus condemns the humanists to failure.

Although humans might well perish, Sperry was sure the universe will continue. Its continuing ensures that the "There" also will continue. Sperry's "There" referred to some vague notion of God: religion "dares to hope, bold as that hope and faith may seem, that we are not lost to the 'There' and that somewhere in the 'There' our joys are confirmed, our sorrows and pains interpreted, our struggles fulfilled."

Religion demands contrast, Sperry maintained, an element he feared humanism would eventually lose. Humanism contrasts the self with an ideal or idealized race; Sperry thought "the element of 'otherness' and the consciousness of belonging to an 'other' seems certain to die a lingering but inevitable death." Underlying Sperry's arguments was a conviction that humanism would eventually lose the dimension of transcendence. Sperry didn't mince words: "A belief in God, in some form or other, must be the main anchor and mooring of our souls, foursquare, substantial, and calculated to bear the full weight of life."

Sperry concluded that the belief "I belong to God" is reinforced by the belief "I belong to a succession or society of men." Both statements attempt to ground humans in the scheme of things. Although humanists may not be able to affirm the first statement, they affirm the second; in doing so, they are "fortifying and interpreting an idea that Christianity must always require."[2]

Walter Marshall Horton

In *Theism and the Modern Mood,* published in 1930, Walter Marshall Horton, who was then on the faculty of Oberlin College, asked, "Whither Humanism?" Like Sperry, Horton was not openly hostile to humanism. In fact, he had no desire to exclude the humanists from Christian fellowship, and he also acknowledged that they were correct in protesting certain forms of moral quietism that had existed in some theological circles before the First World War.[3]

Horton thought "Chicago pragmatism" was the immediate cause of modern humanism. He called John Dewey "the father of this school" and he contended that the central aim of its philosophy was the promotion of social well-being, which included the whole cosmos.

Horton's major criticism of humanism was that it contained a basic dualism: separating the philosophy of values from the philosophy of nature. Its naturalistic view declares that the only way to arrive at truth is through the scientific method. Humanists affirm and promote values, but they do not think the cosmos supports these values. Ultimately, therefore, the humanists will face a dilemma: if they follow the course of scientific naturalism, they will find their values disappearing; if they avoid the danger inherent in naturalism and attempt to work out a position guaranteeing human values, they will discover they have come much closer to theism than they had intended.

Horton thought humanists had attained varying degrees of insight into this dilemma. It appeared to him that Dietrich and Reese were naive in affirming both the scientific method and human values, and were unaware a dilemma existed. He thought Joseph Wood Krutch, having seen the impossibility of holding both views, was in a post-disillusionary state; he had given up on the possibility of values, but bemoaned the loss. Horton thought A. Eustace Haydon had moved slightly beyond Krutch, toward a cautious affirmation of values. Of all the humanists, Horton maintained, Walter Lippmann had progressed furthest. According to Horton, Lippmann was no longer living in a naive, illusionary world, yet he had gone a long way toward affirming values. Horton contended that the next step humanists must take was to embrace a philosophy of organism (along the lines of Alfred North Whitehead) that takes the naturalistic world seriously and also provides cosmic support for values.

Horton thought both Dietrich and Reese were keen and vigorous in their destructive criticisms of orthodox Christianity, but naive in their positive convictions. He saw them as heirs of a critical tradition harking back to Theodore Parker. Horton was convinced that Dietrich relied too heavily on the scientific method and was doomed to disillusionment. If, as Dietrich argued, the scientific method eliminated God and immortality, it was bound also to dissolve Dietrich's faith in humanity. Horton thought that eventually Dietrich would lose his faith in the scientific method, for the logic of his position led in that direction. Ultimately "there will be nothing left for those critical minds but the universal ruin they have created."

Reese, although more skeptical of the use of the scientific method than Dietrich, did not understand its impact on ethical concerns:

...disillusioned in his theology, he has remained entirely naive in his ethics; and neither the war nor its aftermath of disappointment has made the least dent in his social optimism. All the old war-worn slogans and platitudes, about "service" and "sacrifice" for "a sober country and a stainless flag," are preserved unaltered in his pages; and he even dares to tell stories about "soldier boys" dying in the endeavor to "make good for democracy."[4]

Reese believed in the neutrality of the universe, yet seemed to affirm values inconsistent with such a view. Once Reese understood the implications of his view of the universe, Horton thought, he would no longer be able to affirm such naive values.

Horton saw two positive aspects of humanism: its demand that religion be brought into harmony with the scientific spirit of the age, and its demand that religion become "humane" in the best sense of the word. Horton said theism must embrace both these emphases to meet the challenge of religious humanism.

Douglas C. Macintosh

Douglas C. Macintosh, who was Dwight Professor of Theology at Yale University in 1930, compared the religious humanists to the fox who lost his tail in a trap. The fox went around talking about the unprofitableness of tails in general and of foxes' tails in particular. He then tried to get other foxes to follow the new fashion by having their tails amputated. Macintosh thought the humanists were really mutilated Christians: "they are religiously defective, whatever their qualifications, intellectual, aesthetic, moral, or social."[5]

Macintosh was rather tough on the humanists; he even impugned their motives. He accused humanists of avoiding the term *atheist*, which he thought adequately described their position, for propagandist reasons.[6] The public would not be interested in a movement explicitly claiming to be atheistic; the movement therefore hid behind the more ambiguous and acceptable term *humanist*.

The term *God* has traditionally been associated with religion, but although the religious humanists refrain from using the word, they retain the term *religion*. Macintosh asked, "Why not drop the word religion also?" Why not call the humanist position "the democratic way of life"? Again, Macintosh thought that humanists recoiled from the term *atheist* for the same reason that they retained the word *religion*— namely, the exigencies of propagating the new humanism.[7]

Macintosh turned his critical eye to Harry Emerson Fosdick's statement about "religion without God." He disagreed with Fosdick, who had maintained that friendship, poetry, science, and the development of good were irrational without belief in God and immortality. Macintosh argued that if these things have no value in this life, they will not accrue value in eternity. Macintosh affirmed that "these values can stand without the support of religion in the more specific sense...."

On the other hand, denying belief in God and immortality has the psychological effect of depreciating spiritual values. Macintosh believed the first generation of religious humanists were living off the spiritual capital they had brought with them from theism; he doubted that the second generation could continue to be spiritually devoted.

If one must choose between spiritual values, such as truth and beauty, and theological doctrines, such as God and immortality, and if one were certain that spiritual values could be pursued without theological doctrines, then one would be justified in choosing spiritual values over theological doctrines. However, Macintosh argued, it is neither logically nor psychologically necessary to choose one or the other; both can be retained, and each complements the other.

Agreeing with the humanists that one of the ends of religion is to create a good life here on earth, Macintosh also agreed that the good life will be brought about by human effort aided by scientific technology. Such an agreement with the humanists did not preclude God, however; he argued that "a definite act of whole-hearted and truthful self-surrender to the God whose will is regarded as identical in content with the highest ultimate well-being of humanity" led to the right religious adjustment that religion seeks.

Macintosh concluded his remarks about "religion without God" or "this fox without a tail" on the following note:

Still, there are many in our day who, whether from intellectual or religious reasons, honestly find it difficult to be theists, and this being the case, I can see a large place for humanism...in its positive aspects....Humanism has no doubt come to stay...at least for quite a long while...and I for one am glad to see those of this persuasion maintaining churches for the promotion of what are still essentially Christian moral and social ideals.[8]

Louis Harap

In 1933 Louis Harap published a critique of religious humanism entitled "The Paradox of Ethical Naturalism." In this essay, Harap said that various forms of ethical naturalism can be distinguished from any religion in at least one respect: regardless of what else religion may stand for, it maintains "that moral virtues are the very first principles of the universe and that other natural laws in some more or less inscrutable manner subserve moral goodness."[9] In contrast, ethical naturalism denies the reality of cosmic moral principles; they are merely conventions, for nature is impersonal.

Harap contended that ethical naturalism has much to learn from religion. Ethical ideas, in fact, are sufficiently flexible to be embraced by both the ethical naturalist and the religious ethicist. The ethical naturalist may incorporate a religious concept into his moral code, and yet give sanctions that are not religious but "social and rational at their broadest point, and immediately personal in their ultimate justification."

Despite their differences (for example, the religious man "saves" his life for eternity, whereas the ethical naturalist "saves" it for his lifetime), Harap thought that ethical naturalists and religious ethicists can coexist. Ethical naturalists might embrace a statement from religion—for example, that one should love one's neighbor; in doing so, they might even find that the ethical end of life is best served by being loving toward other human beings.

Although some protagonists of religion argue that it is impossible to follow such a tenet as loving one's neighbor without the promise of a supernatural reward or of divine approbation, Harap found no empirical evidence to support such a view. In other words, there are some very decent and moral people who make no appeal to religion whatsoever: "some act done by a 'religious' for love of God or attainment of the kingdom of heaven may be performed by the skeptic for social reasons or because that act appeals to him, however irrationally, as a worthy end in itself."

If both ethical naturalists and religious ethicists have different justifications for ethical conduct, what is the paradox of ethical naturalism? According to Harap, the paradox "lies in the claim of the ethical naturalist that the greatest wisdom is not to be found among the exponents of naturalism, but in the writings of religious teachers of the world." Ethical naturalists often profess that happiness results from following the wisdom of a religious teacher, yet at the same time they replace the religious claim to absoluteness with a naturalistic explanation. Religious conduct often has great appeal to ethical naturalists, yet they find the religious justification inadequate. Harap argued that the religious humanist has turned this paradox into an outright contradiction; that is, the ethical theory of the religious humanist is naturalistic, for he does not appeal to any superpersonal sanction. This naturalistic grounding of ethics breaks with what has traditionally been viewed as the very essence of religion. If Jesus was religious in his appeal to the Heavenly Father, then the religious humanist is not religious; to differentiate and/or separate their views from those they are opposing, religious humanists must drop the word *religious*. Harap argued: "Either they are religious, and hence not humanists, or they are really humanists, in which case they are declaring allegiance to a very old doctrine, a form of ethical naturalism."[10] The point is that the religious humanists claim novelty for their position by combining the words *humanist* and *religious*. Doing so is contradictory; humanists should either drop the word *religious* or incorporate the term *God* into their definition of religion.

Charles Hartshorne

Charles Hartshorne, the well-known "process philosopher" who at the time was on the faculty at the University of Chicago, acknowledged in 1937 that traditional religion often has stood in the way of political and intellectual freedom.[11] He thought that the humanists' attack on the "old supernaturalism" was valid, as was their repudiation of revelation. Having admitted this, Hartshorne went on to describe "The Philosophical Limitations of Humanism."

Hartshorne began with the conviction of theistic religion that abundant life comes from love of God and love of humans "in inseparable unity." Humanism is based on the love of humans alone. Even the humanists, however, are concerned with the problem of controlling nature, and must therefore enter into relationship with it. Hartshorne saw the basis for the humanist's relationship with nature as some form of love: "To say nature is worthy of being profoundly loved and to say there is a God are scarcely distinguishable assertions. For what is God but the cosmos as an integrated whole worthy of love?"[12] Nevertheless, there is a slight difference; namely, the humanist's love of cosmic unity is primarily intellectual, whereas the love of the theist, in addition to being intellectual, is emotional, ethical, aesthetic, and social.

Science indicates that nature has a rational order, but science does not speak of cosmic tenderness. Because the humanists, following the clues of science, see the universe as capable of inflicting suffering and destruction, they cannot easily make the transition from an intellectual to a total religious love of nature. Yet this transition is difficult to avoid, "for if order is not intelligible apart from reason, neither is reason intelligible apart from purpose, and purpose in turn is not to be divested of a social aspect, that is, of love." This somewhat ambiguous statement suggests Hartshorne's answer to the problem of evil: both good and evil can be explained logically, given man's freedom and God's omnipotence; unfortunate events have some greater purpose, and to alter nature for an immediate good diminishes intellectual beauty and the general reliability of nature. Moreover, the presence of evil enhances the individual's ability to exercise "powers of foresight and prevention."

Pushing this argument still further, Hartshorne maintained that the humanist contention that humans have being on their own implies that they have power and cannot be completely coerced by cosmic forces. This means that the concept of divine omnipotence is compatible with the belief that the individual has at least minimal initiative. With intiative goes responsibility. If God does not have all the initiative, he cannot bear total responsibility for what happens; he therefore should not be blamed for the evil humans themselves create. Furthermore, humans are not the only beings who possess the power to cause havoc; so can molecules, cells, bacteria, and reptiles, for instance.

In this early period of his philosophical development, Hartshorne often referred to his position by various terms, but most often used neo-pantheism and theological naturalism. In the main, he thought the humanist criticisms of traditional theological supernaturalism were on target, especially those that focused upon God's nature as supposedly all-loving and all-powerful and yet allowing the existence of terrible pain and suffering. He thought that he could provide a viable answer to the problem of suffering with his neo-pantheistic concept of God and thus, unlike the humanists, retain God in his theology. He acknowledged, however, that people of certain temperaments will always fall back "upon unanalyzed 'animal faith' [rather] than to humanize this faith through reflective theology."

Finally, Hartshorne asked how effectively humanists can bring more compassion to personal relations without any cosmic ties. In other words, is it possible to love people without loving God? Over the long haul it may prove impossible to love if we believe that nature is based on principles "which have no similarity to love." Hartshorne thought that without a belief in God as a conserver of memory or value, humanists would become paralyzed. If humans do not relate to nature as being loving, they may become as brutal as the nature they describe. He reasoned that people will cease to act morally in an indifferent universe, especially as the prospect of humankind's extinction on this planet becomes more imminent.

Hartshorne maintained:

The ultimate ideal of knowledge and of action remains this: to deal with the world as the body of a God of love, whose generosity of interest is equal to all contrasts, however gigantic, between mind and mind, and to whom all individuals are numbered, each with its own life history and each with its own qualitative—enjoying and suffering, more or less elaborately remembering and anticipating, sensing and spontaneously reacting—natures.[13]

David E. Roberts

David E. Roberts, who at the time was associate professor of philosophy of religion and systematic theology at Union Theological Seminary in New York, in 1941 offered a critique of religious humanism in an article entitled "A Christian Appraisal of Humanism."[14] He attacked an interpretation of humanism presented two years earlier by E. A. Burtt in *Types of Religious Philosophy* (Harper Brothers, 1939). As Burtt was interested in a general systematic statement of humanism, not in advancing his own personal view, many of the questions Roberts raised are pertinent to the three pioneers of religious humanism.

Roberts acknowledged that the existence of God could not be proved empirically, but he thought that it could be interpreted in a way that is compatible with both nature and history. Roberts attacked the humanist position from this perspective. He argued that there are "contradictions" in the humanist position and that the humanists have failed to understand Christianity by equating all Christian positions with a literalistic fundamentalism.

The major contradiction Roberts saw in humanism was its naturalistic view of the world, which "does not undermine but fortifies moral effort." Roberts thought, "What the humanist really believes, of course, is that human life, with its capacities for moral and purposive action, has somehow emerged out of a morally indifferent and nonpurposive environment." He thought it contradictory to maintain that the universe is morally neutral while professing that humans should behave morally. If the purposive element lies only in humans, who exist in a purposeless universe, then science applies only to nonpurposive elements and does not tell "the whole story of reality." To insist upon applying the scientific method to human morality is to render illusory all purposiveness in human action, as well as to undermine "that measure of control through scientific knowledge on which the humanist stakes his moral hopes." Roberts thought humanists must either deny that the scientific method is adequate for understanding all areas of knowledge, or admit that morality is an illusion.

Roberts further contended that the conditions that can adequately account for the emergence of moral personality cannot be regarded as irrelevant for understanding the significance of nature as a whole. In other words, if humans are capable of moral purpose, then it might well be that this is a key for understanding the whole universe—namely, it is permeated with purpose. The entire cosmos thus is involved in producing a moral personality. Our distinctive capacities depend upon the physico-chemical and organic factors that produced us. The more one stresses the relationship of humans to their environment, "the less possible...it [becomes] to believe that those qualities have no support other than human volition and appreciation." In other words, moral values cannot exist without belief in God.

Roberts argued that the humanist position was errected on a closed system, based not on empirical inquiry but on faith. For example, whether the environment contributes to human moral effort or hinders it, the humanist claims the environment is morally neutral. Such a system is closed; positive and negative evidence is allowed to point in only one direction. Roberts thought humanists interpreted the evidence on the basis of a presupposition; they did not reach this "atheism" by impartially examining empirical evidence. Roberts attacked humanists not for basing their position on a presupposition, but for refusing to acknowledge this fact by "pretending to reach [this] position through an 'impartial' investigation." Both the Christian and humanist faiths rest upon a "non-philosophical" decision and commitment; the differences between the two reside not in empirical fact but in their different presuppositions.

Roberts thought humanists were insufficiently aware of the ambiguous nature of science, which can help humans achieve evil as well as good ends. Because science does not tell us which ends to pursue, scientific truth is not the whole truth. In other words, science cannot dictate its social uses; that can be determined only by a culture's moral and religious ideals. Scientific knowledge in and of itself will not enhance our moral and social well-being.

Furthermore, humanism provides few criteria for making ethical decisions. Roberts was convinced that this was because humanists had "lost touch with God," the cosmic ground of the moral order. According to Roberts, the humanist estimate of people was based not on an impartial, inclusive, empirical survey; it was an ideal fashioned by the humanists. People's inability to achieve this ideal image, Roberts maintained, was due to more than "a lack of insight." The true lack was an equivalent of the Christian doctrine of original sin. Roberts did not argue against humanist ideals; he disagreed with the humanists' way of arriving at them and with their explanations for failure to attain them.

Although Roberts's main criticism was of the humanist belief in morality without God, he also was critical of the humanist conception of religion and their attitude toward Jesus. Humanists say that religions, including humanism, are culturally determined, yet they imply that humanism is more valid than other religions (such as Christianity). Humanists claim to have a vantage point from which to evaluate other religious doctrines, and to possess criteria for determining religious truth. Roberts saw a contradiction in maintaining the relativity of religious truth and yet making humanism the norm for establishing it. "The disadvantage of relativism is that one cannot affirm its truth either relatively or absolutely without falling into a self-contradiction."

Roberts criticized humanists for placing Jesus in a literal New Testament context, comparing him to an enlightened twentieth-century humanist, and then declaring him an inferior guide for the modern world. In fact, the Christian's claim about the deity of Jesus is based not on his moral code, but on the relationship of the historical personality of Jesus to the divine Word incarnate in him. Unless one takes the incarnation into account, one will never find the Christian's estimate of Jesus adequate. Roberts also thought it inconsistent for humanists to define religious experience as the unification of the self around some controlling idea while objecting to Christians centering their lives around the person of Jesus.

Finally, Roberts simply considered the scientific method inadequate for establishing the truth of a theological system. Empiricism may be adequate for studying the natural world, but not for studying a personal God. Hence theologians rightly refuse to regard scientific truth as the only truth and the scientific method as the ultimate court of appeal; the scientific method cannot settle ethical and religious questions.[15]

Joseph Haroutunian

Joseph Haroutunian of the Presbyterian Theological Seminary in Chicago entered into discussion with the religious humanists at two points: when

"A Humanist Manifesto" appeared, and when Roberts attacked Burtt's interpretation of humanism. In an essay entitled "Humanism and Christianity," Haroutunian compared the humanism expressed in the Manifesto with Christianity as he understood it.[16]

Haroutunian saw the Christian-humanist controversy as having two poles, which he called the "scientific-metaphysical" and the "moral-religious." The former was concerned with the nature of the world, the latter with the nature and attainment of the good life. Little progress had been made in solving the major issues because few have expertise in these areas and because the problems themselves are so complex. For example, the theist affirms that the universe was "created," whereas the humanist believes that it is "self-existing and not created." Few theists or humanists can discuss such a complex subject intelligently; even when they can, it is doubtful they can resolve the problem. The same is true of the mind-body problem; many humanists reject the traditional dualism accepted by theists. Similar difficulties surround value theory and the existence of God.

Haroutunian thought such debates lead only to an impasse; he sought to get beyond "the intellectual symbols," for he was convinced that theism and humanism are religions as well as metaphysical systems. He tried to approach the controversy from the religious point of view, feeling such an approach might foster the mutual understanding that was lacking at the time.

Haroutunian thought he could reach the heart of the matter by focusing on the eighth article of the Humanist Manifesto, which deals with the "end of man's life." Humanists considered the complete realization of human personality, as well as creation of a society in which people work for the common good, as important. They saw the world as consisting of humans and nature, which is indifferent to human efforts. Yet, humans possess consciousness, intelligence, and will, and they seek to realize goals and ideals. Since nature is neutral, humans must control and use it to realize their ideals. When nature retards their efforts, they must continue to work with courage, forcing nature to yield to their will. Because people live in groups, they must experiment in developing social arrangements through which all can obtain happiness. The task of bringing about needed social changes is a human task. Humanism seeks to promote many values, but deems "the Holy" to be unnecessary. Humanism's "primary virtues...are intelligence, courage, manliness, resourcefulness, and justice or equity."

Christianity, in contrast to humanism, focuses on the person of

Jesus of Nazareth. For the Christian, the good life is Christlike, even though the world rejected the way of Jesus and crucified him. The cross is prominent in the Christian mind, for "it has become the symbol of true love or the supreme goodness, the means of salvation from sin and suffering unto the Joy of Christlikeness, and the clue to the understanding of Reality."

For Christians the complete realization of personality means attaining the "stature of the fullness of Christ." The Christians' attitude toward nature is one of wonder and of conscious kinship with it, for they consider God to have created both humankind and nature. Christians believe that God works through them as well as through nature in reaching his goals. Human desire for the good life is therefore subsumed by the desire to glorify God. "Since salvation is joy in God the vision of the glory of God is the last end of man." Although Christianity has a "tragic sense of life," its hope of immortality is based on faith in the love and power of God.

Haroutunian thought that Christianity was deeply rooted in the human constitution and in people's relationship to the world; therefore, it has had a perennial appeal. Humanism, then, was unwise in going "beyond such a many-sided religion as Christianity." On the other hand, Christians must give humanism its due:

[Humanism's] uncompromising distinction between ideals and facts, its determination to be strictly rational and empirical, its purpose of creating maximum welfare here on earth, are good reasons for the wide acceptance it has enjoyed. Courage, resourcefulness, hopefulness, independence, and self-reliance, are virtues which are prized highly by the human mind. The modern man's success in harnessing nature and adding "to the satisfactions of life" are a challenge that the work be continued. The social reforms enacted in the nineteenth century call for further progress in the elimination of social and natural evil. Humanism is a legitimate successor to humanitarianism, Unitarianism, and the reform movements of the past century. It breathes their spirit and often adopts their language.

However, Haroutunian cautioned that in the post–First World War period pessimism had set in, accompanied by doubt about the good will and intelligence of humans. If humanism was to succeed as a religion, its optimism must be tempered with a "tragic sense of life. Otherwise, there is a real danger that humanism will limit its usefulness greatly by becoming unrealistic and unconvincing." He thought Christianity especially could enrich humanism with its acceptance of sin, repentance, regeneration, and grace, as well as with its emphasis on the Christlike life and its theocentric piety. Finally, Haroutunian thought that by repudiating completely the religions of the past humanism was cutting itself off from much wisdom and insight. If humanism is to make its mark, it must develop a "critical wisdom" that can apply principles and convictions to particular problems.[17]

Haroutunian's critique of humanism reveals the influence of neo-orthodox theology. Haroutunian assured Roberts that they probably agreed basically on Christian theology, but he thought Roberts's critique of humanism was ineffective. Instead of attacking humanism for its "contradictions," Haroutunian thought that the best apologetic was to state the strengths of both humanism and Christianity; God would reveal the truth of the Christian proclamation. Haroutunian saw no advantage in setting up humanism as a straw-man, nor did he think argument would convert the humanist. He was convinced that the Christian proclamation would.[18]

The Pioneers Twenty Years after the Manifesto

Twenty years after "A Humanist Manifesto" was first published, the original signers were asked what changes they would make if it were being published in 1953. Among those asked were the three pioneers of this study. Although the thought of these men was more varied and complex than such a brief statement could reveal, the Manifesto represented a consensus of humanist thought at that time.

Dietrich did not have a copy of the Manifesto at hand, but he thought it should stand unchanged as a historical document. He thought that it was dated and represented a dated philosophy; less was known about "the great cosmic schemes" than the document implied, and it was too "dogmatic and arrogant." Dietrich felt that seekers after the truth should be more humble. He believed that he had put too much reliance upon science and reason, and had too much contempt "for any intuitive insights and intangible values." He was convinced that the humanism of the period had been a protest movement and as such served a purpose. The positive side of humanism was its "enrichment of life in its every form"; its negative side was being "short-sighted" in "cutting itself off from all cosmic relationship, and denying or ignoring every influence outside of humanity itself."[19]

In contrast to Dietrich, Reese thought the Manifesto was as valid in 1953 as it had been in 1933. He said, "I would change nothing and add only a more extensive statement of the implications of the scientific method and spirit."[20] However, as there was a great deal of controversy in the United States about communism at that time, Reese defended

Article 14, which criticized our "acquisitive and profit-motivated society" and advocated "a socialized and co-operative economic order." Reese said it was grossly unfair to interpret this article as support for "Soviet Communism." He added: "We must not allow our anti-communistic attitude to swing us out of accord with the world-wide trend toward a more socialized economy."

Potter, like Dietrich, was somewhat more critical of the Manifesto than was Reese. He suggested a number of stylistic changes, as well as changes of attitude (he advocated more "humility and modesty"). Also, he was somewhat apprehensive about the socialized economy proposed by Article 14, which he thought should be rewritten "in the light of recent history." Potter's interest in extrasensory perception tended to come through in his wishing to delete "in the here and now" in regard to "the complete realization of human personality" in Article 8 because it "is an unnecessary limitation of personality."[21] Finally, he suggested adding "more fervor, hope, and enthusiasm."

Summary

Two of the major criticisms leveled against religious humanism were the same ones found in the humanist-theist controversy in Unitarianism: to advocate a religion without God is to change the meaning of religion, and it is doubtful that a morality without God can be sustained. Each thinker approached these problems from a slightly different perspective, but ultimately each came down to these basic points. The one new note that was struck when the controversy spread beyond Unitarianism was the discussion about Jesus. However, it is interesting that many of the liberal Christians never raised this topic in their encounters with the humanists. The first two criticisms, of course, can be raised with all three pioneers of religious humanism; the question of Jesus is relevant to Dietrich and Reese, but not to Potter.

The general tenor of the critiques of religious humanism was that there is an ultimate path and there is a penultimate one. Theism, especially in its Christian form, is the ultimate path, for it embraces not only the natural world, but something else as well. Religious humanism is the penultimate, for it restricts itself needlessly. However, there are people who, for psychological, intellectual, or other reasons, cannot make the ultimate commitment. As long as humanism attempted to meet their needs, the theists were willing to encourage them, despite their conviction that such a way is only second best.

PART III

★ ★ ★

THE LEGACY

OF

RELIGIOUS

HUMANISM

★ ★ ★

CHAPTER 8

American Religious Humanism Today

"Is Humanism a religion, perhaps, the next great religion? Yes, it must be so characterized, for the word, religion, has become a symbol for answers to that basic interrogation of human life, and the nature of things—which every human being, in some degree and in some fashion, makes." Roy Wood Sellars

WE HAVE EXAMINED THE HISTORICAL BACKGROUND OF RELIGIOUS HUMANISM, and studied the lives and thought of three of its pioneers during the formative stage. We are now ready to explore the current expressions and status of this radical religious movement. In order to do this, we must pull together some of the important threads of materials already discussed in much greater detail earlier, and we shall use them as a context for understanding such institutional expressions of religious humanism as Ethical Culture, Humanistic Judaism, the American Humanist Association, the Fellowship of Religious Humanists, and the North American Committee on Humanism. We shall see that religious humanism, which arose about the time of the First World War, has indeed survived and continues to provide a source of moral and spiritual orientation for many Americans who confess that they no longer can accept the traditional faiths of their mothers and fathers, but who are not quite ready to abandon the religious quest altogether.

The Liberal Context

As we have noted, religious humanism has a distinguished and impressive ancestry in both philosophy and religion. In philosophy, it reaches back to Greece in the fifth century B.C.E. and the European Renaissance in the fourteenth and fifteenth centuries; in the twentieth century it finds expression in naturalistic humanism. In religion, its ancestry goes back to the eighteenth century, to the time of the conflict in New England Congregationalism between the orthodox Calvinists and the more liberal "rational Christians," sometimes referred to as "Arians" or "Arminians." In the main, the liberal Congregationalists were opposed to the Calvinist doctrines of the trinity, election, and the excessive emotionalism expressed in the revivals of the Great Awakening. Eventually the conflict led to a schism in Congregationalism, and in 1825 the liberal group formed the American Unitarian Association with its headquarters in Boston.

Later and immediately following the American Civil War, Henry Bellows, minister of All Souls Unitarian Church in New York City, organized a National Conference of Unitarian Churches, whose purpose was to overcome the provincialism of Eastern Massachusetts, and provide a program for the expansion of liberal religion into other regions of the nation. In order to expand, Bellows thought it imperative for Unitarians to commit themselves to a distinctively Christian creed, albeit a liberal one. This attempt to promote a creed caused much controversy in Unitarianism. In fact, those who viewed Unitarianism as a noncreedal religion rebelled and, in 1867, created the Free Religious Association. Although this association brought together two of the more radical factions of Unitarians—the transcendentalists, whose representatives included Ralph Waldo Emerson and Octavius Brooks Frothingham, and the "scientific theists," with such representatives as Francis Abbott and William F. Potter—it also drew into its membership Reform Jews such as Isaac M. Wise, Ethical Culturists such as Felix Adler, and a few Universalists and Quakers. This inclusiveness reveals the noncreedal nature of the Free Religious Association, and it also reveals that it was not even distinctively Christian in its perspective. Those who were Unitarian were saying, in effect, that one could be authentically religious without being a Christian, that one did not have to be a Christian in order to be a Unitarian. As the Unitarian members of the Free Religious Association continued to press for their noncreedal policy in the National Conference of Unitarian Churches, they slowly chipped away at the creed until it was considered no longer binding. By the end of the nineteenth century, Unitarianism in effect was once again a noncreedal religion.

The noncreedal policy allowed those who were not committed to an expression of Christianity, not even a liberal interpretation, to become members of Unitarian churches. When the twentieth century arrived, Unitarianism was a small, rather comfortable denomination with liberal Christians and non-Christians worshipping together within its membership. But this peace and comfort did not last. The subsequent conflict was caused not by the exploding canons of the First World War but by ministers such as John H. Dietrich and Curtis W. Reese preaching a new interpretation of religion from the perspective of naturalistic humanism. They promoted a radical form of religion repudiating both a doctrine of God and of personal immortality. Their ideas ignited a bitter humanist-theist controversy within the American Unitarian Association that lasted from 1920 up to the eve of the Second World War. Once again the creedal question arose, and once again the Unitarians opted for a noncreedal religion. The religious humanists forced Unitarians to raise the question, Must one believe in God in order to be a Unitarian? And after the debate died down, the final answer was no. Thus, the precedent set by the issues raised by the Free Religious Association had provided a means for resolving the outcome for the debate on "religion without God."

From this liberal context we will examine a number of the basic humanist institutions to assess the situation of American religious humanism today. As we have seen, two small segments of the professional population identified with the religious humanist movement during its formative stage: liberal ministers such as Dietrich, Reese, and Potter; and such academics as Roy Wood Sellars at the University of Michigan, Max Otto at Wisconsin, A. Eustace Haydon at Chicago, John Dewey at Columbia, and J.A.C. Fagginger Auer at Harvard. Countless lay persons, of course, whose names are not recorded in the historical documents, made the religious humanist movement much larger than the few persons mentioned here. Although each spokesman might express his views differently and perceive different issues as primary, the basic theology or ideology of the movement was captured and generally lucidly articulated by the pioneers.

The Ethical Culture Societies

Felix Adler, the son of a Reform rabbi, was born in Alzey, near Worms, Germany, and moved with his family to the United States just before his sixth birthday.[1] The Adlers came to America because the father had been chosen to become rabbi of Temple Emanu-el in New York City. Felix was carefully groomed by his father to succeed him as rabbi at Emanu-el. After his graduation from Columbia College he was sent to Germany for graduate study. He studied at the University of Berlin, where he was profoundly influenced by the neo-Kantian thought of Hermann Cohen; yet he transferred to the University of Heidelberg where he received his doctorate in Semitics. Upon his return from Germany, at age twenty-two with his doctorate in hand, he was invited to speak at his father's temple.[2] On 11 October 1873 he addressed the congregation on "The Future of Religion." Those who heard the address noted that he did not mention the word *God,* nor had his discourse been based on a biblical text; he even went so far as to criticize Jewish exclusiveness. He said, "Judaism never claimed to be a religion—not of creed but of deed—and its destiny is to embrace in one great moral state the whole family of man."[3] Several influential members of the congregation were so shocked by the sermon that it soon became obvious that he was not destined to be his father's successor at Emanu-el. Joseph Seligman, a wealthy banker, secured a teaching position for Adler at Cornell University, and even underwrote it. But before long Adler's extreme views became well enough known in the community that some upstate Protestant clergy, along with some leaders of the Jewish community in New York City, complained to President Andrew B. White that such an arch-heretic should not be allowed to represent Judaism on campus. Their voices were heard and Adler's appointment was discontinued.

Adler returned to New York in the spring of 1876 and founded the Society for Ethical Culture. He drew support from some of the more adventurous members of his father's congregation, though they maintained their membership at Emanu-el, from several of the Unitarian churches, and others who were not affiliated with any denomination or religion. At the beginning Adler gave addresses on Sundays in rented halls such as the secular Chickering Hall and later in Carnegie Hall. Finally the society was able to build its own facility, New York's Ethical Society Meeting House, located at 64th Street and Central Park West. It was dedicated in 1910.

Ethical Culture soon began to spread to other large cities. The Chicago Ethical Society was founded in October 1882 with William M. Slater as leader, the Philadelphia society in 1885 with S. Burns Weston as leader, and the St. Louis society in 1886 with Walter L. Sheldon as leader. In addition to these urban areas in the United States, Ethical Culture also took hold in London, where Stanton Coit worked at South Place Chapel; in 1892 Coit established the West End Ethical Society, which took as its official name the Ethical Church. A few societies also sprang up in Germany, and one was established in Vienna.

In the early years of the Ethical Culture movement the influence of the Free Religious Association on Adler was most apparent. Adler, isolated from Reform Judaism, found in the association a support system of professional and ministerial colleagues. Many of the early leaders of Ethical Culture had made contact with Adler through the association, among them William Slater and Burns Weston, both Unitarians and graduates of Harvard Divinity School. Moreover, the transcendentalism of men like Ralph Waldo Emerson reinforced and broadened Adler's neo-Kantian thought. So smitten was Adler with Emerson that he named his first son, born the year of Emerson's death, Waldo. Although influenced positively by the Free Religious Association, Adler also criticized it. The vast majority of its members tended to be intellectuals who were primarily concerned with ideas, and they enjoyed the annual meetings because they provided an opportunity to present well thought out papers, followed by a time for discussion and even debate. But Adler thought the association remiss in failing to translate ideas into social action. Generally the members thought that social action should be carried out through other agencies. For Adler, moral action was not to be separated from moral thought. The lack of action by the association made Adler impatient; he withdrew from active leadership, although he remained a member. As Adler trained men to become leaders of Ethical Culture societies, of course, he began to create his own intimate professional group.

During the late 1870s, when Adler was developing his understanding of Ethical Culture, there were advocates in New York and London of Auguste Comte's "Positivist Philosophy" and his "Religion of Humanity." William Frey and Edward King were its staunches advocates in New York. Because Ethical Culture and the Religion of Humanity were frequently confused in the popular mind, Adler gave an address on "The Religion of Humanity" in which he assessed Comte's thought. He agreed with Comte that labor was important and that the conditions of workingmen must be improved, that society must have a larger role for women, and that the "Golden Rule" was inadequate as a basic moral principle for an ethical theory. However, Adler faulted Comte for idealizing certain facts of science, society, and femininity. He also cautioned against confusing ideals with facts. Idealizing humans as they are Adler saw as a weakness in the Religion of Humanity. Adler advocated "a religion of the ideal" that transcends "the all too human"—

in other words, a neo-Kantian transcendental idealism, which provided an ethical norm for judging human actions in society.

Adler maintained there was an absolute and universal standard, "a Moral Ideal," that provides a norm for living. With this conviction he set out to teach people how to live moral lives, and in the process he became involved in most of the moral issues of his time. He created a free kindergarten for the children of workingmen, to take them off the streets and provide them with a moral environment in which to grow. In time the Workingmen's Kindergarten developed into the Ethical Culture Schools, private schools whose educational philosophy centered on moral education. He also established a visiting-nurse program for sick people who were homebound in poor neighborhoods. He became involved in issues related to race relations, and when the First World War broke out, he advocated the creation of a more just world where war would not be used to settle international disputes. His general slogan was "deeds above creeds." To make the world better you first had to make people better, and the means for doing so was Ethical Culture. Adler insisted upon high intellectual standards for leaders of Ethical Culture, and he urged them to strive for their own "spiritual" self-development and for moral progress in their own lives as well as in society.

At the center of Adler's thought was ethical idealism. In it he combined his understanding of Kant with his understanding of transcendentalism, especially the thought of Emerson. From Kant he gained insight into the problem of epistemology. He believed that the human mind does not simply record isolated sense data, but, due to its structure and ways of operating, the mind imposes order on these data; the mind therefore plays a part in "creating" the truth rather than simply discovering it. As a result of this conviction, as we have noted, he was critical of Comte's positivist philosophy, and later he was unable to agree with the younger leaders of Ethical Culture who embraced naturalism and its correspondence theory of truth. It was Adler's epistemology that led him to religious agnosticism. He accepted Kant's criticisms of the traditional arguments for the existence of God, and he reasoned further that if the term *God* refers to a realm beyond sense experience, there is no way to determine whether the term is an empty concept or corresponds to reality. Even if God is more than a human concept, it is still an empty one, since there is no perception on which it could be founded—the finite mind cannot comprehend the infinite.

Adler also was influenced by Kant in the realm of ethics. He accepted the notion of the inherent worth or value of the individual, which he derived from the various formulations of the categorical imperative, "one ought to treat others as ends in themselves and never as a means only." Often he expressed the imperative as "Elicit the best in others and thereby in yourself." Kant referred to the categorical imperative as the "supreme principle of morality" and Adler agreed, referring to it as "the Ethical Ideal." Where some religions place a concept of a deity or a historical person (such as Buddha or Jesus) at the focal point of their faith, Adler placed an abstract principle. The Ethical Ideal provided a transcendental perspective for living in the world and making judgments of value. The Ethical Ideal functioned in Adler's understanding of Ethical Culture as the concept of God functions in Judaism and Christianity. In other words, it was Adler's "ultimate concern" or ultimate principle. As noted, this is one of the areas where Adler parted company with the advocates of Comte's Religion of Humanity. The Comteans saw outstanding members of the human race as worthy of veneration; Adler thought humans needed an even higher standard.

Adler also was influenced by his transcendentalist associates in the Free Religious Association. Emerson had promoted a belief in "the oversoul," by which he meant that all individuals had a part of the divine within them. Through "intuition" the individual mind could grasp its connection with the divine that permeates the universe, and the understanding gained from this experience could help one to live appropriately. Such a belief supported Adler's conviction of the inherent value of persons. He thought something of intrinsic worth existed in even the most despicable.

Adler became interested in the relationship of Emerson's concept of "the oversoul" to "the Ethical Ideal," which was a universal, objective, and abstract moral principle. Adler was critical of Kant's failure to note the moral worth of a person's uniqueness, to see the importance of those individual characteristics that set one person apart from another. Adler began to see the value of the interaction between different individuals as "an infinite unity of a boundless manifold." This belief led him to repudiate all monotheistic conceptions of God in favor of a social conception of "divinity." Horace Friess explains, "Religiously...it meant substituting for a single 'God' the 'Divine Life'of an infinite 'Spiritual Manifold.'"[4] Adler reasoned that if moral perfection were centered in a single divine being, human morality would lose its primary importance and become secondary. He therefore viewed Hebraic and Christian

177

monotheism as outmoded stages for providing social authority. For him, the divine life became the social interplay between the various members of a group. The greatest good was created by human beings interacting in a group with other unique and diverse human beings. All these ideas were prefigured in his sermon "The Future of Religion" at the outset of his career.

Judaism had become distorted by emphasizing religious doctrine or belief over moral deeds. It had become exclusive rather then inclusive. Adler, believing that diversity as wide as human experience must be included in social interaction, thought exclusiveness deprived Judaism of the ability to create the highest good. Religious creeds were not only impossible to validate in principle, they were sources of unnecessary antagonisms between individuals and groups. Because creedal diversity caused conflict, even mean antagonisms, Adler proposed creating unity through his Ethical Ideal. Once again Adler proclaimed his well-known slogan, "deed before creed." Adler saw diversity as an important ingredient in social interaction. Instead of the concept of a single God, Adler promoted "the divine life" of an "infinite spiritual manifold."

In some respects Adler's moral perspective resembles ancient Zoroastrianism, albeit it without its good god, Ahura Mazda, or the evil god, Angra Mainyu. Both Adler and Zoroastrians viewed the world in terms of a moral dualism in which the major conflict is between the forces of good and evil. This dualism is based not on the simple Manichean notion of a conflict between spirit and flesh, but rather on a moral dualism in which good wars with evil. One might say Adler saw Ethical Culture as a means for making people good so they could reduce the evil in the world. In this context he employed the term "ethical energy" to describe the process enabling moral people to employ their power well in every area of their lives—their families, schools, vocations, state, and world. The concept of ethical energy provided a means for transforming people, and eventually the world. Adler was like advocates of the social gospel, who sought to create "the Kingdom of God," or Dietrich, whose goal was "the commonwealth of man." Despite Adler's skepticism about a deity providing support for the forces of good, he remained optimistic about the outcome. "I believe," he said, "the law of righteousness will triumph in the universe over all evil."[5]

The question we asked about the pioneers of religious humanism we must now pose for Adler: Was Ethical Culture a religion without God? Adler was less explicit on this subject than Dietrich, Reese, and Potter.

First, Adler avowed that he had never been an atheist; therefore, he did not deny the existence of God. Second, in some contexts, Adler referred to "the great All" or to "the unknown God." Adler thought it impossible to know whether a Supreme Being existed because of the limitations of the finite mind, but he proposed "the divine life of an infinite Spiritual Manifold." With this concept, Adler made it clear that it is not by prayer or by acts of a single deity, but by human effort that good comes about. If we are to live in a good world, we must create it ourselves.

We have referred to the thought of Dietrich, Reese, and Potter as religious humanism. Was Adler's? First, was his thought religious? For Adler himself, Ethical Culture was a religion; yet he recognized that some people are incapable of being religious, and he wished to include them as legitimate members of an Ethical Culture society. "The daring thought we had, in beginning the Ethical Movement, was to unite in one group, in one bond, those who had religious feelings and those who cared simply for moral betterment....The Ethical Movement is religious to those who are religiously-minded and to those who interpret its work religiously, and it is simply ethical to those who are not so minded."[6]

Was Adler a humanist? His thought appears to be radically human-istic because he focused on human beings who are responsible for their lives, for the institutions to which they belong, and for the kind of world they live in. Yet, according to Horace Friess, Adler rejected the label "humanist" because he thought the humanist view much too narrow to embrace his wider religious vision. At least in theory, his view embraced "the infinite society" of "all beings capable of intercommunication," not just humans. Adler wished to keep open the possibility of an infinite relationship with "the Godhead" or "the Divine Life," and he thought the humanism of his day truncated that possibility.

Perhaps these thoughts best capture Adler's private faith: "People want a confession of faith, I am told. Hear then mine—a simple one. I believe in the supreme excellence of righteousness; I believe that the law of righteousness will triumph in the universe over evil; I believe that in the law of righteousness is the sanctification of human life; and I believe that in furthering and fulfilling that law I also am hallowed in the service of the unknown God."[7] Yet, lying behind this private creed was the conviction, "Diversity in the creed, unanimity in the deed. This is that practical religion from which none dissents."[8]

As a younger generation of Ethical Culture leaders came into the movement, including Horace Friess, Adler's son-in-law, they embraced the naturalistic and pragmatic humanism promoted by John Dewey and other members of the philosophy department at Columbia University. As Adler approached the twilight of his life, his followers had deviated from his neo-Kantian philosophy of transcendental idealism. When this transpired, the leaders of Ethical Culture embraced a religious humanism that was not unlike that advocated by Dietrich, Reese, and Potter.

Humanistic Judaism

Sherwin T. Wine is the leading spokesperson for a new form of Judaism, called Humanistic Judaism. As the movement grows, he expects it to take its place alongside Reform, Orthodox, Conservative, and Reconstructionist Judaism. Although currently in its infancy as an institution, it may embrace the actual beliefs of more Jews than any other form of Judaism. In the 1960s Wine organized the first congregation espousing the philosophy of Humanistic Judaism, the Birmingham Temple in Farmington Hills, Michigan, just outside Detroit. By 1969 the movement had embraced ten temples and chapters, organized into the Society for Humanistic Judaism and publishing the journal *Humanistic Judaism.*

Wine notes that ancient Judaism arose in a small, pastoral country. Its language was simple, drawing on metaphors from its rural environment: shepherds waching their flocks, farmers sowing their seeds, and fishermen mending their nets. Today the situation is radically different; most Jews live in urban areas greatly influenced by the values derived from science and technology. Wine contends that many well-educated Jews no longer find meaning in the traditional language espoused in the synagogues, even when the rabbis demythologize it by extrapolating contemporary meanings from the old metaphors and symbols. Many contemporary Jews have become secular, and their everyday beliefs and practices have little or no connection with traditional Judaism. Wine thinks it time for the spokespersons of Judaism to accept the contemporary secular situation and to make a complete break with the traditional norms and canon of Judaism: "A religion which was appropriate to hill-country priests in 500 B.C., or to prosperous merchants in agricultural Spain, or to destitute Poland is simply inappropriate to the citizens of megalopolis. No legal fictions, no textual twisting can ultimately hide that reality."[9]

Since early in his career, Wine has attempted to interpret Judaism from a purely secular perspective that he refers to as Humanistic Judaism, believing that contemporary humanism provides the basic ingredients for interpreting Judaism today. In *Humanistic Judaism* (1978) he provides a brief analysis of the situation of the contemporary Jew, and offers some basic tenets gleaned from contemporary humanism as a means for living and coping today. He says, "Judaism changes from century to century. In Solomon's day it was polytheistic; in Hillel's day it was monotheistic; in our time it has, by any behavior standard, become humanistic."[10]

Wine maintains that Jews today are better educated as a group than at any other time in their history. Their education is based not on the religious texts of traditional Judaism, but on the ideas explored in the contemporary secular university. In contrast to a norm based on fixed religious texts, alleged to be founded on divine revelation, the contemporary Jew has adopted the value of "free inquiry"; knowledge is subject to critical scrutiny, and any claim to truth, religious or secular, must pass the standards promoted by "empiricism" to be accepted. Any claims to address problems of humans or the universe that make no discernible difference are meaningless. Values, contends Wine, were not handed from heaven to holy men standing on high mountains, but have been created by humans. In short, the creation of values has shifted from the divine to the human, with a concomitant shift in focus from theism to "humanism." The contemporary secular Jew exempts no claim to truth from critical inquiry, denies the truth of religions whose claims contradict empirical experience, and doubts that values are derived from the divine. Instead, the secular Jew affirms the principle of free inquiry, applies empirical standards for judging truth claims, and believes that humans are the creators of their own values. From this perspective Wine articulates his understanding of secular religion: "Humanistic Judaism starts with the affirmation that the *new* Jew—the mobile, the intellectual, the science-oriented, the skeptical, the innovative, the money-expert, the atheistic, and aggressive Jew—is *real* and *ok*. In fact, he is more interesting and more significant to world culture than any Jew who preceded him."[11]

By now the secular and humanistic components of Wine's interpretation of religion are apparent, so where does Judaism fit? Religion's main concern is the search for meaning and value, a search in which Judaism will be affirmed as the cultural and aesthetic framework. Jewish customs and ceremonies, like poetry, are "capable of embracing a wide spectrum of human values and experiences" and of interpreting them from several philosophical perspectives, including both mystical theism and naturalistic humanism. Jewish religious activity will be

181

completely secularized; nothing in traditional Judaism will remain an untouchable item of reverence. This means God language will be discarded because it is no longer meaningful and is "incapable of redemption." Societies will be organized to provide a sense of community for those who opt for Humanistic Judaism. Members of these societies are aware, especially in the cultural environment of the United States, that Jewishness is a secondary value, merely an aesthetic option.

The first meeting of the Society for Humanistic Judaism was held in Detriot in 1970. At that meeting the Humanist Manifesto of 1933 was carefully studied and discussed as a background for hammering out the purpose and defining the basic tenets of Humanistic Judaism. Where did the advocates of Humanistic Judaism agree and disagree with the Manifesto? Through their deliberations the members reached consensus on twelve tenets. Wine subsequently reexamined these, and has finally reduced them to seven.

The first tenet focuses on *self-respect* as a goal of life. Humanistic Judaism views the goal of life as experiencing self-worth and developing self-esteem, not finding favor with God. (2) It therefore repudiates the doctrine of original sin, which views humans as flawed sinners, and emphasizes the *power of humans* and their capacity for self-discipline. By establishing goals and then assuming responsibility for reaching them, we build self-esteem. (3) Humanistic Judaism emphasizes the paths of *autonomous persons,* who choose the basic directions for their lives and then seek to reach them. (4) Though humans are individuals, *community* is also important, for through contact with others individuals develop their personalities, and through cooperation survival is possible. (5) Humanistic Judaism *repudiates the authoritarian approach* to truth that claims, for instance, that a statement is true because it was uttered by Moses, or Jesus, or Muhammad. Wine considers this a kind of "name-dropping"; he maintains that it is not the author of a statement that determines its truth, but its veracity. A rational person is impressed not by names, but by the facts supporting a statement. Wine, of course, does not deny the importance of emotion, for he realizes "love and empathy are essential to happiness." (6) The religious ingredient in Humanistic Judaism is not belief in God, but "a strong attachment to ritual practices." Wine explains, "The majority of these practices are associated with two calendars: the seasonal calendar of Rosh Hashanah, Sukkot, Hanukkah, and Passover, and the life-cycle calendar of baby-naming, Barmitzvah, marriage, and death. Both calendars together define the nature of Jewish religious behavior."[12] Viewing humans as "the supreme fulfillment of the evolutionary process," Humanistic Jews find meaning in the *celebration of life*. (7) The final tenet returns to the relationship of Judaism to humanism:

The humanistic Jew is an individual, of either Jewish or non-Jewish descent, who believes in the ultimate value of self-respect and in the principles of humanism, community, and rationality. He also finds meaning in the celebration of life as expressed through the historic Jewish calendar and seeks to interpret this calendar in a naturalistic way.... A humanistic Jew, because of a common history and shared religious practices, feels a strong bond to Jews throughout the world. He also feels an important tie with all men who seek to promote individual self-esteem.[13]

When in June 1994 Beth Adam congregation in Cincinnati applied for admission into the Union of American Hebrew Congregations, the national organization of Reform Judaism, it created a problem for Reform Judaism that resembled the humanist-theist controversy in Unitarianism. Like Unitarianism, Reform Judaism is a liberal expression of religion that is noncreedal and upholds the local autonomy of each congregation. However, Beth Adam is a distinctly independent, consciously humanistic congregation. All references to God have been removed from their liturgy.

Beth Adam member Harriet Edwards left a traditional reform congregation because she no longer resonated with its liturgical beliefs. She has belonged to Beth Adam for nine years, and has served as president and as a member of the liturgy committee. She says that traditional Reform Judaism "called upon a God that was a very male person. It was the kind of God that answers prayers and intervenes in the order of the universe. It was not a God concept that I held." Her experience appears to be representative of the other 220 adult members of the congregation.

Joining the Union requires no doctrinal or liturgical tests, only that a congregation promote "the development of liberal Judaism." Although the Jewishness of Beth Adam is not questioned, strong opposition has been expressed to its application on the grounds that a strictly humanistic congregation "would infuse our community and national movement with divisiveness, discord and disharmony."[14]

From the perspective of the humanist-theist controversy in Unitarianism, one can see that the Union is caught between its belief in congregational autonomy and the view that a congregation should retain and express belief in God. In turning down Beth Adam's application, the Union deemed belief in God necessary. This no doubt violates the autonomy of Beth Adam and its members, and perhaps disturbs the consciences of the Union's more liberal members. Having been denied membership, Beth Adam now has two options: to remain an independent congregation or apply for membership in the Society for Humanistic Judaism. Perhaps Sherwin Wine is not far off target in contending that Humanistic Judaism represents the opinions of far more Jews than its membership figures suggest. He also believes that the Union was correct in denying Beth Adam membership, and he hopes the congregation will apply for membership in the Society for Humanistic Judaism. He says, "There is no need for a Humanistic Congregation to seek admission to the Reform movement. Humanistic Judaism is a vital, active international movement within Judaism today."[15]

The American Humanist Association

We have noted that the religious humanist movement in America began with the chance meeting between John H. Dietrich and Curtis W. Reese at the Western Unitarian Conference held in Des Moines in 1917. Both became articulate spokesmen for the movement, and in addition Reese was able to promote humanism from his administrative position as secretary of the Western Unitarian Conference. By 1928 a small group of students at Meadville Theological School and the University of Chicago who embraced religious humanism started a journal entitled the *New Humanist*. First produced on a mimeograph machine, it grew into a journal of serious liberal religious opinion; Harold Buschman and Raymond Bragg were among its early editors. This student humanist group invited Roy Wood Sellars to come and present his views on religious humanism. Following his visit, Sellars was asked to draw up a draft for the *Humanist Manifesto* (1933) in which Raymond Bragg, Edwin H. Wilson, A. Eustace Haydon, and others provided input. The Humanist Press Association was organized to assume the responsibility of publishing the *New Humanist*. When a destructive fire caused it to suspend publication, Edwin H. Wilson picked up the reins and began publishing the *Humanist Bulletin*.

In 1941 the American Humanist Association was established with Curtis W. Reese as president, a position he held for the next fourteen years. One of the main responsibilities of the new association was publishing the *Humanist*, so in a sense the Humanist Press Association evolved into the American Humanist Association, and the *Humanist* evolved from the *Humanist Bulletin*, which in turn had evolved from the *New Humanist*. In the 1940s the American Humanist Association was made up mostly of liberal ministers, notably Unitarians, and academicians, mostly philosophers, among them Edwin Burtt of Cornell University, Max Otto of the University of Wisconsin, and John Herman Randall and John Dewey of Columbia University. In its early years, then, the American Humanist Association was a cozy club for like-minded humanist ministers and academicians.

By the 1950s the Ethical Culturalists had become active in the American Humanist Association, and, as the association began to draw a wider and much more diverse membership, including several well-known people in the sciences, tensions arose. Members held differing views of the nature of humanism; some maintained it was a religion, others that it was a philosophy, and still others that it was simply a way of life. The association embraced both religious and secular humanists; still others were outright atheists, and some strongly opposed the view of humanism as a religion. Some of the atheists and secularists were militantly anti-church, even the liberal church. (One of the gentler atheists said of his more militant colleagues, "One does not have to be hateful to be an atheist.") Fueling the controversy over the nature of humanism were people possessed of strong personalities who had been successful in their chosen professions.[16]

By the early 1960s the "religious humanists" thought that many of their concerns were being pushed to the periphery by the more blatantly "secular humanists." Since their ranks had been drawn primarily from the American Unitarian Association, which became the Unitarian Universalist Association in 1961, and since there had been much passing back and forth between the Ethical Culture societies and Unitarian Universalist churches, especially of ministers/leaders, they formed the core of the group who created the Fellowship of Religious Humanists in 1963. Edwin H. Wilson became administrative secretary and editor of *Religious Humanism*, Lester Mondale was president, and Edward Ericson and Raymond Bragg were some of the better-known members of the board.

Ironically, following the creation of the Fellowship of Religious Humanists, the "secular humanism" of the American Humanist Association began taking on the form of a "religion," or what Paul Kurtz calls "eupraxophy." Kurtz, who derived this word from the Greek words for "good," "practice," and "wisdom," defines it as "good conduct and wisdom in living." Eupraxophy includes both ethics and a world view that provide the foundation for conduct and living.[17] The American Humanist Association sponsors conferences at the national, regional, and local levels. Today "counselors" certified by the association perform duties similar to those of Unitarian Universalist ministers or Ethical Culture leaders, such as preparing weddings and memorial services according to the wishes of their participants. Seventy-five chapters located throughout the United States provide opportunities for active local participation and a sense of community for their members. Members of the association receive subscriptions to the *Humanist* and to *Free Mind*, a newsletter especially for the membership reporting on the American Humanist Association, its leaders, chapters, and humanists around the world.

Generally the American Humanist Association promotes principles related to democratic ideals, humanist values, and the scientific spirit. Its perspective is broadly within that created by Dietrich, Reese, and Potter, brought up to date with the more recent developments in the sciences and addressing new social issues as they arise. One of the tensions within the movement today is whether the AHA should focus on the problem of establishing sound ethical principles for living, and/or whether it should address specific social problems. Those who opt for principles believe that social action should be left to other groups, for example, the American Civil Liberties Union, the National Association for the Advancement of Colored People, or the National Association for Women. Others would like the AHA to become directly involved in such issues as freedom with respect to sexual preference, choice for women seeking abortions, the right to die with dignity assisted by a qualified physician, and specific issues related to freedom of religion and maintaining the separation of church and state. Sometimes members of the AHA are not on the same side of certain issues, and those whose views are not promoted by the association question its right to speak on their behalf. Such instances reveal that the AHA may be more actively involved in specific social and political issues than formerly.

Members of the American Humanist Association generally share the perspective of Dietrich, Reese, and Potter, although it has been updated and its tone is different. A good summary of the views of the AHA today is provided by a pamphlet entitled "What Is Humanism?"

Humanism is a philosophy for people who think for themselves. There is no area of thought that a Humanist is afraid to challenge or explore.

Humanism is a philosophy focused upon human means for comprehending reality. Humanists make no claims to possess or have access to supposed transcendent knowledge.

Humanism is a philosophy of reason and science in the pursuit of knowledge. Therefore, when it comes to the question of the most valid means for acquiring knowledge of the world, Humanists reject arbitrary faith, authority, revelation, and altered states of consciousness; and even religious experience, while not a valid means to acquire knowledge, remains a useful source of ideas that can lead us to new ways of looking at the world. These ideas, after they have been assessed rationally for their usefulness, can then be put to work, often as alternate approaches for solving problems.

Humanism is a philosophy for the here and now. Humanists regard human values as making sense only in the context of human life rather than in the promise of a supposed life after death.

Humanism is a philosophy of compassion. Humanist ethics is solely concerned with meeting human needs and answering human problems—for both the individual and society—and devotes no attention to the satisfaction of supposed supernatural entities.

Humanism is a realistic philosophy. Humanists recognize the existence of moral dilemmas and the need for careful consideration of immediate and future consequences in moral decision making.

Humanism is in tune with the science of today. Humanists therefore recognize that we live in a natural universe of great size and age, that we evolved on this planet over a long period of time, that there is no compelling evidence for a separable "soul," and that human beings have certain built-in needs that effectively form the basis for any human-oriented value-system.

Humanism is in tune with today's enlightened social thought. Humanists are committed to civil liberties, human rights, church-state separation, the extension of participatory democracy not only in government but in the workplace and education, and expansion of global consciousness and exchange of products and ideas internationally, and an open-ended approach to solving social problems, an approach that allows for the testing of new alternatives.

Humanism is in tune with new technological developments. Humanists are willing to take part in emerging scientific and technological discoveries in order to exercise their moral influence on these revolutions as they come about.

Humanism is, in sum, a philosophy of those in love with life. Humanists take responsibility for their own lives and relish the adventure of being part of new discoveries, seeking new knowledge, exploring new options. Instead of finding solace in prefabricated answers to the great questions of life, Humanists enjoy the open-endedness of a quest and the freedom of discovery that this entails.[18]

The Fellowship of Religious Humanists

By the early 1960s several factors gave rise to the organization of the Fellowship of Religious Humanists. First were a number of liberal clergy who considered themselves religious humanists, especially in the ranks of the recently created Unitarian Universalist Association that resulted from the merger of the American Unitarian Association with the Universalist Church of America in 1961. Many of the older Unitarian Universalist clergy had known personally the pioneers of religious humanism, especially John Dietrich and Curtis Reese. Both Edwin Wilson and Raymond Bragg had studied at Meadville Theological

School in Chicago. They knew Reese, an outspoken humanist and secretary of the Western Conference, and they had been active in starting the *New Humanist* journal and in creating and signing the *Humanist Manifesto* (1933). Bragg became Dietrich's associate and succeeded him as minister in Minneapolis.

Second, several leaders of the Ethical Culture movement had repudiated the Kantian Idealism of Felix Adler and had accepted a philosophical naturalism as advocated by Roy Wood Sellars and several of the members of the philosophy department at Columbia University, notably John Dewey and John Herman Randall. Lester Mondale and Eric Erickson had served both Unitarian churches and Ethical Culture societies. Mondale, who had received his theological training at Harvard Divinity School, was one of the original signers of the *Humanist Manifesto*; Erickson received his ministerial training at Starr King School for the Ministry, a Unitarian school in California. Since its inception, the Ethical Culture movement had interacted with the more radical wing of Unitarian ministers, a relationship that dated from the founding of the Free Religious Association. The creation of the Fellowship of Religious Humanists provided a society where both groups could come together again to address mutual concerns.

Third, the recent leaders of the American Humanist Association had moved the organization toward "secular humanism." In contrast, the religious humanists tried to maintain a casual relationship with various types of liberal theists and to remain engaged in the theological dialogue taking place in the United States. If religious humanists were to serve Unitarian Universalist churches and participate effectively in the life of the Unitarian Universalist Association, they needed to develop a *modus operandi* for working with such diverse groups as the Unitarian Universalist Christian Association as well as various types of philosophical theists. Within this context the Fellowship of Religious Humanists also sought to provide a society for Unitarian Universalist religious humanists, representing their concerns and interests within the Unitarian Universalist Association. At the theological and professional level, religious humanists also have joined groups of scholars and have participated in study and dialogue in order to provide religious humanism as a live option for religious liberals, and such participation keeps the thought of religious humanism current. Scholars who embrace religious humanism are involved in such professional groups as the American Academy of Religion, the Society for the Scientific Study of Religion, the American Philosophical Association, and the Highlands

Institute for American Religious Thought. The last, for instance, has an interest in promoting research in the "Chicago School" of American religious thought, which included such liberal theological theists as Henry Nelson Wieman, Bernard Loomer, and Bernard Meland, as well as such religious humanists as A. Eustace Haydon and George Forester. The works of the Chicago School have provided a common canon for contemporary religious thinkers, some of them naturalistic theists and some religious humanists, to engage in common study and fruitful dialogue.[19]

Like the Free Religious Association in the nineteenth century, the Fellowship of Religious Humanists is a noncreedal society, not a denomination; it is primarily concerned with the practice and philosophy of humanism as a religion. The following comments summarize its purpose:

To provide fellowship in association devoted to the cultivation of humanistic religious living which springs from the insights of inner experience that is circumscribed neither by creed nor by ecclesiastical or political authority. In this endeavor the disciplines are such as are required by the pursuit of truth.

To state and restate from time to time, without dogmatism or compromise of the free-mind principle, the basic tenets of humanism as philosophy, ethics, and religion.

To support and preserve the pluralistic character of modern humanism through understanding other emphases in humanism than the religious (rationalist, scientific, secular, etc.) and to help relate the various facets of the movement, including the organized liberal religious, ethical, and humanistic societies, in cooperative endeavors.

To defend and protect freedom of thought in religion.

To develop and apply the scientific spirit and methods in the study of religion.

To encourage among humanists writing that will give voice to those values of religion which can evolve only where there is freedom.

To meet the particular needs of religious humanists by providing inspirational materials, arranging seminars and conferences, and, if possible, publishing in economical form some of the basic writings, past and present, of religious humanism.[20]

Members of the Fellowship of Religious Humanists generally do not view themselves as a social-action group, believing that members should study the issues and participate in other groups whose goal is some kind of social action. They have learned from experience, and contrary to Felix Adler's belief, that moral issues can be as controversial as religious creeds. Although the fellowship itself does not participate in social action, there is general agreement on such issues as racial equality, freedom of speech, separation of church and state, an end to war as a means for solving international conflict, equality between the sexes, and opposition to discrimination based on sexual orientation.

The Fellowship of Religious Humanists publishes a quarterly

journal, *Religious Humanism*, which carries scholarly articles on the thought and lives of humanists, on ethical theory and moral issues, on social movements (such as the death of God theology) with an impact on humanism, postmodernist philosophy, current scientific theory, contemporary movements in religious thought, and feminist issues. It seeks to provide an outlet for ideas about religion, many of them controvsersial, that other religious journals would not touch. In other words, the fellowship views itself as the inheritor of the tradition started by such pioneers of liberal religious thought as John Dietrich, Curtis Reese, and Charles F. Potter. It attempts to do in the religious realm of the present generation what they did in their earlier generation.

The North American Committee on Humanism

When the first English Puritans came to America in the seventeenth century and settled in their homes and villages, they were confronted with a problem that has plagued many groups, namely, obtaining well-trained ministers. Most of the leaders of the puritan villages were university educated, and they naturally did not wish their churches to fall into the hands of the uneducated. Only six years after their arrival at the Massachusetts Bay Colony, they set about establishing a college for educating men to be ministers. That college was soon named after its first benefactor, John Harvard, a puritan minister who died young and left his library and a small share of his estate to the proposed college. Most of the earliest eastern colleges were started to train ministers. After the Civil War, the American Jewish community faced a similar problem. This time Isaac M. Wise was the man of the hour, and he was responsible for founding Hebrew Union College in Cincinnati, Ohio, an Institute of Religion for the training of Reform rabbis.

Once Felix Adler had started the Ethical Culture movement he immediately recognized the need for a school to train leaders for his movement. It was not until 1976 that Paul Beattie, a Unitarian and a dynamic leader of the Fellowship of Religious Humanists, conceived of the idea of the Humanist Institute and shared it with Sherwin Wine, the leader of Humanistic Judaism. In 1982, the Fellowship of Religious Humanists met in Chicago, and at that meeting the North American Committee on Humanism was created with Wine as its first president. At this time humanism was under attack by the fundamentalist religious right, and the alliance provided a vehicle for various humanists to defend themselves against their enemies as well as to seek more effective ways to spread the message of humanism. The alliance was composed of members of the Fellowship of Religious Humanists, the American Humanist Association, the American Ethical Union (the organization of Ethical Culture societies), and Humanistic Judaism.

The Humanist Institute was headquartered in New York City in facilities provided by the Ethical Culture Society. In 1984 Howard Radest, a leader in the Ethical Culture Society, was appointed dean, and a three-year graduate program was devised. Three years later eight people from the first class were graduated. The program provides certification as a professional humanist leader. Generally the three-year program requires thirty units of study in the institute curriculum, thirty units of graduate study at another accredited institution, and thirty units of required fieldwork. Students must also complete a research paper or an approved project.[21]

Though most of the energy of the North American Committee on Humanism has been devoted to creating and overseeing the Humanist Institute, it also, like the Fellowship of Religious Humanists and the American Humanist Association, holds annual meetings at which scholarly addresses are presented, seminars are held, and business is conducted. It also publishes an annual journal, *Humanism Today,* and it periodically mails out a newsletter to its members.

Conclusion

The ideas that gave rise to the conflict in Congregationalism between the Trinitarians and the Unitarians eventually found their way into other Protestant denominations. In time these ideas, along with such others as Darwinian evolution, also began to be felt in other religions, for example, Judaism and Catholicism. Reform Judaism emerged after the American Civil War, and Roman Catholic Modernism at the turn of the twentieth century. Auguste Comte (1798–1857), a Roman Catholic in Paris, had created his "Religion of Humanity," which eventually spread into Victorian England and, to a much lesser extent, into the United States. Shortly thereafter, Felix Adler created his Ethical Culture movement in New York, and an indigenous movement arose in London.

These various liberal religious movements—transcendentalism, scientific theism, Comte's Religion of Humanity, Ethical Culture, the Free Religious Association, and Protestant liberalism—prepared the way for the radical thought of Dietrich, Reese, and Potter. If one adds to this mix the "death of God" philosophy of Friedrich Nietzsche and the death, devastation, and destruction created by the First World War, it is not too difficult to see that the radical theology of "religion without God" might result.

Once Dietrich, Reese, and Potter, along with a number of sympathetic scholars in the academic community, created the perspective of religious humanism, it spread in a variety of directions. The more secular direction has been advocated by the American Humanist Association. The more religious direction has been advocated by the Fellowship of Religious Humanists, the Ethical Culturalists, and the Society for Humanistic Judaism. The North American Committee on Humanism was created in order to coordinate the work of the various humanist groups. As all groups have a need for qualified humanist leaders, it was natural that they all supported efforts to create the Humanist Institute.

No doubt the largest number of people in the United States who are humanists have no contact or membership in any of these groups and remain unaffiliated. The largest number of humanists are members of Unitarian Universalist churches, although certainly not all members of these churches are humanists. Of the specifically humanist organizations, the American Humanist Association is the largest. However, it is not uncommon for one individual to be a member of several humanist organizations—a local Unitarian Universalist church, the Fellowship of Religious Humanists, the National Committee on Humanism, and possibly also the American Humanist Association. Ethical Culture and Humanistic Judaism provide other possible combinations.

Khoren Arisian, for example, is the minister of the First Unitarian Society of Minneapolis, the church where John Dietrich worked out his thought on religious humanism. Arisian also has been a leader in the Ethical Culture Society of New York, the society created by Felix Adler, and is president of FRH, vice-president of the NACH, and a member of AHA. He says, "Humanism subsumes a whole philosophy of life: it suggests a moral stance that includes measureless respect for the individual; thinking for oneself and acting accordingly, as well as in concert with others; adherence to democratic process; a monistic rationalism; ethical striving and spiritual worldliness. It seems to me that these are common denominator dimensions of any humanism worthy of the name."[22] Arisian's sentiments are certainly within the tradition of the pioneers of religious humanism; this reveals that the movement they started is alive and flourishing today. It provides an alternative for those who cannot accept the faith of their fathers, but who desire a perspective for orienting themselves in the world and living according to that orientation.

CHAPTER 9

Conclusion

*"Is there anything that is neither atheism nor faith, something
between belief and unbelief? Atheism and unbelief are grounded in
the absence of an experience of God; the theology of the death of God is grounded
on an experience of an absence. For radical theology there is a hole where God
used to be, and it is the work of that theology to explore that hole—within a
Christian allegiance or, failing that, without it."—William Hamilton*

BY 1964, THE "DEATH OF GOD" THEOLOGICAL MOVEMENT had burst on the American religious scene and was commanding the attention of even the popular press. It had become obvious that Friedrich Nietzsche (1844-1900) was an important influence on the movement through his parable of the "mad man" who proclaimed the death of God. Most of the spokesmen for the death of God theology had studied with well-known neo-orthodox theologians, and several had even been promoters of neo-orthodox theology before advocating the death of God. Moreover, one of the major problems for the death of God theologians was that of theodicy, especially as it related to the Nazi genocide program against the Jews during the Second World War. They asked, if the neo-orthodox God was a transcendent being, yet all-loving and all-powerful, and if prayer has more than a placebo effect, why were six-million Jews annihilated? Of course, the neo-orthodox theologians had spoken of the "silence of God," but they also retained the conviction that God, who was "wholly other," had acted decisively in the past. Rolf Hochhuth's controversial play, *The Deputy,* criticized a pope for being silent in the face of innocent suffering. If God, like the pope, were silent, should he not also be held accountable? The death of God theologians thought not; they excused the divine silence because God was dead! Just as humans

193

are not accountable for what happens after death, a dead God is not responsible either. The point was made: we live in the age of the death of God. When in the early 1960s some of the young neo-orthodox theologians reflected on the human carnage and destruction of the Second World War, they opted for Nietzsche's metaphor of the death of God; it seemed to them to be the most candid explanation for the divine silence.

It was in this context that I became especially interested in liberal theology. Both Karl Barth from his academic post in Switzerland and Reinhold Niebuhr from his at Union Theological Seminary in New York had brutally attacked liberalism, pointing to its naiveté, rationalism, optimism, and excessive faith in the scientific method. Certainly a number of second-generation neo-orthodox theologians went even further, considering a serious study of liberal theology to be a wasted effort. Yet, as I read several of the liberal primary sources themselves, I began to question the legitimacy of the neo-orthodox thinkers' assessments of liberalism. It was in this attempt to understand liberal theology, especially in the United States, that I came across the term *humanistic liberalism.*

Seeking to understand this "humanistic liberalism," I was a bit surprised to discover that although it was a radical movement within theological liberalism, it advocated a "religion without God." As we have seen, it arose during the First World War, also a time of human slaughter and destruction. The pioneers of this movement had some knowledge of Nietzsche's vision of the death of God, and they reasoned that if humans left their problems to divine providence, they would never be solved. Humans themselves must take responsibility and solve their problems to the best of their abilities with the materials at hand.

It became obvious that both the "religion without God" theology and "the death of God" theology, though originating in quite different historical periods and reacting to quite different social factors, had much in common. They arose out of the contexts provided by the two world wars, they were morally and intellectually stunned by the suffering of innocents, and in the background hovered the nagging metaphor of Nietzsche's vision of "the death of God." In many respects, "religion without God" was the final phase of Protestant liberalism, and "the death of God theology" was the final phase of Protestant neo-orthodoxy. Both tried to save religion by disassociating it from notions of God, which they did not believe viable. For the earlier radical the question was how to be religious without belief in God, but for some of the later radicals the question was how to be a Christian without either God or religion.

It is only fair to consider the people in this study, especially the pioneers and their antecedents, in terms of the period in which they lived. Today a rather serious debate centers around the issues of modernism and postmodernism. In the main, the early pioneers were realists and empiricists, which most likely places them in the modernist camp. In addition, they were monists who viewed the world in terms of nature and who thought the best way to understand it was the empirical method. The empirical method enabled them to distinguish between genuine and bogus concepts. They concluded that such concepts as a "transcendent God," an "immortal soul," and "heaven" and "hell" were bogus and could not be justified, so they deleted them from their understanding of religion or their grand narrative. Of course, for those postmodernists who have taken "the linguistic turn," there is no metanarrative with which to determine the claims of these skeptical modernists, nor is there one for the less skeptical theistic modernists. Thus, whether to employ linguistic concepts such as God and soul might well have to be determined on more pragmatic grounds. Had the issues been defined from this more contemporary context, there are a number of indications that the religious humanists would still hold to their beliefs, albeit for pragmatic rather than for empirical reasons.

It would appear that the seeds planted by Dietrich, Reese, Potter, and a whole host of others have taken root and will endure. We see evidences of this in the institutions that promote religious humanism, especially the Unitarian Universalists, the Ethical Culturalists, and the Humanistic Jews. As long as they survive, they are a constant reminder to theists in general and Christian theists in particular that their understanding of existence may be incorrect; humanists are likewise reminded of the risk involved in their commitment. It is not my intention to offer a final resolution of this problem, for it appears to entail more than a disagreement about "facts." It concerns the interpretation of facts based on other prior commitments, such as "grand narratives." Hence I shall conclude by attempting to clarify the nature of the two commitments. To do this, I shall use two short philosophical parables. The first is adapted from John Wisdom's well-known essay, "The Gods."[1]

Two people had been away from home on an extended vacation. When they returned and went into their garden, one of them was surprised to see that some of the plants were doing well—so well, in fact, that he concluded a gardener must have been caring for them. Yet inquiries indicated that no one had seen or heard a gardener. Observing how orderly and purposeful everything looks, he concludes that despite the lack of witnesses, a gardener must have been at work. The second person, examining the same garden, notices some rough places that indicate a lack of order. The first person, hearing this observation, suggests that the gardener may be invisible and inaudible. The second person remains convinced there is no gardener; this is how the garden happens to grow when it is unattended.

Finally everything in the garden area is examined; both people have looked at all the facts. Neither has evidence that the other lacks. Yet the first insists there is a gardener, while the second is equally certain no gardener exists. The two reactions are based not on unknown evidence but on their feelings about the garden. Just so, when we examine the vast garden we call Earth, some feel there is a gardener—God—whereas others do not. We all possess the same facts about the world, but arrive at radically different conclusions.

John Hick also tells a parable, which I will apply to our two people as I attempt to identify them further.[2] The person who believes a gardener has been taking care of things may be called a theist, and the person who doubts the gardener's existence may be called a humanist. The theist believes there is a personal God who supports values and who ultimately will overcome evil with good; the theist also believes humans have the capacity for personal immortality after death. The humanist, on the other hand, believes that humans are alone in the universe, that values are created by people, and that there is no cosmic guarantee that good will overcome evil. All humans are a part of nature, and when they die their minds, which are merely a functional aspect of their brains, will cease to operate; consciousness will pass away and they will return to the elements. The points of view of the theist and the humanist are contradictory; both cannot not be true.

These different points of view colored each person's interpretation of life from young adulthood until old age. As a youth, the theist believed in God and personal immortality, whereas the young humanist denied both these tenets. When the sun shone brightly for them, when they prospered and were happy, the theist said, "God was good to me today." The humanist responded, "I was lucky today." As time passed and both experienced suffering and saw friends die, the theist said, "Suffering is hard and I don't understand it, but in some way God will use this suffering for my own good." The humanist remarked, "Well, my luck seems to be running out." As the two age and near the end of their journey, for death is imminent, the theist remarks, "Soon I shall be discarding this physical body and go on to the heavenly city where the real person never dies." The humanist replies, "I shall be going to my grave, and when the dirt has covered my body that will be the end of me, for there is nothing beyond this natural life."

Which one has the truth? Both possess the same facts about the empirical world, but each interprets these facts differently. It would appear that we will discover which person's story is true only if the theist's interpretation is correct. Otherwise, we shall never know.

Notes

Chapter 1: Religious Humanism and Humanism

1. Charles Francis Potter, *Humanism: A New Religion* (New York: Simon & Schuster, 1930), 63-64. Chapter 4, "The Ancestry of Humanism," is useful in placing religious humanism within the context of humanism.

2. Moses Hadas, *Humanism: The Greek Ideal and Its Survival* (New York: Harper & Bros., 1960), 13. It might also be noted that the one significant study of religious humanism, by Arthur Hazard Dakin, is entitled *Man the Measure: An Essay on Humanism as Religion* (Princeton: Princeton University Press, 1939).

3. John H. Dietrich, *Humanism* (Boston: American Unitarian Association, 1934), 6.

4. Ibid. See also Fred Gladstone Bratton, *The Legacy of the Liberal Spirit* (New York: Charles Scribners Sons, 1943). This work contains a chapter on Renaissance Humanism. See 59-85.

5. "The Literary Humanists" (editorial), *Christian Register* 109 (21 August 1930), 684.

6. O. W. Firkins, "The Two Humanisms: A Discrimination," *New Humanist* 4 (1931): 1-9. In this article Firkins explains the similarities and differences between religious humanism and literary humanism, especially with reference to Dietrich and Babbitt. Also it might be noted that Charles F. Potter referred to literary humanism as "academic" humanism, whereas Dietrich followed Firkins's terminology. See Potter, *Humanism*, 110-14.

7. Irving Babbitt, "On Being Original," *Atlantic* 10 (March 1908): 388-96. This work is representative of Babbitt's position.

8. Friedrich Nietzsche, *Thus Spake Zarathustra*, tr. Walter Kaufman in *The Portable Nietzsche* (New York: Viking Press, 1968), 204.

9. John Herman Randall, Jr., "Epilogue: The Nature of Naturalism" in *Naturalism and the Human Spirit,* ed. Yervant H. Krikorian (New York: Columbia University Press, 1944), 354-82.

10. Ibid., 357.

11. Corliss Lamont, *The Philosophy of Humanism,* 5th ed. (New York: Frederick Ungar, 1967), 22.

12. Randall, *Naturalism,* 359.

13. Ibid.

14. Ibid., 358.
15. Ibid., 381.
16. Ibid., 376.
17. Lamont, *Philosophy of Humanism,* 23-24.

Chapter 2: Religious Humanism and Protestant Liberalism

1. John Dillenberger and Claude Welch, *Protestant Christianity* (New York: Charles Scribner's Sons, 1954), 179-206. See also 207-26, 241-54. It also might be emphasized that the Social Gospel movement was important to liberalism in the United States, and the liberals were concerned with the problem of Christianity to other world religions.
2. Walter Marshall Horton, *Theism and the Modern Mood* (New York: Harper & Brothers, 1930), 96.
3. Kenneth Cauthen, *The Impact of American Religious Liberalism* (New York: Harper & Row, 1962), especially 26-32. In this excellent study of religious liberalism, Cauthen draws a distinction between "evangelical liberalism" and "modernistic liberalism." Also, as we shall do, he identifies Fosdick with evangelical liberalism, but he prefers the term *modernism* for the second division of liberalism, and he locates Wieman within this type. Modernism is obviously a less cumbersome term than "empirical philosophy of religion," which I shall retain for locating Wieman's position in liberalism. Cauthen also makes distinctions within the broad categories of evangelical and modernistic liberalism, e.g., he calls Fosdick's position "personality-centered Christianity" and Wieman's "theological naturalism." Furthermore, Cauthen thinks that religious humanism or humanistic liberalism went beyond the legitimate bounds of Protestant liberalism. Although I agree with Cauthen, I wish to show the relationship of humanism to liberalism, for it sheds light on both. Moreover, most of the pioneers of religious humanism at an earlier time had been Protestant liberals.
4. This contention will become more obvious when we study the biographies of the pioneers, for each was a Protestant liberal before he became a humanist.
5. Harry Emerson Fosdick, "Shall the Fundamentalists Win?" in *American Protestant Thought: The Liberal Era,* ed. William R. Hutchison (New York: Harper & Row, 1968), 170-82.
6. Cauthen, *The Impact of American Religious Liberalism,* 67-69.
7. See ibid., 188-206, for his summary of Wieman's thought. Also see: Bernard E. Meland, "The Religion of Henry Nelson Wieman," *Christian Register* 112 (19 October 1933), 677-79.
8. Henry Nelson Wieman, "This Is My Faith," in *This Is My Faith,* ed. Stewart G. Cole (New York: Harper & Brothers, 1956), 260.
9. A. Wakefield Slaten, "Modernism and Humanism" in *Humanist Sermons,* ed. Curtis W. Reese (Chicago: Open Court, 1927), 79-92.
10. Roy Wood Sellars, *The Next Step in Religion* (New York: Macmillan, 1918), 211-25; *A Religion Come of Age* (New York: Macmillan, 1928), 131-34; 275-89.
11. See Roy Wood Sellars, "The Humanist Outlook" in *The Humanist Alternative,* ed. Paul Kurtz (Buffalo: Prometheus Books, 1973), 133-40. On the creation of the Manifesto, Sellars said, "During the 1930s I was invited by a small group of people, teachers and ministers, to give a talk at the University of Chicago on the situation in

religion. The outcome was that I was asked to formulate basic principles along humanistic lines. I called my formulation A Humanist Manifesto. I sent it back and received suggestions, some of which I incorporated.... It was then published with the signatures of many outstanding persons in the religious field, and is now called an historical document. I have found that many do not know of its origin and that is why I give this account" [137].

12. "A Humanist Manifesto" originally appeared in the *New Humanist* 6:3 (1933), 1-5. It also appeared in the Unitarian publication *Christian Register* 112 (11 May 1933), 303. Moreover, it was published and commented on in *Christian Century* 50 (7 June 1933), 743-45. Finally, a copy of the document appears in the "appendix" of Corliss Lamont's *Philosophy of Humanism,* 285-89.

13. Roy Wood Sellars, "Naturalistic Humanism" in *Living Schools of Religion,* ed. Vergilius Ferm (Patterson, New Jersey: Littlefield, Adams, 1965), 421-23.

14. Sellars, "Naturalistic Humanism," 423.

15. Ibid., 424.

16. Ibid., 429.

17. *Christian Century* 50 (7 June 1933), 743-45.

18. Bratton, *Legacy of the Liberal Spirit,* 74.

Chapter 3: Religious Humanism and Unitarianism

1. Conrad Wright has made a careful study of the factors leading to the rise of Unitarianism in the early nineteenth century. See *The Beginnings of Unitarianism in America* (Boston: Beacon Press, 1955). His study deals with the rise of religious liberalism in New England Congregationalism, where it originated in the eighteenth century. He begins with the Great Awakening in the Connecticut River Valley in 1735, and discusses the developments leading up to the selection of Henry Ware as Hollis Professor of Divinity at Harvard in 1805, an appointment that precipitated the Unitarian controversy. Wright designates the liberal movement Arminianism, and he sees it as the bridge between seventeenth-century Puritanism and nineteenth-century Unitarianism. It would appear that Arminian Unitarianism was the forerunner rather than the product of Protestant liberalism.

2. Octavius Brooks Frothingham's classic study, *Transcendentalism in New England* (Philadelphia: University of Pennsylvania Press, 1972), first published in 1876, provides some valuable insights into Schleiermacher, transcendentalism, and Unitarianism.

3. Paul Tillich, *Perspectives on 19th and 20th Century Protestant Thought,* ed. Carl E. Braaten (New York: Harper & Row, 1967), 7.

4. See Wright, *The Beginnings of Unitarianism in America.*

5. One of the most complete studies of the American Enlightenment is Henry E. May's *The Enlightenment in America* (New York: Oxford University Press, 1976). See especially the chapters on New England and on Philadelphia, 177-96, 197-222.

6. Elmo Arnold Robinson, *American Universalism* (New York: Exposition Press, 1970), 39.

7. The term was derived from Jacob Arminius (1559–1609) who repudiated strict Calvinism in the Netherlands, especially the doctrine of election. He thought that

humans had some choice in determining whether they would be saved or lost. His view was condemned at the Synod of Dort in 1619. Thinkers who questioned Calvinism and advocated some degree of human choice in determining eternal destiny were therefore dubbed "Arminians."

8. Of the many accounts of this story, perhaps Charles Forman's is the most complete. See his "Elected Now by Time: The Unitarian Controversy, 1805–1835" in Conrad Wright, ed., *Stream of Light* (Boston: Unitarian Universalist Association, 1975), 3-32.

9. Ibid., 31.

10. The definitive study of Bellows's life and thought is Walter Donald Kring, *Henry Whitney Bellows* (Boston: Skinner House Books, 1979). See especially 237-39.

11. Stow Persons, *Free Religion: An American Faith* (Boston: Beacon Press, 1963), 41. Persons's study is the most complete work on the Free Religious Association, containing perceptive insights into the people and issues that gave rise to it.

12. Quoted by Conrad Wright in "'Salute the Arriving Moment': Denominational Growth and the Quest for Consensus, 1865-1895" in *Stream of Light,* 90.

13. Ibid.

14. Marc Lee Raphael, *Profiles in American Judaism* (New York: Harper & Row, 1985), 14, 18-19.

15. Carleton Winston, *This Circle of Earth* (New York: G. P. Putnam, 1942), 123.

16. Curtis W. Reese, *A Democratic View of Religion* (Yellow Springs, Ohio: American Humanist Association, Publication No. 218).

17. In order to understand the rise of humanism in Unitarianism, it is helpful to know the kinds of liberal theory in Unitarianism in the nineteenth century. For an overview, see Mason Olds, "Varieties of Nineteenth-Century Unitarianism" in *Religious Humanism* 16 (Autumn 1982): 150-60.

18. John H. Dietrich, "The Religion of Experience," *Christian Register* 98 (13 March 1919), 241.

19. Sidney S. Robins, "What Is a Humanist? This Will Tell You," *Christian Register* 99 (29 July 1920), 739-40.

20. Editorial, *Christian Register* 99 (12 August 1920), 783.

21. Curtis W. Reese, "Do You Believe What He Believes?" *Christian Register* 99 (9 September 1920), 883-84. The entire text of "The Content of Religious Liberalism" also appeared in *Unity* 85 (12 August 1920), 327-29.

22. "Mr. Reese's 'Humanism'" (editorial), *Christian Register* 105 (17 June 1926), 558.

23. Edwin H. Wilson, "The Humanist Controversy Is History-I," *Christian Register* 118 (5 January 1938), 8.

24. Edwin H. Wilson, "The Humanist Controversy Is History-II," *Christian Register* 118 (12 January 1938), 23.

25. George R. Dodson, "Clear Thinking or Death," *Christian Register* 100 (11 August 1921), 750-51.

26. Charles H. Lyttle, *Freedom Moves West* (Boston: Beacon Press, 1952), 247.

27. William L. Sullivan, "God, No-God, Half-God," *Christian Register* 100 (8 August 1921), 775-76.

28. Curtis W. Reese, "The Dead Hand," *Christian Register* 100 (1 September 1921), 826-27. George R. Dodson, "The Right of the Majority," *Christian Register* 100 (22 September 1921), 896.

29. John H. Dietrich, "The Faith That Is in Us," *Christian Register* 100 (27 October 1921), 1015.

30. Ibid. See also "Theist and Humanist" (editorial), *Christian Register* 100 (20 October 1921), 986-987.

31. William L. Sullivan, "The Faith That Makes the Church," *Christian Register* 100 (3 November 1921), 1039.

32. Marion Franklin Ham, "What Is Humanism? Here Are Some Answers," *Christian Register* 107 (15 November 1928), 925-26.

33. John H. Dietrich, "Mr. Dietrich to Mr. Ham," *Christian Register* 107 (20 December 1928), 1046.

34. Marion Franklin Ham, "Concluding a Discussion," *Christian Register* 108 (17 January 1929), 42.

35. Although Dietrich and Ham ended their exchange, the humanist-theist controversy continued within Unitarianism and, with the publication of numerous books, it began to extend beyond the bounds of one church. Through these publications professors who were representatives of the more traditional denominations became interested in the discussion. Douglas C. Macintosh engaged Roy Wood Sellars; Joseph Haroutunian engaged J. A. C. Fagginger Auer; Andrew Banning engaged Sellars; the perennial exponent of theism, Dodson, engaged A. Eustace Haydon, professor of comparative religion at the University of Chicago. A few years later David E. Roberts of Union Theological Seminary in New York City engaged the humanist professor Edwin A. Burtt of Cornell University, and even later, J. A. C. Fagginger Auer and Julian Hartt of the Yale Divinity School debated the subject of humanism versus theism. (Actually John L. Calhoun debated Auer personally at Antioch College, but the published text for the position of theism was written by Hartt.)

36. Leslie T. Pennington, "The Humanist Manifesto" (editorial),*Christian Register* 112 (25 May 1933), 334. For George R. Dodson's response, see "What the Manifesto Lacks," *New Humanist* 6 (1933): 28-32. For a more detailed study of the creation of the manifesto, involving such areas as the context, people involved, and the issues, see William Schultz, "Making the Manifesto" in *Religious Humanism* 17 (Spring 1983): 88-97, 102.

37. Lyttle, *Freedom Moves West,* 254-55.

38. Lon Ray Call, "Humanism in England," *Christian Register* 112 (14 September 1933), 604.

39. "The Humanist Manifesto" (comments by some who did not sign), *Christian Register* 112 (25 May 1933), 330.

40. David Rhys Williams, "Humanism and Mysticism," *Christian Register* 112 (30 November 1933), 775.

41. Roy Wood Sellars, "Humanism or Theism," *Christian Register* 112 (30 November 1933), 777.

42. Lyttle, *Freedom Moves West,* 256-57.

43. Wilson, "The Humanist Controversy Is History-II," 25.

44. Walter D. Kring and Raymond D. Sabin, "Humanism, Theism and Unitarianism," *Christian Register* 127 (May 1948), 34-37.

45. Charles E. Park, *Why the Humanism-Theism Controversy Is Out of Date* (Boston: American Unitarian Association, 1954), 1-8.

46. Ibid., 8.

Chapter 4: John H. Dietrich, the Father of Religious Humanism

1. The Unitarian Universalist Association keeps a personal file on each of its ministers. Although controversial material is removed from the file after their death, the facts remain. Dietrich's ministerial file provided some of the biographical details in this chapter, which is also indebted to Carleton Winston's *This Circle of Earth,* the biography written by Dietrich's second wife. See Chapter 3, n. 4.
2. O.W. Firkins, "The Two Humanisms," 2-3.
3. For a more detailed study of Dietrich's life from the perspective of "faith development theory," see Mason Olds, "John H. Dietrich: A Pilgrim's Progress, Parts I and II" *Religious Humanism* 18 (fall 1984): 156-67 and 19 (winter 1985): 2-10.
4. Winston, *This Circle of Earth,* 66-82. Chapter V, entitled, "Heresy," provides details of Dietrich's differences with the Reformed Church on Christian doctrine.
5. Ibid., 121-22. Frederick James Gould was primarily an advocate of Auguste Comte's philosophy of Positivism and his "Religion of Humanity." In his religious development, he moved "from evangelical Anglican faith through a period of vague theism to Secularism before finding in Positivism the creed which came closest to his independent views." However, he assisted Stanton Coit in starting the East London Ethical Society and the publication *Ethical World.* Yet it was always Comte's though that influenced his philosophy of life. See T. R. Wright, *The Religion of Humanity: The Impact of Comtean Positivism on Victorian Britain* (Cambridge: Cambridge University Press, 1986), especially 245-47.
6. Ibid., 136.
7. For an understanding of the situation in Minneapolis during Dietrich's early ministry there, see Frank M. Rarig, "John H. Dietrich," *Minneapolis Unitarian* 21:15 (Summer 1957).
8. John H. Dietrich, "What I Believe," *Humanist Pulpit* 7 (1934): 165.
9. The most readily available primary source for Dietrich's thought is John H. Dietrich, *What If the World Went Humanist? Ten Sermons,* selected by Mason Olds (Yellow Springs, Ohio: Fellowship of Religious Humanists, 1989).
10. John H. Dietrich, "New Universes for Old," *Humanist Pulpit* 4 (1930): 81.
11. Ibid., 83-84. See also: John H. Dietrich, "What the Bible Really Is," an address given 8 November 1925 (Minneapolis: First Unitarian Society), 6.
12. Dietrich, "What I Believe," 167.
13. Roy Wood Sellars, *Religion Coming of Age* (New York: Macmillan, 1928), 141-42.
14. John H. Dietrich, "What Do You Give in Place of What You Take Away?" *Christian Register* 103 (8 May 1924), 438.
15. Dietrich, "What I Believe," 167.
16. Ibid., 166.
17. John H. Dietrich, "Will Science Destroy Religion?" *Humanist Pulpit* 2 (1928): 166.
18. John H. Dietrich, "The Supreme Discovery of the Ages," *Humanist Pulpit* 4 (1930): 129. Dietrich acknowledged that he had taken the title from the physicist Robert A. Millikan.
19. John H. Dietrich, "Is There a Moral Law?" *Humanist Pulpit* 2 (1928): 102.
20. Dietrich, "The Supreme Discovery of the Ages," 137.
21. Dietrich, "What I Believe," 166.

22. Dietrich, "What the Bible Really Is," 17.

23. John H. Dietrich, "New Bibles for Old," *Humanist Pulpit* 4 (1930): 98.

24. Dietrich, "What the Bible Really Is," 16.

25. John H. Dietrich, "What Is an Atheist?" *Humanist Pulpit* 2 (1928): 5.

26. Ibid., 10-11.

27. John H. Dietrich, "Thankful—for What and to Whom?" *Humanist Pulpit* 4 (1930): 69.

28. Dietrich, "What Is an Atheist?" 4.

29. John H. Dietrich, "How the Gods Were Made," *Humanist Pulpit* 1 (1927): 5.

30. John H. Dietrich, "Is the Universe Friendly or Unfriendly?" *Humanist Pulpit* 5 (1931): 19.

31. John H. Dietrich, "Can the God-Idea Be Saved?" *Humanist Pulpit* 5 (1931): 73-74.

32. John H. Dietrich, "Is Atheism a Menace?" *Humanist Pulpit* 2 (1928): 19-20. See also *Humanist Pulpit* 7:172.

33. John H. Dietrich, "What Is Happening to the Individual?" *Humanist Pulpit* 7 (1934): 180.

34. John H. Dietrich, "Individualism vs. Socialism," *Humanist Pulpit* 7 (1934): 20.

35. John H. Dietrich, "The Chief Danger in Our Civilization," *Humanist Pulpit* 3 (1929): 30.

36. John H. Dietrich, "Can Human Nature Be Changed?" an address given 22 March 1925 (Minneapolis: First Unitarian Society), 4.

37. John H. Dietrich, "The Superstition of Sin," *Humanist Pulpit* 3 (1929): 187.

38. John H. Dietrich, "When Death Comes," *Humanist Pulpit* 6 (1932): 53.

39. Dietrich, "What I Believe," 175.

40. John H. Dietrich, "The Kind of Salvation Man Needs," an address given 3 January 1926 (Minneapolis: First Unitarian Society), 45.

41. John H. Dietrich, "What Does It Mean to Be Spiritual?" *Humanist Pulpit* 4 (1930): 5.

42. John H. Dietrich, "The Advance of Humanism," *Humanist Pulpit* 2 (1928): 46.

43. John H. Dietrich, "The Relation of Religion to Morality," an address given 9 January 1921 (Minneapolis: First Unitarian Society), 3.

44. John H. Dietrich, "Do We Need a New Morality?" *Humanist Pulpit* 2 (1928): 85.

45. John H. Dietrich, "The Ethics of Birth Control," *Humanist Pulpit* 4 (1930): 163.

46. John H. Dietrich, "Do We Need a New Moral Outlook?" an address given at the Iowa Unitarian Association and the Illinois Unitarian Conference meeting jointly on 18 October 1922 in Davenport, Iowa.

47. John H. Dietrich, "Is There a Moral Law?" *Humanist Pulpit* 2 (1928): 108.

48. Dietrich, "Do We Need a New Moral Outlook?" 5.

49. John H. Dietrich, "My Religion," *Humanist Pulpit* 3 (1929): 73.

50. John H. Dietrich, "Is This Life Preparation for Another?", an address given 17 January 1926 (Minneapolis: First Unitarian Society), 5-6.

51. John H. Dietrich, "Has Man a Soul?", an address given 27 December 1925 (Minneapolis: First Unitarian Society), 5-6.

52. John H. Dietrich, "The Immortal in Man," an address given 4 April 1920 (Minneapolis: First Unitarian Society), 6.

53. Dietrich, "What I Believe," 173.

54. John H. Dietrich, "What the Liberal Church Must Do to Survive," an address given 30 July 1944 (Berkeley, California: First Unitarian Church), 11.

55. John H. Dietrich, "What Are We Trying to Do?" *Humanist Pulpit* 3 (1929): 4-5.
56. John H. Dietrich, "Do Humanists Worship?" *Humanist Pulpit* 7 (1934): 6.
57. John H. Dietrich, "After Prohibition—What?" *Humanist Pulpit* 7 (1934): 143.
58. John H. Dietrich, "The Origin and Development of Religion," an address given 30 January 1921 (Minneapolis: First Unitarian Society), 13.

Chapter 5: Curtis W. Reese: The Statesman of Religious Humanism

1. Curtis W. Reese, "My Life among the Unitarians" (1961), 1. This unpublished manuscript is the source of much of the biographical information in this chapter, which also relied on Reese's ministerial file.
2. Curtis W. Reese, "How the Fundamentalists Met Defeat," *Christian Register* 101 (29 June 1922), 612.
3. Ralph E. Bailey, "Had Chaucer Only Known C. W. R.," *Unity* 139 (November-December 1953), 60.
4. Curtis W. Reese, "Conditions in Camps," *Christian Register* 96 (7 December 1917), 1211- 12.
5. Curtis W. Reese, "The Scope of the New Iowa State Housing Law," *American City* 21 (September 1919): 204.
6. Curtis W. Reese, "Travel Notes—On to India!" *Unity* 102 (26 November 1928), 175-76.
7. Curtis W. Reese, "Brahmo Celebrations," *Unity* 103 (15 April 1929), 107.
8. Reese, "Travel Notes—On to India!" 175.
9. Jessie E. Donahue, "Lombard College Enters New Era: Unitarians Share in Management," *Christian Register* 107 (5 April 1928), 275-77.
10. Curtis W. Reese, "The Glory of a Great Unitarian Centre," *Christian Register* 117 (5 May 1938), 300-301
11. "Curtis W. Reese at Lincoln Centre to Carry on Free Spiritual Ideals," *Christian Register* 108 (1929): 765. See also: Curtis W. Reese, "Abraham Lincoln Centre," *Meadville Theological Journal* 25 (October 1930): 42-51.
12. "Dean of Lincoln Centre Has Varied Experience," *Christian Register* 115 (6 August 1936), 484.
13. For Levinson's views on this subject see: Curtis W. Reese, "The Outlawry of War," *Unity* 98 (14 February 1927), 378-80.
14. Ernest W. Kuebler, "Curtis W. Reese—Liberal Statesman," *Unity* 142 (May-June 1957): 36-42.
15. Curtis W. Reese, *Humanist Religion* (New York: Macmillan, 1931), 12-13.
16. Curtis W. Reese, *The Meaning of Humanism* (Boston: Beacon Press, 1945), 20-21.
17. Curtis W. Reese, "The Faith of Humanism," *Open Court* 41 (May 1927), 272.
18. Reese, *Humanist Religion,* 18.
19. Curtis W. Reese, ed., *Humanist Sermons* (Chicago: Open Court, 1927), vi.
20. Reese, *Humanist Religion,* 23.
21. Reese, *The Meaning of Humanism,* 8.
22. Curtis W. Reese, *Humanism* (Chicago: Open Court, 1926), 1.
23. Reese, ed., *Humanist Sermons,* xi.
24. Reese, *The Meaning of Humanism,* 22.

25. Reese, ed., *Humanist Sermons,* xi.
26. Reese, *The Meaning of Humanism,* 25.
27. Reese, *Humanist Religion,* 30.
28. Ibid., 31.
29. Reese, *Humanism,* 4.
30. Reese, *Humanist Sermons,* 40.
31. Reese, *The Meaning of Humanism,* 22.
32. Reese, *Humanist Religion,* 38.
33. Curtis W. Reese, "Democratizing Human Nature," *Open Court* 58 (July 1924): 428.
34. Curtis W. Reese, "Democratize Human Nature," *Christian Register* 99 (15 January 1920), 49.
35. Reese, "Democratizing Human Nature," 429.
36. Reese, "The Faith of Humanism," 276.
37. Curtis W. Reese, "Changing Opinions, Ideals, and Values in Religion and Life," *Unity* 134 (July-August 1948): 46.
38. Reese, *Humanism,* 34.
39. Reese, *Humanist Religion,* 33.
40. Reese, ed., *Humanist Sermons,* vii-xi.
41. Reese, *Humanism,* 32.
42. Curtis W. Reese, "The Social Implications of Humanism," *Humanist* 8 (June 1948): 2. This same article appeared in Vol. 21 (July-August 1961), the issue announcing Reese's death.
43. Reese, *Humanism,* 11.
44. Curtis W. Reese, "Our Corporate Life Moves to New Goals," *Christian Register* 108 (17 October 1929), 836.
45. Reese, *Humanism,* 63.
46. Reese, *The Meaning of Humanism,* 12.
47. Reese, *Humanist Religion,* 52.
48. Reese, *Humanism,* 53.
49. Reese, *Humanist Religion,* 55.
50. Curtis W. Reese, "The Function of a Radical Church," *New Humanist* 6 (January-February 1933): 13.
51. Reese, *Humanism,* 65.
52. Curtis W. Reese, "The Function of a Modern Minister" in *Contemporary Accents in Liberal Religion,* selected by Bradford E. Gale (Boston: Beacon Press, 1960), 161.
53. Reese, *Humanism,* 66.
54. Reese, "The Function of a Radical Church," 15.
55. Reese, ed., *Humanist Sermons,* vii.
56. Curtis W. Reese, "A Plea for Discrimination," *Christian Register* 105 (18 March 1926), 266.
57. Curtis W. Reese, "Theism and Other Theories of God," *Christian Register* 105 (14 October 1926), 929.
58. Reese, *Humanism,* 62.
59. Ibid., 62. See also Curtis W. Reese, "The Content of Religious Liberalism," *Unity* 85 (12 August 1920), 328.
60. Elmo A. Robinson, *American Universalism* (New York: Exposition Press, 1970), 158.

Chapter 6: Charles Francis Potter

1. Biographical details in this chapter are drawn from Potter's ministerial file with the Unitarian Universalist Association and from his autobiography, *The Preacher and I* (New York: Crown Publishers, 1951).

2. Potter wrote an article about his work at the mission church in Alberta. See Charles F. Potter, "Our Work in Alberta," *Christian Register* 95 (6 July 1916), 628.

3. Potter, *The Preacher and I,* 360.

4. Ibid., 360-61.

5. For the text of this debate see John Roach Straton and Charles F. Potter, *Battle over the Bible* (New York: George H. Doran, 1924). See also "Rev. Charles F. Potter Wins First Debate," *Christian Register* 103 (3 January 1924), 20.

6. For the text of this debate see John Roach Straton and Charles F. Potter, *Evolution versus Creation* (New York: George H. Doran, 1924). See also Jenkin R. Hockert, "Sidelights of the Second Debate," *Christian Register* 103 (7 February 1924), 149-50.

7. For the text of this debate see John Roach Straton and Charles F. Potter, *The Virgin Birth—Fact or Fiction* (New York: George H. Doran, 1924).

8. For the text of this debate see John Roach Straton and Charles F. Potter, *Was Christ Both God and Man?* (New York: George H. Doran, 1924). See Edwin Fairley, "Fourth Debate Is on Deity of Jesus," *Christian Register* 103 (15 May 1924), 472; and C. F. Potter, "Debates Prove One Thing," *Christian Register* 103 (5 June 1924), 551.

9. Potter, *The Preacher and I,* 137-244.

10. Ibid., 258. Potter wrote five articles for the *Christian Register* on the Scopes Trial. See Vol. 104: "A Unitarian in Dayton, Tennessee" (30 July 1925, 741-42); "The Real Origin of the Dayton Trial" (6 August 1925, 765-66); "The Unassuming and Obliging Mr. Scopes" (13 August 1925, 792-93); "Mr. Bryan at the Dayton Trial" (20 August 1925, 818-19); "They Called Them the Three Infidels" (27 August 1925, 839-40).

11. "Mr. Potter's Resignation," *Christian Register* 104 (14 May 1925), 490. See also "Why Mr. Potter Resigns," ibid., 487.

12. "Now—a Creedless Cult," *Literary Digest* 16 (November 1929): 23.

13. Potter, *The Preacher and I,* 356-68.

14. "Charles Potter, Clergyman, Dead," *New York Times,* 5 October 1962.

15. This article was reprinted in the *Christian Register* 105 (29 April 1926), 396-97.

16. John C. Wilson, "Introduction," in Charles F. Potter, *The Lost Years of Jesus* (New York: University Books, 1963), 7.

17. Harry Elmer Barnes, "Dr. Potter and American Humanism," *Humanist* 12:1 (1952): 40.

18. Wallace P. Rusterholtz, *American Heretics and Saints* (Boston: Manthorne and Burack, 1938), 302. Chapter 16 is entitled "Charles Francis Potter: Scientific Religionist."

19. "First Humanist Assembly," *Christian Register* 113 (1 November 1934), 665.

20. Barnes, "Dr. Potter and American Humanism," review of *The Preacher and I* in the *Humanist* (no. 1, 1952), 39-42.

21. Charles F. Potter, *Humanism: A New Religion* (New York: Simon & Schuster, 1930), 10. Also see Potter's *Humanizing Religion* (New York: Harper & Brothers, 1933), 29.

22. Charles F. Potter, *Creative Personality* (New York: Funk & Wagnalls, 1950), 129. See also Potter, *Humanizing Religion,* 107.

23. Potter, *Humanizing Religion,* 249-50.

24. Charles F. Potter, "Life," an address (New York: First Humanist Society, Easter 1930), 8.

25. Charles F. Potter, *Beyond the Senses* (New York: Doubleday, Doran, 1939), 188.

26. Potter, *Creative Personality,* 32, 186.

27. Ibid., 9.

28. For the extended details of this first crisis see ibid., 21-34.

29. Ibid., 12.

30. Potter, *Humanizing Religion,* 21-27.

31. Potter, *Creative Personality,* 132-34.

32. Potter, *Humanizing Religion,* 44.

33. Potter, *Humanism: A New Religion,* 59.

34. Potter, *Beyond the Senses,* 132-33.

35. Potter, *Creative Personality,* 187.

36. Potter, *Humanism: A New Religion,* l.

37. Potter, *Humanizing Religion,* 225.

38. Potter, *Creative Personality,* 191.

39. Ibid., 192. See also *Humanism: A New Religion,* 2, 4.

40. Potter, *Humanizing Religion,* 207.

41. Potter, *Creative Personality,* 61.

42. Charles F. Potter, *Technique of Happiness* (New York: Maculay, 1935), 183.

43. Potter, *Humanism: A New Religion,* 24.

44. Potter, *Humanizing Religion,* 210.

45. Potter, *Technique of Happiness,* 172; see also *Creative Personality,* 82.

46. Potter, *Humanism: A New Religion,* 41.

47. Potter, *Humanizing Religion,* 131.

48. See, for example, Charles F. Potter, "The Influence of Personality," *Christian Register* 94 (23 December 1915), 1211-12.

49. Potter, *Humanism: A New Religion,* 20.

50. Ibid., 28.

51. Potter, *Creative Personality,* 122.

52. Ibid., 138.

53. Potter, *Humanism: A New Religion,* 87.

54. Potter, *Humanizing Religion,* 217.

55. Potter, *Humanism: A New Religion,* 88.

56. Potter, *Humanizing Religion,* 221, 223.

57. Potter, introduction to *Technique of Happiness.*

58. Potter, *Creative Personality,* 88. See also *Technique of Happiness,* 112.

59. Potter, *Humanizing Religion,* 180.

60. Potter, *Humanism: A New Religion,* 12.

61. Potter, *Humanizing Religion,* 125.

62. Potter, *Creative Personality,* 196.

63. Potter, *Humanizing Religion,* 67.

64. Potter, *Humanism: A New Religion,* 121.

65. Potter, *Humanizing Religion,* 27.

66. Ibid., 28.
67. Potter, *Creative Personality,* 202.
68. Potter, *Humanism: A New Religion,* 99.
69. Ibid. See also 39.
70. Potter, *Humanizing Religion,* 102.
71. Potter, *Technique of Happiness,* 205.
72. Potter, *Humanism: A New Religion,* 7.
73. Potter, *Creative Personality,* 171–72.
74. Potter, *Creative Personality,* 180.
75. Potter, "Life," 9.
76. Potter, *Humanizing Religion,* 247.
77. Potter, *Creative Personality,* 113-14.
78. Potter, *Humanizing Religion,* 111, 166. See also *Creative Personality,* 202-3, and *Humanism: A New Religion,* 9.
79. Potter, *Humanism: A New Religion,* 62. See also 8.
80. Ludwig Feuerbach, *The Essence of Christianity,* tr. George Eliot (New York: Harper & Brothers, 1957), 21.
81. Potter, *Humanism: A New Religion,* 48-49.

Chapter 7: Critics of Religious Humanism

1. Willard L. Sperry, *Signs of These Times,* (Garden City: Doubleday, Doran , 1929), 105.
2. Ibid. Although Sperry was critical of humanism, in *Religion and Our Divided Denominations* (Cambridge: Harvard University Press, 1945), he divided the faiths of Americans into four and included statements from representatives of each. The four faiths were Judaism, Roman Catholicism, Protestantism, and Humanism. He included an essay by the humanist Archibald MacLeish. His argument for including an essay by a humanist was "a recognition of the fact that outside formal organized churches there is a great body of persons, mainly, perhaps, in our educational institutions and in the professions or in the arts, who are idealists and loyal servants of their fellow men, but who find themselves intellectually unable to profess the traditional faith in God," viii.
3. Walter M. Horton, *Theism and the Modern Mood* (New York: Harper & Brothers, 1930), 48.
4. Ibid., 69-70.
5. Douglas C. Macintosh, "The Fox without a Tail," *New Humanist* 3 (January 1930): 1.
6. Ibid., 2. See also Macintosh's "Contemporary Humanism" in *Humanism: Another Battle Line!,* ed. by William P. King (Nashville: Cokesbury Press, 1931), 55.
7. Ibid., 2. See also "Contemporary Humanism," 56-57.
8. Macintosh, "Contemporary Humanism," 67. See also Macintosh's "Humanism Viewed and Reviewed, II," *New Humanist* 4 (July-August 1931): 16-19. For A. Eustace Haydon's response to Macintosh's "Contemporary Humanism," see Haydon's "Modernism versus Humanism," *New Humanist* 4 (May-June 1931): 1-4.

9. Louis Harap, "The Paradox of Ethical Naturalism," *Christian Register* 112 (21 September 1933), 611.

10. Ibid., 612. For two reactions to Harap's critique, see "Two Comments on Ethical Naturalism" by John Dewey and Edgar Sheffield Brightman, *Christian Register* 112 (21September 1933), 612-14.

11. Charles Hartshorne, *Beyond Humanism* (Chicago: Willett, Clark , 1937), 10-11.

12. Charles Hartshorne, "The Philosophical Limitations of Humanism," *University Review* 3 (Summer 1937): 240.

13. Charles Hartshorne, *Beyond Humanism,* 12-16.

14. David E. Roberts, "A Christian Appraisal of Humanism," *Journal of Religion* 21 (January 1941): 8.

15. Ibid., 18. Roberts' critique brought five responses: from Howard B. Jefferson, Curtis W. Reese, A. Eustace Haydon, Edward Scribner Ames, and Joseph Haroutunian. See "Notes and Communications," *Journal of Religion* 21 (April 1941): 173-86. In the next issue of the same publication, E. A.Burtt responded and Roberts gave a rebuttal. (21:300-307).

16. Joseph Haroutunian, "Humanism and Christianity," *Christian Register* 112 (26 October 1933), 691-93.

17. Ibid. For J. A. C. Fagginger Auer's response to Haroutunian's critique, see Auer, "Comment on Humanism and Christianity," *Christian Register* 112 (2 November 1933), 709-10. For Haroutunian's response, see "In Reply to Professor Auer," *Christian Register* 112 (9 November 1933), 726-27.

18. Joseph Haroutunian, "Christianity and Humanism," *Journal of Religion* 21 (April 1941): 181-86.

19. John H. Dietrich, "Comments on the Humanist Manifesto," *Humanist* 13:3 (1953): 137.

20. Curtis W. Reese, "Other Comments," *Humanist* 13:2 (1953): 68.

21. Charles F. Potter, "Other Comments," *Humanist* 13:2 (1953): 67.

Chapter 8: Religious Humanism Today

1. The two major sources for understanding the life and thought of Adler are Horace L. Friess, *Felix Adler and Ethical Culture: Memories and Studies,* ed. Fannia Weingartner, (New York: Columbia University Press, 1981) and Benny Kraut, *From Reform Judaism to Ethical Culture: The Religious Evolution of Felix Adler* (Cincinnati: Hebrew Union College Press, 1979). Friess taught both religion and philosophy at Columbia and was Adler's son-in-law. Kraut traces the evolution of Adler's thought and explains its repercusions on Adler as well as the Jewish community in New York and the American Jewish community at large.

2. Robert Hemstreet, "Felix Adler: Artist of the Ideal Good," *Religious Humanism* 28:4 (Autumn 1984): 146-55, 167; see esp. 149-51.

3. Ibid., 149.

4. Friess, *Felix Adler and Ethical Cullture,* 212.

5. Ibid., 125.

6. Ibid., 221.

7. Kraut, *From Reform Judaism to Ethical Culture,* 122.

8. Ibid, 109.

9. Sherwin T. Wine, *Humanist Judaism* (Buffalo, NY: Prometheus Press, 1978), 13. For an article placing Humanistic Judaism within the broader context of modern Judaism, see Seth Kulick, "The Evolution of Secular Judaism," *Humanist* 53:2 (March/April 1993): 32-35. Kulick interprets the Congress of Secular Jewish Organizations and the Society for Humanistic Judaism, both in North America, as being embraced within the umbrella of the International Federation of Secular Humanistic Jews, which is based in Israel.

10. Ibid., 10.

11. Ibid., 15.

12. Ibid., 119-20.

13. Ibid., 121.

14. David Gonzalez, "Temple with No Place for God Seeks a Place: Reform Judaism's Liberalism Is Tested," *New York Times,* 11 June 1994, p. 8.

15. Sherwin Wine, *NACH Newsletter* 11: 2 (Summer 1994): 5.

16. A helpful essay documenting some of the early history of the humanist movement is "Fifty Years of Humanist Publication," by the AHA Editorial Board, *Humanist* 39:1 (Jan./Feb. 1979): 1619. See also Edwin H. Wilson, "The History of American Humanism: What Worked; What Did Not Work," *Religious Humanism* 27:3 (Summer 1993):141-51.

17. Paul Kurtz, *Eupraxophy: Living without Religion* (Buffalo, NY: Prometheus Press, 1989).

18. "What Is Humanism?" is a promotional pamphlet published by the American Humanist Association. For an explanation of the doctrines contained in the pamphlet, see Frederick Edwards, "The Humanist Philosophy in Perspective," *Humanist* 44:1 (Jan./Feb. 1984): 17-20, 42. Edwards is the national administrator of AHA.

19. See, for example, Creighton Peden, *The Chicago School: Voices in Liberal Religious Thought* (Bristol, IN: Wyndham Hall Press, 1987), and William Dean, *American Religious Empiricism* (Albany: State University of New York Press, 1986).

20. The FRH statement appears from time to time in its journal, *Religious Humanism.* For instance, this was copied from the inside cover of the spring 1989 issue.

21. An announcement about the opening of the institute—"Worth Noting: At Last! A Humanist Institute," *Humanist* 44:3 (May/June 1984):31. See p. 31.

22. "At Last! A Humanist Institute." Arisian's words are quoted in this article announcing the opening of the Humanist Institute.

Chapter 9: Conclusion

1. John Wisdom, "Gods," Logic and Language, first series, ed. A. G. N. Flew (Oxford: Basil Blackwell, 1960), 192-94.

2. John Hick, Faith and Knowledge (Ithaca: Cornell University Press, 1957), 150-51.

Selected Bibliography

WORKS BY JOHN H. DIETRICH

Books

The Present Crisis in Religion. Minneapolis: First Unitarian Society, 1922.
The Fathers of Evolution. Minneapolis: First Unitarian Society, 1927.
The Humanist Pulpit, vol. 1. Minneapolis: First Unitarian Society, 1927.
"Unitarianism and Humanism." *Humanist Sermons,* edited by Curtis W. Reese. Chicago: Open Court Publishing Co., 1927.
The Significance of the Unitarian Movement. Boston: American Unitarian Association (1st printing, August 1927; 6th printing, April 1929).
The Humanist Pulpit, vol. 2. Minneapolis: First Unitarian Society, 1928.
The Humanist Pulpit, vol. 3. Minneapolis: First Unitarian Society, 1929.
The Humanist Pulpit, vol. 4. Minneapolis: First Unitarian Society, 1930.
"The Advance of Humanism." *A Free Pulpit in Action,* edited by Clarence R. Skinner. New York: Macmillan, 1931.
The Humanist Pulpit, vol. 5. Minneapolis: First Unitarian Society, 1931.
The Humanist Pulpit, vol. 6. Minneapolis: First Unitarian Society, 1932.
Humanism. Boston: American Unitarian Association (1st printing, October 1934; 3rd printing, April 1939).
The Humanist Pulpit, vol. 7. Minneapolis: First Unitarian Society, 1934.
"Humanism." In *Varieties of American Religion,* edited by Charles S. Braden. Chicago: Willett, Clark, 1936.

Addresses

"Is the Bible the 'Word of God'?" Pittsburg: St. Mark's Memorial Reformed Church, 16 October 1910.

"The Undying Fire." Minneapolis: First Unitarian Society, autumn 1919.

"The Ethics of Violence." Minneapolis: First Unitarian Society, 15 February 1920.

"The Immortal in Man." Minneapolis: First Unitarian Society, 4 April 1920.

"The Cooperative Movement and Industrial Democracy." Minneapolis: First Unitarian Society, 9 May 1920.

"The Relation of Religion to Morality." Minneapolis: First Unitarian Society, 9 January 1921.

"The Origin and Development of Religion." Minneapolis: First Unitarian Society, 30 January 1921.

"Is There a World-wide Jewish Peril?" Minneapolis: First Unitarian Society, 27 February 1921.

"The Business of a Church in These Days." Minneapolis: First Unitarian Society, 18 September 1921.

"The Faith That Is in Us." (Given to the General Conference of Unitarian Churches meeting in Detroit). Minneapolis: First Unitarian Society, 5 October 1921.

"Forty Years of Truth Seeking." Minneapolis: First Unitarian Society, 13 November 1921.

"The Life of Jesus— 1. The Birth Stories." Minneapolis: First Unitarian Society, 5 January 1922.

"What to Read and Why." Minneapolis: First Unitarian Society, 26 February 1922.

"What Did Jesus Really Teach?" Minneapolis: First Unitarian Society, 5 March 1922.

"Do We Need a New Moral Outlook?" (Delivered at Davenport, Iowa, before joint sessions of the Iowa Unitarian Association and the Illinois Unitarian Conference). Minneapolis: First Unitarian Society, 18 October 1922.

"Shall It Be Again?" Minneapolis: First Unitarian Society, 12 November 1922.

"Westward of Forty-Five—How to Grow Old." Minneapolis: First Unitarian Society, 14 October 1923.

"An Imaginary Conversation." Minneapolis: First Unitarian Society, 28 October 1923.

"The Human Thanksgiving." Minneapolis: First Unitarian Society, 25 November 1923.

"The Human Christmas." Minneapolis: First Unitarian Society, 21 December 1924.

"The General Break-up of Orthodox Christianity." Minneapolis: First Unitarian Society, 4 January 1925.

"The Failure of Protestantism." Minneapolis: First Unitarian Society, 1 February 1925.

"Science and the Future of Man." Minneapolis: First Unitarian Society, 8 March 1925.

"Can Human Nature Be Changed?" Minneapolis: First Unitarian Society, 22 March 1925.

"Christian Science and New Thought." Minneapolis: First Unitarian Society, 26 April 1925.

"Religious Reaction and Fundamentalism." Minneapolis: First Unitarian Society, 24 May 1925.

"What and Where Is God?" Minneapolis: First Unitarian Society, 18 October 1925.

"What the Bible Really Is." Minneapolis: First Unitarian Society, 8 November 1925.

"Has Man a Soul?" Minneapolis: First Unitarian Society, 27 December 1925.

"The Kind of Salvation Man Needs." Minneapolis: First Unitarian Society, 3 January 1926.

"Is This Life Preparation for Another?" Minneapolis: First Unitarian Society, 17 January 1926.

"The Problem of Clear Thinking." Minneapolis: First Unitarian Society, 24 January 1926.

"Democratic Rights and Responsibilities in War Time." (Delivered at the Triennial Session of the Pacific Coast Conference-Free Church Fellowship in San Francisco). Berkeley: Starr King School for the Ministry in cooperation with the Pacific Coast Conference-Free Church Fellowship, 15 April 1942.

"What the Liberal Church Must Do to Survive." Berkeley, Calif.: First Unitarian Church, 30 July 1944.

"Humanism—Its Background and Meaning." (Given at the Bay Area Humanist Conference at Oakland, Calif.). Oakland, Calif.: American Humanist Association, 7 August 1945.

Articles

1. The Christian Register

"Will the Old Order Return?" 97 (7 November 1918), 1065.

"The World Not Yet Made Safe." 97 (28 November 1918), 1140-41.

"Gallio Cared for None of Those Things." 98 (23 January 1919), 82-83.

"The Religion of Experience." 98 (13 March 1919), 241.

"The Faith That Is in Us." 100 (27 October 1921), 1014-15.

"The Holiday of Humanity." 100 (22 December 1921), 1205-6.

"What Do You Give in Place of What You Take Away?" 103 (8 May 1924) , 437-39.

"Can Human Nature Be Changed?" 104 (10 September 1925), 897.

"Humanism." 105 (18 February 1926), 158.

"Christian or Humanist." 105 (4 March 1926), 205.

"Important Explanation." 105 (27 May 1926), 492-93.

"Do Not Fear Denominationalism." 105 (18 November 1926), 1045-46.

"Growing Literature of Humanism." 110 (22 October 1931), 808-9.

"Sermons They Like Best." 111 (28 January 1932), 52.

"Impressions of the Oxford Group." 114 (21 February 1935), 118.

2. Miscellaneous

"My Idea of God." Unity 99 (28 March 1927), 62.

"Forward" to Humanism as a Way of Life by Joseph Walker. New York: Macmillan, 1932.

"What Is Humanism?" New Humanist 6 (1933), 1-10.

"The Inevitability of Humanism." University Review 3 (summer 1937), 243-44.

"Can a Humanist Be a Theist or a Christian?" Arbitrator 23 (August 1941), 1.

WORKS ABOUT DIETRICH

1. The Christian Register

Hosmer, James K. "An Uncompromising Radical Church." 98 (15 May 1919), 469-70.

"Humanism the Next Step for Liberal Religion." 104 (20 August 1925), 828.
"Dietrich in Boston." 108 (10 January 1929), 36.
"Mr. Dietrich Participates in 'Symposium on Religion'." 108 (6 May 1929), 419.
"John H. Dietrich Has Written an AUA Tract." 106 (22 September 1927), 749.
"Minneapolis Unitarian Center Dedicated." 106 (26 May 1927), 431.
"Dietrich at 'Church School Institute'." 106 (28 July 1927), 612-13.
"Western Conference News." 111 (28 April 1932), 275.

Miscellaneous

Firkins, O. W. "The Two Humanisms: A Discrimination." *New Humanist* 4 (1931), 1-9.
Rarig, Frank M. "John H. Dietrich." *Minneapolis Unitarian* 3 (summer, 1957).
Winston, Carleton. *This Circle of Earth: The Story of John H. Dietrich.* New York: G. P. Putnam, 1942

WORKS BY CURTIS W. REESE

Books

Humanism. Chicago: Open Court Publishing Co., 1926.
Editor, *Humanist Sermons.* Chicago: Open Court Publishing Co., 1927.
Editor, *Friedrich Nietzsche* by George Burman Foster. New York: Macmillan, 1931.
Humanist Religion. New York: Macmillan, 1931.
"The Faith of Humanism." In *The World's Great Sermons,* edited by S. E. Forster. Garden City: Halcyon House, 1943.
The Meaning of Humanism. Boston: Beacon Press, 1945.
"Priorities of Spiritual Conversion." In *The Voices of Liberalism,* vol. 1. Boston: Beacon Press, l947.
"Time for Liberal Action." In *The Voices of Liberalism,* vol. 2. Boston: Beacon Press, 1948.
"The Function of a Modern Minister." In *Contemporary Accents in Liberal Religion,* selected by Bradford E. Tale. Boston: Beacon Press, 1960.
"My Life among the Unitarians." Unpublished Manuscript, 1961.

Articles

1. The Christian Register
"The Function of the Preacher." 95 (23 November 1916), 114-15.
"Good-Will." 96 (15 March 1917), 252-53.
"The Matter with Mysticism." 96 (23 August 1917), 811-12.
"Conditions in Camps." 96 (20 December 1917), 1211-12.
"The Cult of Superman." 97 (23 May 1918), 494-95.
"The 'Iowa Idea' in Unitarian Polity." 98 (16 January 1919), 59-60.

"A True Story." 98 (6 February 1919), 126.
"Religion—Committal to a Cause." 98 (22 February 1919), 500.
"Mr. Reese's Stirring Salutatory." 98 (11 September 1919), 882.
"Meaning of the Great Change." 98 (11 September 1919), 886, 910.
"Letter." 98 (25 September 1919), 934.
"We Shall Renew Our Youth." 98 (16 October 1919), 1002-3.
"Preparing the Church for a Prepared Ministry." 98 (20 November 1919), 1113-14.
"Unitarian Day of Small Things Past." 98 (25 December 1919), 1246.
"Democratic Human Nature." 99 (15 January 1920), 49.
"The Church of the Democratic Movement." 99 (12 February 1920), 163-64.
"Do You Believe What He Believes?" 99 (9 September 1920), 883-84.
"The New Mysticism." 100 (3 February 1921), 114.
"The Dead Hand." 100 (1 September 1921), 826-27.
"How the Fundamentalist Met Defeat." 101 (29 June 1922), 611-12.
"Facts the Liberals Must Face." 101 (7 December 1922), 1165-66.
"A Plea for Discrimination." 105 (18 March 1926), 253, 266.
"Theism and Other Theories of God." 105 (14 October 1926), 929-30.
"What No One Else Can Do." 105 (15 April 1926), 347-48.
"What the 'Outlawry of War' Means." 106 (27 January 1927), 65-66.
"How Laymen and Ministers Can Help Each Other." 106 (28 April 1927), 338-39.
"Pacific Not a Quiet Sea." 108 (10 January 1929), 26-27.
"On Their Way." 139 (14 February 1929), 139.
"Dr. Reese Meets Bishop Gregoris Aglipay..." 108 (7 March 1929), 190, 204.
"Travel Notes of a Memorable Journey." 108 (18 April 1929), 320-21.
"The General Situation in India." 108 (23 May 1929), 425-29.
"Our Corporate Life Moves to New Goals." (17 October 1929), 835-36.
"Four Significant Trends in Modern Religious Developments." 109 (26 June 1930),
    539, 562-63.
"Asks for Clear Thinking." 109 (21 August 1930), 109, 683.
"Whither Humanism?" 110 (5 March 1931), 188, 203.
"Jane Addams—World Patriot." 114 (10 October 1935), 583-84.
"Would We 'Indoctrinate'?" 115 (4 June 1936), 384-85.
"A Church for Radicals." 116 (6 May 1937), 295-96.
"The Western Unitarian Conference." 119 (1 June 1940), 218-19.
"The Church and Propaganda." 120 (21 March 1941), 166-67.
"Presuppositions of Democracy." 121 (July 1942), 244-45.
"The Liberal Position and Movement." 126 (June 1947), 235-36, 264.
"Can a Unitarian Be a Real Communist?" 126 (October 1947), 594.
"Unitarianism Becomes Muscular." 129 (June 1950), 29-30.
"Let the Churches Confess Their Sins." 131 (July 1952), 22-24.
"The Hundred Year Revolution. 132 (September 1953), 17-19.
"A Mess of Ecumenical Pottage." 135 (April 1956), 11, 35.

2. The Humanist
"Should We 'Indoctrinate'?" 4 (summer 1944): 70-72.
"The Social Implications of Humanism." 8 (June 1948), 1-6. Reprinted in 21 (July-
    August 1961), 195-201.

"Scientific Religion and Human Economy." 10 (March-April 1950): 41-45.
"Globaloney." 13 (July-August 1953): 148.

3. The New Humanist
"Theism." 4 (November 1930): 16-20.
"The Function of a Radical Church." 6 (January-February 1933): 10-16.
"The Humanist Tradition." 7 (January-February 1934): 27-30.

4. Open Court
"The New Mysticism." 36 (February 1922): 125-28.
"The New Religion." 36 (May 1922): 188-92.
"The New Liberalism." 38 (April 1924): 247-51.
"Democratizing Human Nature." 38 (July 1924): 427-31.
"Outline of Liberal Fundamentals." 39 (May 1925): 170-75.
"The Faith of Humanism." 41 (May 1927): 270-77.
"Theism Distinguished from Other Theories of God." 41 (August 1927): 507-510.
"The Outlook for Religion." 41 (August 1927): 677-83.
"The Idea of Purpose." 43 (July 1929): 411-21.
"Humanist Trends in Modern Religious Developments." 44 (November 1930): 647-56.

5. Unity
In addition to the items listed here, through the years Reese also wrote a number of editorials for Unity; *over sixty appeared from vol. 127 (September 1941) through vol. 251 (November-December 1955).*

"Spiritual Slackers." 80 (12 February 1918), 395-96.
"The Content of Religious Liberalism." 85 (12 August 1920), 327-29.
"World Democracy." 86 (7 October 1920), 44-46.
"Industrial Democracy." 86 (25 November 1920), 154-55.
"Booker T. Washington." 86 (30 December 1920), 236-37.
"Religion at the Cross-roads." 89 (30 April 1922), 120-22.
"Religion and the New Philosophy." 91 (8 March 1923), 28-29.
"Liberal Churches Need Socially Minded Ministers." 92 (20 December 1923), 221.
"The New Church." 94 (25 January 1925), 247-48.
"A Social Confession of Faith." 95 (23 March 1925), 51.
"Tabloid Reviews." 95 (4 May 1925), 165.
"The Five Greatest Men in History." 96 (2 November 1925), 110.
"Essentials of Humanism." 96 (28 December 1925), 233.
"Humanism Grows." 96 (29 January 1926), 78.
"The Negative Aspects of Humanism." 97 (29 March 1926), 71-72.
"Tabloid Reviews." 97 (5 April 1926), 93.
"Naturalistic Metaphysics." 98 (15 November 1926), 173.
"Tabloid Reviews." 98 (13 December 1926), 238.
"The Outlawry of War—an Interview with S. 0. Levison." 98 (14 February 1927), 378-80.
"Ponsonby and Peace." 99 (16 May 1927), 173.
"Book Notes." 100 (24 October 1927), 114.

"Book Notes." 100 (13 February 1928), 370.

"From the Editor." 101 (5 March 1928), 22.

"College Medicine Lien." 102 (24 September 1928), 33.

"On to India." 102 (26 November 1928), 175-76.

"From San Francisco to Honolulu." 102 (26 November 1928), 206.

"From Honolulu to Japan." 102 (27 January 1929), 271-72.

"Seeing Japan through a Hospital Window." 102 (7 January 1929), 287-88.

"A Humanist Philosophy of Life." 102 (27 January 1929), 318-20

"In Tokyo." 102 (11 February 1929), 352-53.

"Shanghai and Beyond." 103 (4 March 1929), 9-10.

"Brahmo Celebration." 103 (15 April 1929) , 106-8.

"In Egypt." 103 (1 July 1929), 279.

"Major Attitudes toward the Problem of War and Peace." 106 (10 November 1930), 139-42.

"These Things Shall Be." 107 (16 March 1931), 37-38.

"Historical Background of Humanism." 107 (20 July 1931), 308-9.

"The Political Situation in India." 108 (23 November 1931), 161-62.

"Science—a World Method." 109 (21 March 1932), 37-38.

"A World Language." 110 (13 February 1933), 341-42.

"Thomas Paine." 112 (5 February 1934), 104.

"The Religion of Abraham Lincoln." 112 (19 February 1934), 221-22.

"Unitarians: Background and Foreground." 115 (6 May 1935), 87-89.

"The Basic Principles of Adult Education." 115 (21 October 1935), 71-72.

"Summary of the Humanist Position." 116 (3 February 1936), 241.

"A Peace Platform." 116 (17 February 1936), 230.

"Should We 'Indoctrinate'?" 117 (18 May 1936), 110.

"Why I Support the Roosevelt Administration." 117 (18 May 1936), 6-8.

"Social Practices in India." 118 (5 October 1936), 50-51.

"Education." 118 (4 January 1937), 175.

"Thomas Paine: Λ Tribute." 118 (18 January 1937), 193-94.

"Toward Organic Humanism." 119 (19 April 1937), 70-71.

"Modern Unitarianism." 119 (17 May 1937), 117-20

"Consideration of Civil Liberties." 119 (16 August 1937), 225-226.

"The Social Function of a Free Church." 120 (21 February 1938), 190-91.

"Politics in Kentucky." 122 (5 September 1938), 3-4.

"Editorial." 122 (3 October 1938), 35-36.

"The Need for Clear Thinking on the Question of War." 124 (20 November 1939), 94-95.

"Proposition of Democracy." 125 (4 March 1940), 6-7.

"A Provocative Volume." 125 (15 April 1940), 63.

"A Practical Philosophy." 125 (6 May 1940), 79.

"Emma Goldman." 125 (3 June 1940), 102.

"Toward Clarification of Thought on the War Situation." 125 (1 July 1940), 136.

"No Concession to Hitlerism." 125 (13 July 1940), 160.

"The Policy of *Unity*." 125 (5 August 1940), 166.

"Tribute to Great Britain." 126 (16 December 1940), 199.

"Editorial." 126 (17 February 1941), 179.

"Aid to Great Britain." 126 (17 February 1941), 188.
"The Policy of *Unity* Restated." 127 (April 1941), 19.
"The Meaning of Outlawry." 127 (May 1941), 34.
"The Beginning of a New World." 127 (July 1941), 74-77.
"National Unity." 127 (August 1941), 87.
"The New Allied Front." 127 (July 1941), 69.
"Free India Now." 128 (March 1942), 1.
"Background of the Situation in India." 128 (October 1942), 122-26.
"The New Front." 128 (December 1942), 145.
"American Purpose." 129 (July 1943), 67.
"Goodness without Power." 129 (November 1943), 142.
Unitarian Advance. 130 (May 1944), 35.
"Dumbarton Oaks." 130 (January 1945), 163.
"Tribute to F.D.R." 131 (May 1945), 33.
"Emma Goldman." 131 (July 1945),70-71.
"Expanding Patriotism" 132 (May 1946), 33.
"The Role of America in World Affairs." 132 (July 1946), 67-70.
"Palestine." 132 (August 1946), 83.
"Lynching." 132 (September-October 1946), 97.
"Liberty Unlimited." 132 (November 1946), 115.
"Book Notes." 132 (December 1946), 142.
"The Liberal Position." 133 (May-June 1947), 23-25.
"Changing Opinions, Ideals, and Values in Religion and Life." 134 (July-August 1948, 46-48.
"Modern Unitarianism." 134 (November-December 1948), 85-88.
"Memorial Issue of Curtis W. Reese." 147 (September-October 1961), 69-96.
"Consideration of Civil Liberties." 147 (Jan.-Feb., 1962), 68.

6. Miscellaneous
"Abraham Lincoln Centre." *Meadville Theological Journal* KV (October 1930), 42-51.
"A Democratic View of Religion." Yellow Springs, Ohio: American Humanist Association, Pub. No. 218.
"Christianity and Humanism." *Journal of Religion* 21 (April 1941): 175-77.
"Principles Undergirding Unitarianism." Boston: American Unitarian Association, April 1946.
"Toward Organic Humanism." *Journal of the Liberal Ministry* 2 (autumn 1940): 75-83.

WORKS ABOUT REESE

---

1. The Christian Register
"Editorial." 100 (1 September 1921), 818-19.
"Large Society in Chicago Joins Western Conference."101 (11 March 1922), 280.

"Mr. Reese's Humanism." 105 (17 June 1926), 558.
"Is It Positivism?" 106 (13 October 1927), 798
"Dr. Reese Made Chairman." 107 (26 January 1928), 66.
Donahue, Jessie E. "Lombard College Enters New Era." 107 (5 April 1928), 275-77.
"Lombard College Confers 47 Degrees." 107 (21 June 1928), 523.
"Dr. Reese's Journey to India." 107 (2 August 1928), 630.
"Dr. Reese Resigns." 108 (1929), 633.
"Curtis W. Reese at Lincoln Centre to Carry on Free Spiritual Ideals." 108 (1929), 765.
"Western Conference Directors' Tribute to Dr. Curtis W. Reese." 109 (20 March 1930), 246.
"Church to Resume, Lincoln Centre, Chicago, Uniting Activities in Religious Meetings:" 111 (7-14 July 1932), 443.
"Dean of Lincoln Centre Has Varied Experience." 115 (6 August 1936), 484.
"The Glory of a Great Unitarian Centre." 117 (5 May 1938), 300-1.
"The Lincoln Centre Murals." 120 (21 March 1941), 165.
"Abraham Lincoln Centre, One of the Most Notable Unitarian Institutions, Acquires a New Dean." 136-138 (April 1957), 26.
"Unitarian Award Winner." 136-138 (May 1959), 17.

2. Unity
Backus, Burdette E. "Beyond all else...the Man Himself. " 139 (November-December 1953), 60.
Bailey, Ralph E. "Had Chaucer Only Known C.W.R." 139 (November-December 1953), 60-61.
Ruehrcr, Edwin T. "A Salute to 'Mr. Western Conference." 113 (May-June 1957), 58.
Hilton, Randall S. "Editorial Comments." 150 (May-June 1964), 35-36.
———. "He Can Never Retire from Our Hearts." 150 (November-December 1953), 58.
"Editorial Comments." 147 (September-October 1961), 68.
Kuebler, Ernest W. "Curtis W. Reese—Liberal Statesman." 143 (May-June 1957), 36-42.
Lyttle, Charles H. "The Statesmanship of Curtis W. Reese." 139 (November-December 1953), 58-59.
Silliman, Vincent B. "A Tribute to Courage." 143 (May-June 1957), 57.

WORKS BY CHARLES FRANCIS POTTER

Books

The New Unitarian Statement of Faith. Boston: George H. Ellis, 1920.
With John Roach Stratton. *The Battle over the Bible.* New York: George H. Doran, 1924.
Evolution Versus Creation. New York: George H. Doran, 1924.
The Virgin Birth—Fact or Fiction? New York: George H. Doran, 1924.

Was Christ Both God and Man? New York: George H. Doran, 1924.
The Story of Religion. New York: Simon & Schuster, 1929.
Humanism: A New Religion. New York: Simon & Schuster, 1930.
Humanizing Religion. New York: Harper & Brothers, 1933.
Is That in The Bible? (1st published in 1933). New York: Fawcett Crest Books, 1970.
Technique of Happiness. New York: Macaulay, 1935.
Beyond the Senses. New York: Doubleday, Doran, 1939.
Creative Personality. New York: Funk & Wagnalls, 1950.
The Preacher and I. New York: Crown Publishers, 1951.
The Faiths Men Live By. New York: Prentice-Hall, 1954.
The Lost Years of Jesus. (1st published in 1958). Hyde Park, New York: University Books, 1963.
The Great Religious Leaders. New York: Washington Square Press, 1962.
Did Jesus Write This Book? (1st published in 1965). New York: Fawcett Crest Books, 1967.

Articles

1. The Christian Register
"The Influence of Personality." 94 (23 December 1915), 1211-12.
"To Lincoln." 95 (10 February 1916), 128.
"The Godlikeness of Service." 95 (30 March 1916), 301.
"A Great Temperance Victory in Alberta." 95 (27 April 1916), 398.
"Our Work in Alberta." 95 (6 July 1916), 628.
"Opposition." 97 (20 June 1918), 594.
"At High Noon." 97 (18 July 1918), 689.
"Camp beyond the Bridge." 97 (18 July 1918), 691.
"Is the Sunday-School a 'Non-Essential'?" 97 (3 October 1918), 960.
"The Valley of Achor." 97 (24 October 1918), 1024-25.
"The Christian Register in 1918." 98 (2 January 1919), 9-11.
"A Parish Program That Worked." 98 (23 January 1919), 84-85.
"Laymen Embody Their Life in the Unitarian League." 98 (17 April 1919), 366-68.
"Construction." 98 (26 June 1919), 601.
"The Renaissance of the Apocrypha." 98 (31 July 1919), 725-27.
"The Liberal Spirit Speaks Plainly for Industrial Democracy and Church Unity." 98 (26 October 1919), 1014-17.
"To Be a Real Church—That Is the First Thing." 98 (30 October 1919), 1039-43.
"Folk-Lore in the Old Testament." 99 (2 September 1920), 866.
"The Fruit of a Leaflet in Hayti." 99 (11 November 1920), 1098.
"A Forward Step in New York." 100 (15 December 1921), 1196-97.
"Dean Sperry's Little Brush-Fire." 102 (28 June 1923), 605.
"Debates Prove One Thing." 103 (5 June 1924), 551.
"Unitarians, Awake!" 104 (9 July 1925), 669-70.
"A Unitarian in Dayton, Tennessee." 104 (30 July 1925), 741-42.
"The Real Origin of the Dayton Trial." 104 (6 August 1925), 765-66.
"The Unassuming and Obliging Mr. Scopes." 104 (13 August 1925), 792-93.

"Mr. Bryan at the Dayton Trial." 104 (20 August 1925), 818-19.
"They Called Them the Three Infidels." 104 (27 August 1925) , 839-40.
"Roman Catholics One with Liberals." 104 (3 September 1925), 867.
"A Sermon That Was Never Preached." 104 (24 September 1925), 933-34.
"Humanism—Theism." 105 (29 April 1926), 396, 408.
"Mr. Potter Replies." 108 (28 November 1929), 963.

2. Miscellaneous
"Should Legal Barriers against Birth Control Be Removed?" *Congressional Digest* 10
     (April 1931): 113-15.
"Has This Woman Supernatural Power?" *Liberty* 47 (21 November 1936): 16-18.
"Fun among the Fundamentalists." *American Mercury* 47 (1939): 37-42.
"Time in Bible Times." *Journal of Calendar Reform* 10 (1940): 110-13.
"Boston Accredits a Counselor." *Humanist* 11 (June 1951): 124-25.
"Roy Wood Sellars." *The Humanist* 15 (May-June 1955): 109-12.
"The Qumran Library." *Publishers Weekly,* 25 February 1956, 1132-37.
"The Qumran Community." *Humanist* 17 (March-April 1957): 75-76.

WORKS ABOUT POTTER:

1. The Christian Register
"After the 'Truce,' On with the Controversy." 103 (10 January 1924), 41.
Hockert, Jenkin R. "Sidelights of the Second Debate." 103 (7 February 1924), 137-38.
Schaick, John Van, Jr. "l Should Have Voted for Potter." 103 (14 February 1924), 149-
     50.
"Do We Need a New Bible?" 103 (20 March 1924), 272.
Hockert, Jenkin R. "At Mr. Potter's Bible Class."103 (10 April 1924), 342-43.
Fairly, Edwin. "Fourth Debate is on Deity of Jesus." 103 (15 May 1924), 479.
"Mr. Potter's Resignation." 104 (14 May 1925), 490.
"Why Mr. Potter Resigns." 104 (14 May 1925), 487.
"Mr. Potter's Remarkable Farewell." 104 (8 November 1925), 999.
"Mr. Potter to be State Supply at Church of Divine Paternity." 106 (1927), 569.
Vrooman, W. A. "Agnostic Humanism." Review of *Humanism: A New Religion* by
     Charles Francis Potter. 109 (3 July 1930), 566.

2. Miscellaneous
"Now—A Creedless Cult." *Literary Digest* 103 (16 November 1929), 23.
Rusterholtz, Wallace P. "Charles Francis Potter: Scientific Religionist." In *American
     Heretics and Saints.* Boston: Manthorne & Burack, 1938.
Barnes, Harry Elmer. "Dr. Potter and American Humanism." Review of *The Preacher
     and I* by Charles Francis Potter. *Humanist* 12 (1 November 1952), 39-42.
"Charles Potter, Clergyman, Dead." *New York Times,* 5 October 1962, 33.

OTHER SOURCES

Books

Auer, J. A. C. Fagginger. *Humanism States Its Case*. Boston: Beacon Press, 1933.

Auer, J. A. C. Fagginger, and Julian Hartt. *Humanism versus Theism*. Yellow Springs, Ohio: Antioch Press, 1951.

Barnes, Harry Elmer. *The Twilight of Christianity*. New York: Vanguard Press, 1929.

Bratton, Fred Gladstone. *The Legacy of the Liberal Spirit*. New York: Charles Scribners Sons, 1943.

Burtt, Edwin A. *Types of Religious Philosophy*. New York: Harper Brothers, 1939.

Cauthen, Kenneth. *The Impact of American Religious Liberalism*. New York: Harper & Row, 1962.

Cole, Stewart G., ed. *This Is My Faith*. New York: Harper & Brothers, 1956.

Dakin, Arthur Hazard. *Man the Measure: An Essay on Humanism as Religion*. Princeton: Princeton University Press, 1939

Dewey, John. *A Common Faith*. New Haven: Yale University Press, 1934.

———. *The Influence of Darwin on Philosophy*. Bloomington: Indiana University Press, 1965.

Dillenberger, John. *Protestant Thought and Natural Science*. Garden City: Doubleday, 1960.

Dillenberger, John, and Claude Welch. *Protestant Christianity*. New York: Charles Scribners Sons, 1954.Ferm, Vergilius, ed. *Living Schools of Religion*. Patterson, N. Y.: Littlefield, Adams, 1965.

Feuerbach, Ludwig. *The Essence of Christianity*. Translated by George Eliot. New York: Harper & Brothers, 1957.

Flew, A. G. N., ed. *Logic and Language* (1st series). Oxford: Basil Blackwell, 1960.

Fosdick, Harry Emerson. *As I See Religion*. New York: Grosset & Dunlap, 1932.

———. *The Modern Use of the Bible*. New York: Macmillan, 1961.

Frothingham, Octavius Brooks. *Transcendentalism in New England*. Philadelphia: University of Pennsylvania Press, 1972. (1st published 1876).

Hadas, Moses. *Humanism: The Greek Ideal and Its Survival*. New York: Harper & Brothers, 1960.

Harnack, Adolf. *Outlines of the History of Dogma*. Translated by Edwin Knox Mitshell. Boston: Beacon Press, 1957.

———. *What Is Christianity?* Translated by Thomas Bailey Saunders. New York: Harper & Brothers, 1957.

Grattan, C. Hartley, ed. *The Critique of Humanism*. New York: Brewer & Warren, 1930.

Hartshorne, Charles. *Beyond Humanism*. Chicago: Willett, Clark, 1937.

Haydon, A. Eustace. *Biography of the Gods*. New York: Frederick Ungar, 1941.

———. *The Quest of the Ages*. New York: Harper & Brothers, 1929.

Hick, John. *Faith and Knowledge*. Ithaca: Cornell University Press, 1957.

Horton, Walter Marshall. *Theism and the Modern Mood*. New York: Harper & Brothers, 1930.

224

Hutchinson, William R., ed. *American Protestant Thought: The Liberal Era.* New York: Harper & Row, 1968.

Huxley, Julian. *Religion without Revelation.* New York: New American Library of World Literature, 1958.

Jones, Howard Mumford. *American Humanism.* New York: Harper & Brothers, 1957.

King, William P., ed. *Humanism—Another Battle Line!* Nashville: Cokesbury Press, 1931.

Koch, G. Adolf. *Religion of the American Enlightenment.* New York: Thomas-Crowell, 1969. (1st published as *Republican Religion,* 1933).

Krikorian, Yervant H. *Naturalism and the Human Spirit.* New York: Columbia University Press, 1944.

Krutch, Joseph Wood. *The Modern Temper.* New York: Harcourt, Brace & World, 1929.

Lamont, Corliss. *The Philosophy of Humanism.* New York: Frederick Ungar, 1967.

Lippmann, Walter. *A Preface to Morals.* Boston: Beacon Press, 1960. (1st published 1929).

Lyttle, Charles H. *Freedom Moves West.* Boston: Beacon Press, 1952.

Mercier, Louis J. A. *The Challenge of Humanism.* New York: Oxford University Press, 1933.

Otto, N. C. *Things and Ideals.* New York: Henry Holt, 1924.

Parks, David B. *The Epic of Unitarianism.* Boston: Beacon Press, 1960.

Randall, John Herman, Jr. *The Meaning of Religion for Man.* New York: Harper & Row, 1968.

———. *The Role of Knowledge in Western Religion.* Boston: Starr King Press, 1958.

Rauschenbusch, Walter. *A Theology of the Social Gospel.* Nashville: Abingdon Press, 1917.

Robinson, Elmo A. *American Universalism.* New York: Exposition Press, 1970.

Russell, Bertrand. *Why I Am Not a Christian.* New York: Simon & Schuster, 1957.

Sartre, Jean Paul. "Existentialism Is a Humanism." In *Existentialism from Dostoevsky to Sartre,* edited by Walter Kaufmann. New York: World Publishing, 1956.

Schleiermacher, Friedrich. *The Christian Faith,* vols. 1 & 2. Translated by H. Macintosh & J. S. Stewart. New York: Harper & Row, 1963.

Sellars, Roy Wood. *The Next Step in Religion.* New York: Macmillan, 1918.

———. *Religion Coming of Age.* New York: Macmillan, 1928.

Shapely, Harlow. *Of Stars and Men.* Boston: Beacon Press, 1958.

Sheen, Fulton J. *Religion without God.* New York: Longmans, Green, 1928.

Sontag, Frederick, and John K. Roth. *The American Religious Experience.* New York: Harper & Row, 1972.

Sperry, Willard L., ed. *Religion and Our Divided Denominations.* Cambridge: Harvard University Press, 1945.

———. *Signs of These Times.* Garden City: Doubleday, Doran, 1929.

Stiernotte, Alfred P., ed. *Frederick May Eliot: An Anthology.* Boston: Beacon Press, 1959.

Tavener, Wallace B. *The Challenge of Humanism.* London: Lindsey Press, 1933.

Tillich, Paul. *Perspectives on 19th- and 20th-Century Protestant Thought.* Edited by Carl Braaten. New York: Harper & Row, 1967.

Webb, Clement C. J. *Religion and Theism.* London: George Allen & Unwin, 1934.

Wieman, Henry N. *The Source of Human Good*. Chicago: University of Chicago Press, 1946.

Wright, Conrad. *The Beginnings of Unitarianism in America*. Boston: Beacon Press, 1955.

Articles

Atwood, John Murray. "The Church and the Humanist Controversy." *Christian Leader* (18 January 1930), 75-77.

Auer, J. A. C. Fagginger. "Comments on Humanism and Christianity." *Christian Register* 112 (2 November 1933), 710, 726.

"The Humanist Manifesto." *Christian Register* 112 (11 May 1933), 30

Babbitt, Irving. "On Being Original." *Atlantic* 101 (March 1908), 388-96.

Banning, Andrew. "Confidence in Values." *Christian Register* 112 (6 July 1933), 437-39.

———. "Humanism and Subjectivism." *Christian Register* 112 (7 September 1933), 587.

Braden, Charles S. "Is Humanism Dead?" *University Review* 3 (summer 1937): 247-49.

Buschman, Harold. "Humanism and Positivism." *New Humanist* 1 (March 1929): 1-2.

———. "Mr. Fosdick's Philosophy of Religion." *New Humanist* 3 (December 1929): 1-2.

Call, Lon Ray. "Humanism in England." *Christian Register* 112 (14 September 1933), 604.

Cole, Walton E. "Humanism 'Makes' The Congregationalist." *New Humanist* 1 (February 1929), 1-2.

Davis, Earl C. "Three Questions on Humanism." *Christian Register* 111 (21 April 1932), 252.

———. "Neo-Humanism—What Is It?" *New Humanist* 1 (summer 1928): 1-2.

———. "The New Humanism and the Modern Temper." *New Humanist* 3 (January 1930): 4-6.

———. "What Is Humanism?" *University Review* 3 (summer 1937): 237-40.

"A Humanist Manifesto." *New Humanist* 6 (1933): 1-5.

"The Humanist Manifesto." *Christian Century* 50 (7 June 1933), 743-45

"The Humanist Manifesto: 1. Comments by Some Who Signed; 2. Comments by Some Who Did Not Sign." *Christian Register* 112 (25 May 1933), 330.

Hutcheon, Robert J. "The Central Problem of Contemporary Philosophy of Religion." *New Humanist* 3 (April 1930), 1-4.

———. "Humanism and Theism—Their Arguments and Differences." *Meadville Theological School Quarterly Bulletin* 21 (April 1927): 3-25.

———. "Humanism in Religion Restated." *Meadville Theological School Quarterly Bulletin* 23 (January 1929): 3-34.

Kring, Walter D., and Raymond A. Sabin. "Humanism, Theism and Unitarianism." *Christian Register* 127 (May 1948), 34-37.

Macintosh, Douglas Clyde. "The Fox without a Tail." *New Humanist* 3 (January 1930): 1-4.

Park, Charles E. "Why the Humanism-Theism Controversy is Out of Date." *Christian Register* 133 (July 1954): 18-l9, 35.

Pauck, Wilhelm. "The Validity of the Idea of Revelation in an Empirical Age." *New Humanist* 3 (February 1930): 1-7.

Pennington, Leslie T. "The Humanist Manifesto." *Christian Register* 112 (25 May 1933), 334.

Pratt, James Bissett. "The Transiency of Humanism." *University Review* 3 (summer 1937), 245-46.

"Professor Sellars Again." *Christian Register* 99 (12 August 1920), 783.

Robins, Sidney S. "What Is a Humanist? This Will Tell You." *Christian Register* 99 (29 July 1920), 739-40.

Rombotis, Gabriel. "Haydon's Philosophy of Religion and His Method." *New Humanist* 6 (1933): 15-24.

———. "Scientific Method in Haydon's Religion." *New Humanist* 6 (1933): 33-38.

Roth, John K. "William James, John Dewey, and The 'Death-of-God'." *Religious Studies* 7 (March 1971): 53-61.

Schaick, John Van, Jr. "What about Humanism?" *Congregationalist,* 14 February 1929, 206-7.

Sellars, Roy Wood. "Does Humanism Support Confidence in Values?" *Christian Register* 112 (7 September 1933), 586.

———. "Humanism or Theism." *Christian Register* 112 (30 November l933), 777-78.

———. "Nature and Naturalism." *New Humanist* 7 (1934): 1-8.

———. "A Naturalistic Interpretation of Religion." *New Humanist* 3 (March 1930): 1-3.

———. "Religious Humanism." *New Humanist* 6 (1933): 7-12.

———, and Douglas Clyde Macintosh. "Humanism Viewed and Reviewed." *New Humanist* 4 (1931): 12-19.

Sullivan, William L. "The Faith That Makes the Church." *Christian Register* 100 (3 November 1921), 1039-40.

———. "God, No-God, Half-God." *Christian Register* 100 (18 August 1921), 775-76.

"Theism and Humanism." *Christian Register* 117 (20 October l938), 600-l.

"Theist and Humanist." *Christian Register* 100 (20 October 1921), 986-87.

Williams, David Rhys. "Humanism and Mystictsm" *Christian Register* 112 (30 November 1933), 775-76.

Wilson, Edwin H. "Humanism, Theism and Denominational Unity." *Christian Register* 117 (17 March 1938), 175-77.

———. "The Humanist Controversy Is History, Part I." *Christian Register* 117 (5 January 1938), 8-9.

———. "The Humanist Controversy Is History, Part II." *Christian Register* 117 (12 January 1938), 23-25

———. "Positivism and Humanism: Some Needed Distinctions." *New Humanist* 1 (January 1929): 1-2.

Index

humanist-theist controversy: 38-48; extent of, 153; and Free Religious Association, 173, 188-89; and God, 48-49; major points of dispute, 168, 195-97; mentioned, 183
Humanizing Religion by Charles F. Potter, 130, 132
human nature: Dietrich's view of, 76-77; Potter's view of, 137-39; Reese's interest in bettering, 114-16
human responsibility: Dietrich's view of, 81-82
humans: Dietrich's view of, 73-79; Potter's view of, 137-39; Reese's view of, 113-17
Huxley, Thomas, quoted, 113
Hymns of the Spirit, publication of, 47

idealism, ethical, Adler's, 176
idealists, defined, 10
Illinois State Baptist Association, mentioned, 100
immortality: Christian view of, 166; Dietrich's view of, 72, 88-93; and fear of death, 78; Fosdick's view of, 17; and Humanist Manifesto, 21, 24; humanists' rejection of, 173; and naturalistic humanists, 10-11; Potter's view of, 146-48; Reese's disavowal of, 123-24; and Renaissance, 5; Sellars's view of, 35
individual: Adler's view of, 177; relationship to society, 144; sacredness of, 115
individualism: Dietrich's stress on, 73-76; and socialism, 115-16
industrial revolution, Dietrich's view of, 74
institutions, religious, purpose of, 23
intellect: humanists' reliance on, 160
intellectuals, and Ethical Culture, 175
intelligence, Reese's description of, 113
intuition, Adler's view of, 177; Potter's view of, 136, 142
Is That in the Bible? by Charles F. Potter, 130

Jesus: as champion of personality, 16-17; Christianity's focus on, 165-66; introduction into humanist-theist controversy, 168; liberals' view of, 14, 28-29; and Pauline view of salvation, 89; and traditional view of salvation, 79; Dietrich, Reese, and Potter's views of, compared, 152-53; Potter's interest in, 130-31; Potter's view of, 142-43, 147-48; Sellars's, view of, 35; Wieman's view of, 19
Jones, Jenkin Lloyd, and *Unity,* 104
Joy, Charles R., and American Unitarian Association presidency, 46-47
Judaism: and Adler, 174, 178; as aesthetic option, 181-82; humanistic, 180-84; Reform, controversy within, 183-84; Reform, efforts to organize, 33; secular, 181-82
Judeo-Chritian tradition, and religious humanists, 25

Kant, Immanuel: and Ethical Culture, 175-77, 188; and existence of God, 68; mentioned, 117
King, Edward, 175
Kring, Walter D., and humanist-theist controversy, 47-48
Krutch, Joseph Wood, and "Futilitarian" view, 72; Horton's view of, 156
Kuebler, Ernest W., description of Reese, 106-7
Kurtz, Paul, and eupraxophy, 185

Lamont, Corliss: and naturalistic humanism, 9; quoted, 11
leadership: and progress, 118; religious, Reese's view of, 121; training, 190-91
Levinson, S.O., mentioned, 106
Levy, J. Leonard, mentioned, 55
liberalism, Protestant: characteristics of, 13-15; Tillich on, 27
liberal religious movements, summarized, 191-92
liberals, religious: Fellowship of Religious Humanists option for, 188
life, purpose of, Reese's view on, 110
Lippman, Walter, Horton's view of, 156
literary humanism, 5-7
Lombard College, Reese presidency, 104
Loomer, Bernard, mentioned, 189
Lost Years of Jesus by Charles F. Potter, 130
Lupton, Dilworth, mentioned, 42
Lyttle, Charles, and Humanist Manifesto, 45

Macintosh, Douglas C., criticism of religious humanists, 157-58
Mangasarian, M.M., mentioned, 38
Manifesto, Humanist: see Humanist Manifesto
Maritain, Jacques, and humanism, 3
Marxism, Reese's criticism of, 117-18
Marxists, and humanism, 3
Mason, Walter L., mentioned, 55
materialism: definitions, 82; Dietrich's, 60-61; Reese's criticism of, 108, 110
Matthews, Shailer, mentioned, 103
Mayhew, Jonathan, and revivals, 28; mentioned, 30
Meadville Theological School: and Reese, 103, 104, 107; mentioned, 184, 187-88
Meaning of Humanism by Curtis W. Reese, mentioned, 105
mechanism, Reese's view of, 108
Meland, Bernard, mentioned, 189
Mercersburg Academy, mentioned, 53
Michelangelo, 5
mind-body dualism: and *Christian Century,* 24; rejected in Humanist Manifesto, 21
mind vs. soul, 90-91
ministers: role of, 35, 122-23; training of, 190
Minneapolis, Dietrich's career in, 57-58
miracles, impossibility of, 64

233

234